CHRISTINE HASSING

For Bette &
Booner
N Lafer, Editor

BALBOA.PRESS

A DIVISION OF HAY HOUSE

Balboa Press books may be ordered through booksellers or by contacting:

Balboa Press
A Division of Hay House
1663 Liberty Drive
Bloomington, IN 47403
www.balboapress.com
844-682-1282

Because of the dynamic nature of the Internet, any web addresses or links contained in this book may have changed since publication and may no longer be valid. The views expressed in this work are solely those of the author and do not necessarily reflect the views of the publisher, and the publisher hereby disclaims any responsibility for them.

Scripture quotations marked NIV are taken from the Holy Bible, New International Version®. NIV®. Copyright © 1973, 1978, 1984 by International Bible Society. Used by permission of Zondervan. All rights reserved.

The author of this book does not dispense medical advice or prescribe the use of any technique as a form of treatment for physical, emotional, or medical problems without the advice of a physician, either directly or indirectly. The intent of the author is only to offer information of a general nature to help you in your quest for emotional and spiritual well-being. In the event you use any of the information in this book for yourself, which is your constitutional right, the author and the publisher assume no responsibility for your actions.

Any people depicted in stock imagery provided by Getty Images are models, and such images are being used for illustrative purposes only.
Certain stock imagery © Getty Images.

Print information available on the last page.

ISBN: 978-1-9822-5528-2 (sc)
ISBN: 978-1-9822-5530-5 (hc)
ISBN: 978-1-9822-5529-9 (e)

Library of Congress Control Number: 2020917945

Balboa Press rev. date: 09/28/2020

To Peppi, who first taught me hope
and
To Yana. Namaste

TABLE OF CONTENTS

Dear Reader,

When asked to share in a class who I most admired and why, I sat thankfully and fretfully in the back row of the classroom pondering my answer. I was thankful I was sitting in the back row and would not have to answer first so that I had the additional time to reflect. I was fretful trying to narrow my list down to one person.

When it became my turn to answer, my reply was something like this: *I stopped telling people to watch the movie* Extremely Loud and Incredibly Close *when the overwhelming response I would receive was that the movie was so sad. I didn't see the sadness when I had watched the movie. Instead I saw the purpose of each encounter between the little boy and the individuals he met. I watched the gifts that came from tragedy. I found that I, too, desired to find and build 427 people into my scrapbook, twenty-fold. Throughout the entire movie I saw hope. What do I most admire? The strength and beauty of the human spirit.*

I communicated that in class sitting next to a student who exemplified these two traits of those whom I most admire. Both of us were in an organizational leadership program and learning about servant-leadership. Both of us were now learning how we could take our leadership to next levels and he had far surpassed me in his experiences and capabilities to serve and lead in his career up to this point. His career involved the willingness and the vow to lay down his life for others in service to our country. And he was in class with his service dog who was supporting this veteran's journey with PTSD.

As our journey with this class progressed, this student gave me one of his most valuable assets for a final class project. He gave me his trust to write his life story. He dug deep within to find his courage to share this story with someone who had zero experience in or with the military. Because he was being asked to bravely share his story with a stranger rather than close friend, he needed to decide to put aside fears that his story would be judged. He had to assess his willingness to verbally share a story that is very hard to give voice to. He was facing a requirement to take a significant risk that he would be stronger than the painful memories that might resurface by sharing his story.

Yet, stronger than these fears in my classmate was his inherent desire to continue to serve. His vow to lay down his life for others is a lifetime oath. He is no longer living out this vow deployed in a war zone; now he is living this vow as a civilian, a veteran, and a lifetime brother who does not want to see his armed forces brothers and sisters lose their lives now that they, too, are civilians.

We don't always know in the moment we take a step that we are entering a path we are being called to travel. Writing this veteran's life story was the first step to this book you now hold.

Emily Dickenson wrote: *Hope is the thing with feathers, that perches in the soul, and sings the tune without the words, and never stops—at all.* From an unknown author, a quote reads: *In my darkest hour, I reached for a hand and found a paw.*

Hope Has a Cold Nose, is a compilation of veteran life stories written to increase awareness and understanding about the positive impact service dogs make in the support and recovery of those who journey with pain, trauma, sorrow, and despair (PTSD). It is a book unlike any of its kind, for it is authored by not just one individual. It is written by twenty-three additional coauthors who hope and pray that by bravely sharing their stories they will inspire their brothers and sisters in arms not to give up. It is a book of extraordinary stories of resilience, despair, survival, dignity, hope, and the power of fur and cold noses to aid healing in place of traditional treatments such as prescription medicines.

Much of the information communicated indicates that twenty-two United State veterans die by suicide daily. At certain points in time, the number was as low as twenty. As Shannon Walker, CEO of Northwest Battle Buddies, shares in her Mount Hood TEDx talk from November 2019, that is 7,300 lives per year. This is in comparison to 548 US military combat deaths per year. The current statistic is not as critical as the absolute reality; if even one life ends in suicide, the number is too high.

I am someone who believes so deeply that there is purpose in the emotional and mental anguish and grief that comes with life, and that we are called to make tragedy matter through the choices we make in how we respond. Because I believe that amid life's darkest pains are beautiful gifts, my heart aches to think one person reaches a point in which living becomes too unbearable. Let alone twenty or twenty-two per day!

The number of suicides rise when we factor in first responders and others who serve humanity who reach a point where the weight of the pain, trauma, and grief becomes too great for them to bear.

The veteran stories you will read are from several branches of the military and from varying experiences—Afghanistan, Saudi Arabia, Iraq, Kuwait, Vietnam, Israel. Yes, Israel too. For on this journey of seeking stories of the positive impact of service animals in the lives of veterans journeying with PTSD, my path was led to two individuals who served in the Army in Israel. Their stories are affirmation that pain, trauma, sorrow, despair, and grief are not unique. At least one of these components of suffering we have all experienced and survived.

These two Israeli stories are also representative of something else to ponder, and perhaps ultimately learn from—that we in the United States may adopt and apply to our own healing journeys. According to an article from 2014 written by Marissa Newman in the *Times of Israel*: "7 [suicide] cases reported in 2013, down 50% from last year and 75% from 2010." Friends residing in Israel affirm the suicide rate is still this considerably low. In the words of a dear friend, *We are an entire country that has PTSD*, for Israel has been a country of war for many generations. And yet, it is a country in which few are reaching a self-chosen decision that life should end. Unstoppable resilience? It would seem so. Unwavering hope? Absolutely.

Two of the twenty-three stories you will read are from authors whose dogs are not certified service dogs. Their dogs are what we would consider an emotional support animal. Yet their stories are inspiring and extraordinary. And their stories represent something else that is key. Best-selling author Cheryl Richardson wrote: *People start to heal the moment they feel heard.* I also have a personal belief that there is a significant positive ripple effect that occurs from any healing moment. Healing breaks painful generational cycles that need not be replicated, helps another who can see in someone's else's story a piece of themselves, and heals history in which there may not have been community support for those returning from service, such as during the Vietnam War era.

There is also a story shared by an individual who is a spouse of a military veteran, and the storyteller is also a first responder. Like the two stories mentioned above, this person's story is equally inspiring and extraordinary. It affirms, as all the stories from this book do, that pain, trauma, sorrow, and despair do not discriminate. It is a story of healing to inspire others who may see into the mirror of their hearts a reflection of themselves. And it is a story to demonstrate that one person's pain is not for that person only. There is a tie binding to loved ones, to friends, and to the surrounding community who hurt when someone they love is deeply hurting.

It is community that can help individuals on their journeys, a support system that can serve as a complement to those in fur with cold noses. To look someone's pain or grief in the eye is one of the hardest things to do. We find ourselves uncomfortable listening to the content of the story. We don't want to hear about death, depression, addiction, or wanting to die. We'd rather avoid having to make a choice that taps into our ethical systems of belief. We are fearful to feel that deep-down feeling—*what if that was me?* We judge, either out of naivety or because judging is our self-protection against our fears—fears we may not even know. It can feel safer if we critique another's story so that we can avoid looking into a mirror at our own pain we try to hide. A veteran who enters a public setting with a service dog is exhibiting a courage to communicate they know emotional pain. Often, these veterans face judging public eyes. The stories you will read in *Hope Has a Cold Nose* are written with a tone of beauty to serve as a bridge to you, the reader. The intent is that the tone will provide you the opportunity to not want to push away, but instead "hear" the stories with compassion and without judgment. *People begin to heal the moment they feel heard.* And, so does humanity.

Though you will find similarity across all of the stories, you will also find that each story differs. Sure, there is the obvious reason in that no two of us experience life exactly the same way. My approach as a life-story writer is not to ask questions. I do not have a script or template that guides what to ask. As I tell storytellers, my approach is to listen for the story you wish to share with me as it is the story that is meant to be shared. When we can listen not from a place of what we want to know but from a place of what others wish to share, we are providing that nonjudgmental, compassionate space for healing. We are allowing others in pain the freedom to be. It is through this approach that you will find the stories vary in length, in which ones share about deployment, and in which ones focus only on their time postwar. *People begin to heal the moment they feel safe* to share their stories.

On this journey to develop *Hope Has a Cold Nose*, I have been blessed to learn about many organizations that embody giving purpose to life's tragedies, fostering dignity, and enabling healing for those whose voices are quiet or hard to hear. These organizations are courageously looking into eyes of pain, trauma, sorrow, despair, or grief to offer a supporting hand. You can read about these organizations at the end. May these "communities" of support inspire you, just as they find inspiration to keep living their missions and purpose through each individual—human and fur—they serve.

2020 has proven to be a year in which the entire world found itself seeking hope and faith in, or perhaps despite, the vulnerabilities and traumas that are an essence of life's flow. As more uncertainty became an hour-by-hour norm, each person was being asked to choose their reactions and their actions. The more that was perceived as slipping away, the greater the gifts of connecting and reconnecting were found. It's that fundamental truth of life that we learn through opposites and it is how well we dance in the middle—and in the choices we make—that give us grace.

As you read the stories on the next pages, may you find the grace and heart to listen with the same kind of unconditional acceptance as those with fur do. And if you are one journeying with significant pain, trauma, sorrow, or despair, may you find a community of grace holding out their helping hands.

Indeed, I can think of no greater admiration than the strength and beauty of the human spirit, and the spirits that come in fur coats.

Sincerely,

—Christine Hassing

PROLOGUE

Ad astra per aspera: through difficulty to the stars

—Latin Phrase

When you fall, but fall forward. When you stop, to only catch your breath. And when you face the unknown.

March 24, 2016

I had let the demons of war and the struggles of life allow me to forget I was a husband and a father. A son and a brother. A veteran and a friend.

Within minutes of no longer being here, through a series of miracles and a small army of friends, and a medical staff that was not ready to give up on me...

I AM still here.

And proudly I stand

—-M. Ortiz, US Army, Airborne, 2019 Commencement Speech

Dear me, four years ago,

Today is March 24, 2020 and it has been four years since you attempted to take your life.

Within minutes of no longer being here I look back onto that day and want to tell you, you got through it.

As I sit here and rub the scars you left me, scars I will forever have, I will forever struggle to take any kind of medication in remembrance of the pills that day.

I am still here.

M. Ortiz

JACOB AND TRACER

In racing, they say that your car goes where your eyes go. The driver who cannot tear his eyes away from the wall as he spins out of control will meet that wall; the driver who looks down the track as he feels his tires break free will regain control of his vehicle.

—Garth Stein, *The Art of Racing in the Rain*

His war and my war different, yet both of us experienced the same. Both of us have known loss and inescapable pain. He may not have held the hand of a comrade taking his last breath. Yet he knew the feeling of a shield starting to cover his heart when a cage was his bed. He may not have longed for silence when the spray of ammo was deafening. But he knew the pain of silence when his neighbors stopped their lonely howls for sleep. We both knew the struggle to close our eyes for fear of memories; both of us with images that reinforced we weren't "good for anything." On one level, I knew I was fulfilling my sacred oath to serve and protect. Yet on another, I felt I was failing for each heartbeat that would not know what it was to resurrect. On one level, his purpose to love unconditionally would not let him lose the faith; but not being wanted was eroding his spirit away.

Voices he couldn't shake screamed "NO!", "Bad!", and ultimately "We surrender him to you. Good riddance; he is yours!" Voices I couldn't shake yelled, "Help me, please," "Don't let me die," "Tell my family I bravely fought the war." His way of speaking is through his body in its wiggles and shakes; the more to be happy about, the more movement he makes. As words sharper than a knife snapped his heart in two, his eyes grew dim and his body subdued. I had once spoke in a voice so charismatically, surrounded by family and friends once my top joy and priority. As one life, then two, then...*turn off, oh God, please, let me find that off button immediately.* I, too, grew dim, so very dim inside. Both of us encountering nothing but darkness as we reached for life.

Before our souls would find each other, before hope would nudge us both, I needed to partner with despair upon returning home. *What right do I have to be alive?* or *In this chair, in this room, is the only safe place for me.* These were the types of messages in my mind's relentless repeat. The power of three G's, my armor laying across my chest—grief, guilt, and gutless trying to steal my breath. Death had rubbed against me over and over—during deployment it just wouldn't leave. It had shown me it placed no value on good people—a dirty rotten thief! I was no longer at war, but I was at war every day. Emotions once buried threatening to no longer stay at bay. Those hands I held or wished I could have had they still been attached now keep reaching out when I try to sleep. *Okay, buddies, cheers to you. This fifth of Absolut is on the house, courtesy of me. Down the hatch, one, two, three. Another bottle, another day, oh, sweet oblivion thanks you for your mercy. And yes, Doc, I don't mind if I do. Pile on the prescriptions—twenty-five feels too few.*

Before we were meant to join as one, guardian angels were sent our way. They were the orchestrators as our beacons of faith. My guardian angel was named Teresa and his was a right-arm extension of an angel called Shari. Both were determined they would not give up on him nor me. One step at a time, but steps forward nonetheless we were both taking. Step one for me, no more drink. Step one for him, another veteran and a planned meet and greet. Step two for me, an application acceptance to be partnered with a service dog. Step two for him, a veteran cancellation with one phone call. Step three for me, a six-month waiting period shortened to eight weeks. Step three for him, a veteran named Jacob he was about to meet.

Hello Tracer, I am Jacob. What do you say—shall we give this a try?

Hello Jacob, I am Tracer. And just so you know—I will never leave your side.

I had already been blessed with two gifts to make my life complete. My son Tommy and my daughter Ava, two additional angels inspiring me. Now I have a third gift, a third child to make me whole. Tracer and I inseparable for 99 percent of where I go. Tracer gave me my life back not just once, but twice. Truth be told, he has probably given me many lives back each time he comforts me in the night. He gave me a lifeline the day he and I became a cohesive team. He also was the catalyst for paths intersecting. A dog trainer kindly told me I had a wealth of knowledge that needed to be shared and not kept under lock and key, so, becoming a leader of a youth organization called the Sea Cadets would become my destiny.

Slowly, steadily, with the softest black fur held tightly in my clutch or I held tightly in his; the prescriptions continue to decrease their grip. With a wisdom and an encouragement that he speaks volumes through his eyes, I continue to step forward with my arms open to life. Memories still knock in a menacing way and I'm certain they won't disappear. Actually, I hope they don't fade completely, for it is important my fellow comrades I keep near. For each youth cadet I help, I am giving purpose to a fellow soldier whose time on earth was through. Goodness is paid forward in the community a cadet serves, and in the self-confidence he builds too. It is a slow healing process, and I know I can't erase what deployment revealed about a dark side of life. But with Tracer by my side, I can listen closely when I close my eyes. I take a deep breath, and I hear my comrades say, "Thank you for making it matter in how you are fighting for me. Because you bravely chose hope, you are a beacon of light for others in need. We know it is hard to keep going, but you are doing exactly what we need you to do. The enemy doesn't win because of the courage you choose."

I am not a hero; medals go to Tracer, to my children, to my wife. Medals go to men I proudly served with side by side. Medals go to those who save lives like Tracer's and who teach others like Tracer to save lives like mine. Medals go to my friends who found it too hard once they returned back home to stay alive. Medals go to the Sea Cadets who give me the honor to believe I am teaching them when, in reality, they are teaching me. Medals go to my friends who also journey with PTSD. Medals go to four-legged souls who also fight to survive, trusting that the one they are meant to unconditionally love, they will soon find.

I made many a wish upon a star the nights I was deployed. Like *Please, oh please, stop the noise.* Our prayers get answered but not always in the way we are thinking when we reverently beg and plea. A perfect example is the way that the gift of silence came to me. By my side all the time, silent, yet continually he speaks. Of the most incredible love, a four-legged soul in answer to my plea sent to me from above. I have known what it means to give your all to your team, to give your heart and your soul. It is an entire new level of team with Tracer who makes me whole.

Well, Tracer, my boy, what do you say?

I think you have done well diverting your eyes away.

Diverting my eyes? What do you mean?

You kept your eyes on the track and let your tires break free. We are a pretty good team, aren't we? You and me. Oh, and one more thing. By your side, I will never leave.

JENNIFER AND ONYX

*Sometimes God will put the Goliath in your
life to find the David within you*

—Unknown

I, Jennifer Norris, entered this life vowing to fulfill two things: that I would serve and that I would lead. Like the missions I promised to give my all to, to the death if need be, my soul also promised into all of life I would lean. Life is lived one moment at a time, yet the moments stitch together into a large tapestry. Moments that, had they not been experienced, would leave the canvas incomplete. I've had times I longed to take scissors to a section, to rip it away clean. I've also come to understand that these sections are an essence of me.

I raised my hand and I turned over my soul for safe keep. I proudly embraced the goals of the military. I would lead for the greater good of all. I would sacrifice limb and life, and if deemed necessary, I'd fall. For fifteen years my pledge I did uphold. A lifetime career my original goal. I had my own mind, body, and soul, poised and ready to sacrifice all three. My own wholeness was secondary. My words became not my own but part of a collective vocabulary. Duty, honor, dignity; *I will die for my country.* I was not afraid and trusted I was ready for battle if need be. I knew there was an enemy; thankfully the enemy did not walk beside me. Or so I believed.

Each of us experiences trauma in memories we can't erase. It could be from war, with the image of a comrade's face. It could be a car accident that didn't occur holding enemies at bay. Yet, over and over, and nonstop, that accident replays. I vowed that any mission I was ordered to fulfill, I would most certainly do. That I might not be able to quiet my mind while my voice slipped away could be a reality I also knew. I also believed that any post trauma I might endure would be the result of war I would bravely fight. I didn't yet know that the biggest battle of all would be on this side of the enemy line.

Fear is a powerful weapon, mightier than the heaviest artillery. Fear clouds judgment and blurs the ability to clearly see. It holds the soul at gunpoint, it holds one's truth at the end of a knife blade. It tortures personal ethics and a sense of universal right gets misplaced. Two people can hear *I will obey.* Two different choices can be made. Both hold allegiance to authority. One earns trust while, for the other, trust becomes obsolete. I was the one to lose trust at the hands of others who earned prestige. My soul held at the end of a barrel as the essence of me was stabbed in two. No longer trustful of military virtue.

Some describe a life-changing moment as one in which the world grew dark and still. That moment in life when the ability to feel becomes nil. I have known this cavern, one in which I resided for several years. I couldn't see it at the time, but light was still near. I stayed in the cocoon of this cave, the only place in which I felt safe. I lived in this cave, and I lived outside in the surroundings. Outside I moved through the motions of a reality I could not touch or reach. Outside of this cave, I heard *dishonor, undignified, a promise you did not keep.* Inside of this cave, faintly I heard *warrior, fight, there is purpose you are meant to achieve.*

Cut in two, I would first need to know two more slices with the knife. One occurred when a request of leave was denied. My father was given six months to live; cancer his Goliath, he would not be able to defend against its might. I was not allowed a leave of absence to be by his side. My father had given his armor to me to wear in court when I sought legal justice for the crime of my stolen soul. Into the cave I retreated further as I could not give that armor back to my father because he died alone.

The fear from sudden attacks, death on our home soil out of the blue, led to only one priority of leadership, only one option they saw to choose. Fight for the honor of 9/11, country over family. I was already a dissenter in the making per the eyes of the military; certainly, my request was only another form of my trickery. Another blade inserted to stop the beating of my heart now; breathing for myself second behind loyalty to my military vow.

A next cut would come with a gift, though at the time, I did not readily see it would be. A confrontation took me to my core, bringing my soul back to me. In 2008, another slice took the form of a nervous breakdown. Into the deepest part of the cave I moved, certain I would no longer be found. I thought I knew silence when that first knife cut me in two. In the back of this cave it was the loudest stillness I'd ever been exposed to. It deafened me and was a thief taking from places where I didn't know I had more that could be stolen away. I was safest in this cavern, and yet I longed to escape. Words filling pages, rapidly turning through my mind, reams and reams of paper capturing what I was trying to hide. Yet, if someone stepped inside the doorway willing to listen to me speak, all the words were gone, a fleeting retreat.

One does not know courage until one has decided to rise from where one lies. When a blanket and a bed are the only safe refuge, walking to the couch requires enormous fortitude. You may not understand how someone who fought a war so bravely found it her biggest win to say no to anxiety. My hope is that you never have to know this intimately. And for those who have walked a similar journey or perhaps you are still peeking your head out of the cave, I am here to tell you, "Here is my hand; it will be okay."

I do not say, "It will be okay" lightly to you, my friend, for I know at the bottom of this rope, it feels like an end. I know how words can be said but hold no meaning. All the dictionaries in the world cannot begin to describe how you are feeling. Add the well-intentioned expression of *I care* and that feeling of isolation grows ten-fold. Now there is expectation, of which you feel you are not meeting, leading you further toward alone.

I mentioned that in that darkness there is a light you cannot see. A force mightier than us is busy orchestrating. It is lining up messengers who each hold a locked box awaiting a key. Inside the locked box is hope that is ours for the taking. Only one person holds the key that can open as many boxes as one wishes to look into. That person who holds the key is—you. In that cavern, I did not realize that as fear was reaching for me, I in turn, was reaching courageously. The warrior within me that had vowed I would fight at any cost had not abandoned me. I had to tend to her warrior wounds for a bit until she was ready. But oh, when I put back on my uniform of self-worth, of honor and dignity, beside my tags was a large key. It opened the first box which contained the words *I have the ability to be free.*

My freedom came in the form of fur and four feet. She, too, a warrior, like me. Onyx, too, had been fighting her own war of survival, a desire to serve and lead. She entered my life in 2013 with three things I had lost along the way. An open heart to love without fear, to grab hope, to feel faith. Onyx understands what my heart is unable to communicate. She knows better than I do when I feel unsteady and not safe. Onyx has given me the ability to leave the cave for extended periods of time. If I have moments that feel better to reenter the cavern, she enters with me until again I find my fighting spirit to step back outside. She doesn't need me to tell her where she should sit, or lay. In a vehicle, in a store, in a national park—Onyx has my back at every place.

Like me who entered this life with purpose to achieve, Onyx, too, had reasons for her being. What adds to the gift of my soul-restorer in a fur coat is that she is my comrade with mutual goals. Now we both strive to fulfill our mission to save lives who face a new deadly war. An assault on wills to live, attacks at individual cores. Onyx and I both had to experience what it felt to lose trust and hope and then find it renewed. Otherwise it is only lip service if it isn't something we've gone through. A quote from an unknown author reads, "Sometimes fear won't go away, so you will have to do it afraid." Ask Onyx and she will speak on my behalf that fear is a partner to my every day. It hasn't been removed as a foundation in which I stand. It's just that now I have four helping pawed hands.

I gave a part of my heart away by choice when I said *I do* to my husband Lee. The other half of my heart was stolen from me. I thought I would never recover it, that shame would be the only feeling I could embrace. Yet, that force bigger than us all was putting another plan in place. On the day I met Onyx, she walked toward me carrying a treasure bag gently between her teeth. I looked into her eyes as she carefully dropped this bag at my feet. With shaking hands, I pulled apart the drawstring to look inside. I have moments still, five years later, when

I can't quite believe my eyes. In stillness I looked, in silence I listened as the rhythm began to evenly beat. For in that bag was my heart that Onyx had brought back to me.

With Onyx by my side I have stood in front of others sharing my story in an effort to bring atonement to things that have taken place. My purpose, I knew, was to influence and lead change. Advocating to congress and major news agencies, spent to points broke of money and time. Nonstop promotion for laws almost passed and factual investigation of sexual assault crimes. In each interview, anger and bitterness walked out the door as forgiveness and worthiness slowly entered the doorway. Amidst judgment, hate, and disbelief, I found the courage to not shy away. That my story could inspire others to fight my aim.

Now my mission has expanded to new territory. Now it is time to inspire those who are searching for their key. I know what it is to enter the cavern looking for dynamite to create the rock collapse. I also know it is possible from that darkest place to start crawling back. Crawling may seem slow, but each handprint forward is a gigantic leap. Each inch forward is to the cadence *I cannot be beat*. I have known a life without joy, I have known a fear of sunrises and sunsets. The sunset a reminder that the dark will only grow darker and the sunrise that a long day lies ahead. I also know what it is to rediscover that every twenty-four hours of new beginnings is friend, not foe. To relish laughter that springs forth from the happiness of one's soul. I have known what it is to feel numb and yet feel the most searing pain. I have known what it is to will the next glass on the rocks to keep torturous memories at bay. I also know what it is to no longer need a drink, that leaning into what hurts the most is mutually benefiting. When I am willing to share my story without embarrassment, shame, or guilt, others who are struggling find in my story their own strength and will.

One step at a time or a puzzle piece that connects link by link. I opened one box that contained the next key. The next key opened another box that reinforced *you can do this, in yourself believe*. The next support system or lifeline available each time I opened another lock. I shifted from *I'm not sure* to *I cannot not*. Many messengers have been put on my path, angels sent from God up above. Next to me, spelled backward as D-O-G, is the best one with wings of unconditional love. Onyx loves me, her honor to serve and lead. She loves me not despite of, but because of my story.

I can stand at an entryway into any one of our spectacular national parks where the eyes cannot begin to absorb the beauty to take in. I can watch the sun set over a mountain or listen to the lyrics of the wolves as the evening begins. In the space there is no worry—there only *is* and *be*. Before Onyx, I couldn't come to a park, to the vast space surrounding me. Now it is the majestic expansiveness of these national parks I seek. I know that somewhere at the base of one of the mountains is a tiny cave, but I no longer feel the need to run to its cold walls and hide. Onyx reminds me I have within me a light that needs to shine. In these parks is a natural rhythm, a beat that hums in harmony. Like Onyx and my heart, in unison, a warrior team. Duty, honor, dignity, *I would give my life for you*. Dear Onyx, for guiding me to live again, my unending gratitude.

KRISTOPHER AND SHERA

And then my soul saw you and it kind of went
"Oh, there you are. I've been looking for you."

—Iain S. Thomas

Nine hundred miles, give or take, separated she and I physically; yet, space could not keep us from our destiny. She took her first breaths of life in Tennessee while I was feeling squeezed until I could scarcely breathe in New York City. She entered this life quickly learning she was not worthy while I, once worthwhile, was finding my sense of value fading. Not yet knowing love, she began traveling northeast to find belonging. It is said opposites attract, though I think that it is more opposites find each other to form a whole. Soon we would meet, knowing in that instant our souls had just found home.

Shera was five months old when my eyes met hers, and her eyes whispered *I am meant for you, and you are meant for me.* She knew before I did what her role in my life was meant to be. I saw her as companion while she saw her ability to service my journey with PTSD. Two years after her adoption, we began our certified training. The certified training was the formality. For Shera already knew how to listen to the rhythm of my heart when in irregular beat. If I was anxious, Shera was my mellow presence and her body on which I could lean. Her touch my reassurance that I was in safe keep. Or, if night gripped too tight, Shera the warrior to chase away the horrific dreams. Tap, tap, tap she would gently nudge until I would awake from those dark realities. Her beating heart my comfort until I could bring my entire being back into the bedroom. Until I could remove myself from the engraved and chiseled memories I knew.

I struggle to adequately describe the bond that Shera and I share—not because I am afraid or because I doubt that you will care. I struggle two-fold, maybe three. Let me do my best to explain though it's challenging for me. First, when one spends years "just" living with night terrors, hypervigilance, and public anxiety, one starts to accept it is part of daily living. Second, one learns that the public is uncomfortable hearing military stories that aren't filled with highlights of our victories and our bravery. If I share that I get afraid, I may not meet the images you desire to have and hold on to of the military. And third, have you ever had something that your heart struggled to find the words for because it was a feeling no words could adequately convey? Perhaps like hearing your unborn child's heartbeat for the first time when your breath was absolutely taken away.

I am blessed to be married to my best friend, and I love my stepchildren as if they were of my blood since they were conceived. Yes, now that *but* of what Shera has that my dear family is missing. Though I know my family accepts me as I am, in all my anxious sensitivity, a part of me worries about what they think. Through my ears I hear their judgments and through my eyes, I see their concern at what feelings are rising in me. They might not be thinking anything negative at all, but in my mind that is what I perceive. Shera's unconditional love and her ears—and heart—hear my voice when I can't find my own words to speak. Shera is the safety net that helps me feel completely free to be…me.

I mentioned earlier that I "lived with" PTSD in that "it just is what it is" mode. Prescription medications to sleep and to briefly enter crowded areas were part of what would help me cope. In 2015, a psychiatrist with the Veterans Administration gave me a prescription of a different kind. *Have you considered a service dog to accompany you by your side?* Shera was already filling that role—unofficially—at this time. I didn't need another service dog; I needed Shera to now earn her service stripes. Shera and I filled that script through AKC Canine Good Citizen training. With the passing of her Public Access Test, now Shera goes everywhere with me. And, very infrequently now is prescription medication a necessity.

I should qualify "everywhere," for there are certain situations in which Shera does not go. It is a choice I make that she should stay home. Just as Shera has my back and is ever vigilant at what is best for me, I, too, watch out to make sure Shera is not put into situations that aren't for her well-being. If a hike is the day's plan, but the outside temperature is nearing triple-digit degrees, Shera stays home so as not to be submerged in grueling heat. Shera may momentarily begrudge not going, for she wants to make sure she is there if I become in need. Yet, just as I know she is **always** keeping watch over me, Shera knows I have her back equally.

I know that Shera cannot fill the shoes of my comrades I had the honor of serving with for our country. Those can only be filled by the finest of men and women I have had the privilege of knowing. Yet, when Shera lays down behind my back when I am in a grocery story line, I can feel myself protected from all sides. I like to think that Shera can hear my comrades' heartbeats from distant spaces, wherever those spaces may be. Shera has a wisdom like that, a keen "knowing."

It isn't easy to be in a crowd longing for silence's sweet reprieve. And it isn't easy to be in silence with your thoughts screaming loudly. It is easy to be home because public places feel unsafe. And it isn't easy to be home because there is fear that can't be kept at bay. It is easy to feel better staying up for two or three days straight so that there can be one solid night of sleep. And it can be easy to long for staying asleep to avoid anxiety's reality. In this tug and pull, this stretch, this war that rages within that I don't always have the training to fight, Shera is the one who keeps me centered, moving forward, and upright.

Shera was our flower girl, best man, maid of honor, and I would argue the one to also give us away. Walking down the aisle and then next to my wife and I, Shera sat as we said *I do* on our wedding day. Once again, as Shera stood beside me, I could feel myself surrounded by so many more I couldn't see. Those I had once known were there in the shadows with raised hands in salute. *Kris, way to go man, this girl is most definitely the right one for you!*

Shera is an extension of my right arm, her mission to serve my needs. Her purpose is to support me as I journey with PTSD. Yet, when Shera heard me vow *to have and to hold*, Shera made this vow her own. If my wife is not feeling well, Shera is watchful of her as well as me. Guardian of my wife, too, while keeping me her top priority.

Shera has a second purpose—actually, we both do as a team. Our story is not just about hope, nor dignity. We also feel our story matters for the education we can provide. Dear public, please know some wounds are invisible to the naked eye. I may not be blind, deaf, nor missing of limb, but that does not mean I am not in need. I will never wish the kind of anxiousness and terror I feel near you, yet sometimes I wish you could walk in the footsteps of my feet. And please know, it is not you personally that nearly paralyzes me and threatens to take me to my knees fighting for breath or not to feel like I might explode. I won't have words that will make sense to you, but please know, I don't want to scare you when the walls feel like they are closing in around me. I also recognize that perhaps for you dogs are scary. Because I believe you know that the military places the highest value on one word—honor—which means everything. I promise you I will never put you in harm's way with Shera next to me. Please give her a chance, please withhold your judging, feel free to ask questions for better understanding. Just please don't pet her without first talking with me. I know there are some who abuse the service-dog system, which is unfortunate, but I also kindly ask you not to generalize. For the sake of twenty-two brave and honorable veterans who are daily fighting for their lives. A service dog could help a veteran live independently—and that is the key—*living*.

I have mentioned Shera's wisdom, her keen intuitiveness that isn't just to get my attention when she senses I need to remove myself from a large crowd before anxiety takes the lead. There are moments like when we visited a Starbucks in New York City. Dear Shera loves all ethnic backgrounds, not a discriminatory bone does she have. I can walk with her in my home city full of diversity and she will not negatively react. Anyway, into a Starbucks we walk passing a gentleman who appeared down on his luck, and who Shera immediately did not like. That Shera started to communicate in a low growl took me by surprise. A few minutes later, police arrived due to an incident that took place prior to us entering the door as customers that day. Shera had known something wasn't right immediately upon us entering that place.

If you see Shera jump up and put her paws on my chest, you might think she is not being a "good" dog because she is not staying down. This is how Shera communicates that she can hear how my heart is starting to rapidly pound. When anxiousness is starting to grip me, Shera lets me know it is time for us to find a quieter place, like going for a walk outside. Her other tactic if we are sitting is to put her paw on my leg, look for her leash, and will me to look into her eyes. Shera has a stubborn streak, too, if I am not paying attention as she speaks. For fifty pounds, give or take, she is very strong when she sits refusing to move her feet. I must say, I didn't know it possible to find anyone who knew the shape of my back as if it were their own, ever vigilant in their watch of me, I feel blessed that I have found another soul who is as diligent in guarding against what I may not immediately see.

These moments of anxiety in which Shera wills me outside are not life-and-death emergencies. Yet, in the depths of anxiety's grip, these times can feel like I am being pulled from life toward an ending in which I may no longer be able to breathe. I know sometimes Shera grows in her own anxiousness if she can't be by my side, yet she bravely hides it ever my calmer *Dad, it's all right.* A line had to be drawn in which she couldn't be in pre-op as I prepared for minor surgery. I can still see her excited greeting when I awoke in recovery. I confess, I'm not sure who was happier when our eyes did meet. Shera might be more expressive outwardly of what my heart is inwardly communicating. *I have missed you girl, oh have I missed you so. You are the biggest part of my heart, as I know you already know.*

Dad, I have missed you too, though I knew you were in safe keep. Through rooms and through space, I listen for your heartbeat. I would lay down my life for you, as I know you would lay down yours for me. Did I ever tell you, Dad, that I could hear you from all the way in Tennessee? Your voice was faint, but I could hear what your heart was trying to speak. Humility and pride, not wanting to burden people with your pain. Oh, how you were striving to be so brave. I was too, Dad, trying to be courageous and have faith. I knew I needed to get to you and that there would be a way. Even when I felt I wasn't wanted I would be quiet and listen to what my own heart was beating in rhythm to. It kept repeating your souls will reunite soon; he is looking for you. Dad, thank you for calling out to me loud enough for me to hear so that I would know North and East was the direction I needed to go. When my eyes looked into yours, my heart beat excitedly...HOME.

DESIREE AND CHUNKY

You never know how strong you are until
being strong is the only choice you have.

—Bob Marley

irror, mirror, on the wall, who is the fairest is certainly not me. For the longest time, this is what I believed. That *I am worthy* extinguished within me the moment I learned that trust is not always as it seems. Innocence has a bright side and it can suddenly find itself in the darkest of night. It can leave in an instant, a blink from sparkling eyes to loss of sight. The flame of wisdom that will come is not yet in reach; a journey through darkness alone until hope holds out a hand—or four tiny feet.

Mirror, mirror, self as you look back at me. We just didn't know, did we, when we were nineteen? I had faith in the goodness of people; I had faith in our country. I proudly served, I honored, and I respected authority. I felt safe in the embrace of family—both those of blood and those I would give my life for if need be. I was part of a very large team that "had my six" without question. This I knew to my core. Likewise, there is nothing I wouldn't do to protect my comrades and commanders against any enemy coming through the door.

What I didn't know was that the enemy could be on the same side of the door as me. I didn't realize when I vowed to give my all to my country, it would include giving up all rights to my body. Brotherhood and sisterhood in arms don't always translate to meaningful sibling bonds when outside a war zone. There is a line that can get crossed where there is a deafness to the word *no.*

Mirror, mirror, I thank you, though, for your bravery. Even though your spirit was crushed and slipping away, you didn't let go of me. You were in shock, but you continued listening. *Something isn't right, though*

I don't know what I need. Yet, I will find someone who can help; I will not retreat.

At the Balboa Naval Hospital, my first greeting was a handshake of shame. Certainly, my nineteen-year-old breath hinting at beer meant I was to blame. Though I wasn't new to labels as self-definition, on this night I began expanding my identity. I was handed labels I had not before seen. Daughter, niece, and naval servicewoman were labels I proudly wore. I was now also liar, rebellious, and, well, I anticipate you can imagine the label that begins with *wh* and contains the word *or*.

Life is about duality, like good and evil, or truthfulness and lies. For each person who didn't believe me, someone was brought to stand by my side. Of course, the first call was to the person who has always given me her unconditional love. My mom was the first voice to assure me she would not let go. A kind soul from NCIS helped me retain my dignity, and another female officer held my hand so graciously.

My dear aunt was brought to a crossroads that evening—a crossroads that would test her personal beliefs. Perhaps even more that my military training was her reverent respect of authority. Fear is a powerful force, sometimes stronger than the love held for family. Equally powerful too, is the devastation when one realizes that not all authority exemplifies high integrity. Both these feelings were coursing through my aunt as she picked me up from the hospital realizing I did not plan to go back to the ship though they were expecting me. She was angry at what had happened and angry at me for my consideration of not returning. Through her shock and disbelief was her equally strong wish to support and help me.

And, such is the ripple effect of a moment in time that does not impact only one person or two. That moment cascades from the violated to their loved ones now hurled into powerlessness to know what to do. It can also trigger a third powerful force called guilt—*if only I could have met you at the ship for your weekend leave. Perhaps you wouldn't have experienced this if it wasn't for me.* My aunt was not responsible being unable to meet me while our ship was at port in her home state. That is what helplessness can do, though—such is the grappling with heartache.

After the final report, one communication was I could go home on temporary leave. Yet, communication to my aunt consisted of a different plan for me. The "true" plan was I would return to the ship having the same job responsibilities, the same job, with the same individual who had just taken an essence of me. I needn't worry, for there was a chaplain available for any issues that might arise. My intuition said if I did not change this course of action, my safety would be compromised. Mirror, mirror, yes, you looking back at me. I need to reiterate my gratitude that you could hear that voice from down deep.

There was a long layover in which terror became my twin shadow walking beside me. *Oh, please let me make it home without being stopped, please, PLEASE.* Snares and lies guided my trip as text messages played detective in the name of friendship trying to see where I might be. For the sake of my well-being and others, too, I met lies by planting a divergence seed until I could surround myself with others who knew best what to do. I am not an advocate of lying; please don't misunderstand me. Yet, for the greater good of many involved, sometimes bending truth is the only choice seen.

My mother was a guardian angel and a fighter, especially when it came to me. Making sure I got the help I needed while rallying news coverage. Her boyfriend guided me to a VA facility where I could begin counseling. A painful trial in which I was handed affirming labeling; *admit it, Desiree, look into that mirror and then tell me. Come on, you lied and made up this whole thing.*

Oh mirror, mirror, you inside there, thank you for standing beside me. The truth can win out if we can hold strong without breaking. This time his violation would not be quietly tucked away. We did it, mirror, we ended a pattern of abusing rank. I know, mirror. I know you know the truth we managed to hide from the jury staring with their intent eyes. If only they could see just how shattered I was inside. I courageously voiced my truth and I adorned my armor against the hate and shame aimed at my heart. Dear mirror, is that a crack in my shield, just to the right of my left arm?

The arrow of self-hate can penetrate deep, oh so very deep. Depression, prescription medications, hopelessness inch-by-inch as it pierces one's heartbeat. Twelve hours in bed become fifteen, twenty, twenty-three. What is there to get up for? I'll just lie here and sleep several hours—or days—more. Mirror, mirror, self I am choosing to look the other way today, tomorrow, and the next day. It is these voices that I am hearing play, and replay, and replay. *Stupid, you should be ashamed, how could you not know better, you are worthless, you know that, right? Let's repeat this like a mantra until it is the only label you keep in your sights.*

Mirror, mirror, I see you looking at me. Don't give up on me, please. Dear soul, I see you, behind my mind and my body. I'm going through these tests and I'm taking these medicines…please know I'm trying. I could use an extra hand, though, who sees me for more than my labeling. Someone who can look past the chart that reads *addict* and see past this scar across my cheek. I've nearly died from head injuries in an accident that I know I am responsible for, yet soul, you know it also wasn't completely me. I'm trying to make my way out of this house of mirrors that is only showing me *everything about you is ugly.* I can steer in a new direction; I know I can. Dear soul standing back in that mirror, can you bring me that hand?

Hello, little one, welcome to this thing called life. My, look how big you are…oh, wait, please, fight, come on big guy, fight. One, two, three, four, breathe. In you, big guy, I believe. Well, look at you reaching out for me. I think I have just found a hand, in the form of four furry feet. Hello, Chunky Dunky, I sure am grateful that it is life you chose. I didn't know it until now, but I've been waiting for you and your cold nose.

Determination; where there is a will, there will always be a way. And twenty-three of those twenty-four hours—wait let me rephrase, for no longer is staying in bed how I pass the time away. For my waking hours, Chunky keeps me laughing continually. If he wasn't Chunky, he could have easily been named Goofy. Seventy-five pounds of strength, and not just physically. His spirit is my courage and my calming. Perhaps you've heard the expression where something ends and something begins is not easily distinguished. That is how to describe the bond between Chunky and me.

Chunky my eyes, my ears, the rhythm of my heart when it is calm and when it is afraid. Through him I have found self-respect and I have found a renewed faith. Faith in others, faith in life, faith in myself without prescriptions as my coping strategy. Belief in the power of listening, not just hearing and trust to allow feeling. No longer do I want to miss a day of living, numb in the goodness a day can contain. After all, there is a certain someone counting on me to fill most of each day with play...goofy, silly, unconditionally loving...play.

Sincerity is important to me. Genuineness. Authenticity. Doing what is right for the right reasons, no matter how hard it might be. I have admiration for individuals who exhibit these traits. I'd like to be like them someday.

What is that, mirror, mirror, that you speak? Yes, I see that there is someone standing there with you looking at me. I see a woman and I see what looks like someone in a fur coat with four feet. I can't quite hear what is being said but know that I am listening. Could you speak just a touch louder for me? Um, I'm not sure I know what to say. I think I need time to absorb your words, if I may. I think I'll sit down here next to Chunky, and yes, I see that the reflection in the mirror is doing the same thing. Chunky, can you hear what they are saying to me? That I am well on my way to being the person I admire for courageously doing the right things with the right reasoning? Including choosing life, self-worth, forgiveness, and dignity?

Mom, I hear what the mirror whispers, and it is true. You made a choice to make it matter what you experienced by pushing through. Mom, when I entered this world, I heard you call to me to choose life, even if it wouldn't be easy. In that moment, I found purpose because you needed me. You may not have known your strength at that point, but I could hear it in your voice as you called "Big Guy, don't leave." I knew my mom was not only so very strong, but she also genuinely and unconditionally loved me. And together we would take this life by storm with open hearts, determined, and...rather goofily. I love you, Mom. Where I begin, and you end, no seams between.

BRYAN AND ROXY

Yet there be certain times in a young man's life,
when, through great sorrow or sin, all the boy in
him is burnt and seared away so that he passes at
one step to the more sorrowful state of manhood.

—Rudyard Kipling

Some might say I grew up too quickly, thrust into adulthood that even wise elders would hope to never experience in advanced age. For me, it is as simple as I was fulfilling a commitment and a vow I had made. I enlisted in the Marine Corps at the age of seventeen. By age twenty-one, I was a "pro" at living overseas.

My first deployment to An Nasiriyah, Iraq ushered me into the ripe "ole" age of nineteen. My second deployment to Fallujah, Iraq celebrated my "rite of passage" to adulthood with me. *Cheers to twenty-one, my fellow comrades, oh, and I'll have another, if you please. Keep 'em coming, my friend, no need to keep me thirsty.*

I entered Boot Camp in February 2001 just out of twelfth grade. In December, tents anchored in sand were my main stay. I returned home after the ground invasion that took place in March 2003. I came home with the abundant support of my best friend to see friends and family. Your mind may now have an image of a fellow Marine and me, how our friendship formed and grew when times were most challenging. Before you continue with that image, let me make sure to set you straight. My best friend I brought home was the comfort of being in a drunken state.

If only it was as simple as a young man sowing his wild oats as some youth tend to do. Sure, we can say that is what it was, but at the deepest—and darkest core—of me, I know the truth. I look back on that time now and refer to is as a train already starting to crash. It would take a few more years to play out the aftermath. The happily drunk part of me was on an Amtrak train speeding through the days. Memories I was trying to obliterate were always at the bottom of each bottle I drank.

Thankfully, after about ten months, I was given a gift to escape, a second tour of duty for me in Kuwait. After all, it was not only my commitment and my vow as a Marine, it was a comfort of home not found in the safety of civilian surroundings. Serve, protect, push away the threat of hangings; after all, it is contractors in Fallujah, and not us Marines. One more swallow will wash away any fear or pain. *Ah, yes, there, a moment's peace once again I gain.*

Once again, I traveled back to the United States with my best friend by my side. This time we welcomed ourselves home by really doing it "right!" We earned a DUI our first night back from the desert sands. *Ah, yes, a night behind steel bars is sure grand! Well, my friend, we are going to be a little thirsty until we can leave this joint and get ourselves another drink. But I promise, as soon as we get out of here, it's straight to the store or bar—just you and me!*

The thing about our friendship was that we were an inseparable pair. Wherever I went, I could be assured my friend was always there. That was actually a positive thing, contrary to what you might think. Because I was never not drunk, I was not acting out inappropriately. My best friend and I preferred beer over liquor—we knew what we could hold without getting ourselves into trouble we couldn't undo. From sunrise to sunset to sunrise again we had our drinking groove.

The first time a door started to crack open to reveal what I was choosing not to see was on a date for my favorite cuisine when my hand began shaking as I tried to eat. There is nothing better than that big scoop of salsa with a nice salty tortilla chip. Salsa was being wasted, spilling everywhere, as I strived to take a bite after that chip was dipped!

My best friend and I got lonely, though we didn't realize we were at the time. A broken arm was the matchmaker for us to gain a trio at our sides. Prescribed pain medication joined our daily routine. *Ah, yes, twice the addiction if you please. Why, thank you, I don't mind if I do; I will gladly chase these down with a swig or two.*

Of course, you can see it coming, can't you? Before you receive the news. Headlines read "Train Derailment Leaves Debris Scattered Far and Wide." Not really headline news as in I'm famous—just an analogy for what started to feel like an out-of-control life. Another visit behind steel bars and the feeling that I was slipping away from my mind.

Have you ever come to a bridge spanning across a wide gorge a long way below your feet? Though a part of you can see that the bridge is sturdy, your eyes are drawn to the empty space that has no ropes for security. Perhaps like how you might feel a little dizzy if afraid of heights. Part of you is drawn to move toward the edge, though you are petrified you will fall and die. There are no words to describe the movement I made from the train to the rollercoaster to begin a new way of traveling through my life. I will simply say no amusement park has such a twisting, turning, harshly up-and-down ride. Thank your lucky stars, too, for I would not want you to ever be tempted to visit and see for yourself. To be on a violently rapid ride to want to die *and* to want to live is nothing short of hell.

It's funny—not in a humorous way, but in that way we use the phrase when we are in awe—you can think you have a best friend until you meet the one who is truly best of all. This is a good time in my story to introduce you to the one who completes me. She is sweet, a tad pushy when she knows what she wants, and is impeccable in listening. And she is so smart—did I mention, she's earning a college degree? This might sound kind of silly, but we celebrate the gift of allergies. No, not ours, but because of someone else's she found her way to me. She is my best friend and the savior of my life—literally.

My dear service dog, Roxy—and my loved ones such as my beautiful fiancée and my children—struggle when I share this part of my story. Yet, to not share dilutes what is an essence of me. Sure, sometimes I'd like nothing more than to unwrite a couple of chapters, burn the pages as if they didn't exist as part of my history. Yet, I'm coming to understand that the vow I made in 2001 is even more important now, thus my sharing.

More than once I've tried to take my life, and truth be told, the thoughts haven't been magically erased from my mind in entirety. I guess, just like war, fighting for one's life is a continual priority. It is hard to share this for I don't want friends and family to feel they are not enough in their love for me. It **IS** because of the love given to me that I am here to tell you my story.

Perhaps I can best explain it if you were to think of a pie chart made up of your favorite things. Each of the pieces of that pie add up to 100 percent complete. My friends, my fiancée, my children, my membership with Wounded Warrior Project, earning my college degree—all of these add up to, let's say 75 percent of what makes me whole. The remaining 25 percent comes from one who holds up a mirror to me to reflect the strength of my soul.

It is said that when us humans listen to each other speak, each of us is listening in at least two ways to what the other person has to say. We listen from the other's perspective and we listen from our own, true. Each of us hears from our experiences, our fear points, and our values, too. We also listen from a place of anticipating what the other person is thinking. This can greatly influence our speaking. *How will they respond if I say it this way?* A continual internal dialogue that influences the conversation taking place. As if this wasn't complicated enough, there is yet a third way we listen to each other speak. *What they must think of me!* And often that it must not be good is our certainty.

And we wonder why each of us as humans find it hard sometimes to "talk" about what we are feeling! That is a lot of layers for unconditional listening! I think that is why Roxy holds such a large percent of the pie to complete me. She can hear my heart without any preconceiving. I don't worry that I am letting her down or what she might be thinking. I don't perceive she is seeing the parts of me that I am certain in my own perceptions are unworthy.

My affection for a dog was not new with Roxy; a love for dogs has always been a part of my soul. My fiancée was less immediately sold on the idea of fur entering our home. In that nothing-is-coincidence way a fundraising event planted the first seed to finding Roxy. We met a couple in which a service dog was his centering. My fiancée looked into a mirror when she looked into this veteran's wife's eyes; I resonated with the personal story of this veteran's life.

Both my fiancée and I saw possibility in the mirrors this couple were holding. We could move from rough to good on our way to even better and great based on what they were sharing. Patience and gracious acceptance among my fiancée's strengths whenever I resisted leaving home—which was pretty much any time she mentioned, "Hey, let's go." More than the fact she was ready to do some things out and about in public where I felt so unsafe, my dear fiancée desired for me to find within myself what she knew was lying in wait. My fiancée not only felt she and I could find some fun adventures—and that good Mexican cuisine! My fiancée felt people were missing out on value I could bring.

We began exploring service-dog options, finding an eighteen-month to two-year wait. I couldn't predict tomorrow, let alone what felt a lifetime away. These options didn't feel like they had viability. The noes that lead us to the yes, or in this case, as mentioned above, the gift of allergies. My fiancée found a four-year-old black Lab in need of a new home when a new child in the family became sensitive to Roxy's fur coat. We didn't see this "small" bundle staring back at us as a service dog, per se. Remind me to come back to my italics for "small"— translation, Roxy, in reality, was twice her perceived weight.

In that way the heart communicates *this is it* before we understand *it,* Roxy was on her way to our home. I must say, acquiring a fluent traveler made me nervous about how much she'd want to be on the go. Joking aside, Roxy was born in Wisconsin, yet had visited California and Alaska, enjoying the frequent new scenery. In fact, I should show you a picture sometime of her poised in front of the Hollywood sign so regally! Roxy had been part of a Coast Guard family, so changing home base was something she knew how to do. A little over one year ago, our home became hers, too.

Two miles from our home is a dog trainer whose training includes— yes, you guessed it, service-dog accrediting. Now Roxy is my service dog, going 99 percent of the time with me. Ah, yes, I owe you an explanation about "small" before I continue with my story. My dear fiancée was the first to see Roxy on the computer screen, excitedly asking me, "What do you think?" Now remember, my fiancée was the one uncertain about fur, our furniture, and oh, most certainly fur everywhere on our bedding. She immediately saw Roxy as thirty pounds, which meant in my fiancée's eyes, she could manage the shedding. Let's just say, Roxy found a way to convince my fiancée that sixty pounds is made for one thing—cuddling!

I was going to be gone for a few days on a Wounded Warrior Project trip in which I couldn't take Roxy with me. For my absence, I decided to make a perch next to my side of the bed for Roxy to sleep. I left with the assurance that Roxy would not be in our bed when I returned home. After all, there is not room for fur on a comforter, as you know. I'm laughing as I say that because, see, I'm fortunate to be surrounded by two very determined women in my life. As I walked out the door, Roxy gave me a wink of her eye.

Let me fast-forward to my return home from my trip. That there would be room for me on my own side of the bed was the trick. Whining and pacing can do wonders for getting attention that something is amiss. It crumbles even the strongest willed souls after a few hours of this! *Okay Roxy, fine, come to bed and stop that relentless pace! You can come into bed this night, and this night only, okay?* These were my fiancée's exasperated words that first night I was away. Roxy jumped into bed, and immediate sleep was both their embrace. Well, needless to say, it has been the longest "one night" several weeks and months later as we sleep. There is now plenty of room in our bed for fur scattered across the comforter and sheets!

Hearts communicate through space no matter the physical distance that separates. Roxy needed to keep my side of the bed protected and safe. Roxy "owns" our bed, each room of our house, my car, and the space next to me in any public setting. Where she begins and where I end is blended seamlessly. I like these two quotes for they seem to capture the bond between Roxy and me. How for each other we are the 50 percent to make us complete. One is from Roger Caras who writes a truth I know: *Dogs are not our whole lives, but they make our lives whole.* The other is from an unknown author: *They might be here a part of our lives, but to them we are their whole life.* Where Roxy begins and where I end does not have a dividing line. Roxy fuels my strength of will not to give up because I know equally she needs me by her side.

I mentioned above how we as humans—because we are human— spend our lives trying to learn unconditional love and listening. Or perhaps it is that we spend a portion of our lives trying to unlearn from the experiences that taught us conditional accepting. It wasn't easy when Roxy and I first became a team. Going out in public with her was incredibly distressing. See, the thing is, I put aside how I can hear you in three ways—my perception, my thinking what you are thinking, and my consideration of what you are thinking of me. I also have an intuition that notices when your scowls are disapproving.

I know it isn't "normal" to be in a public setting with a canine, even more uncertain when you can't see I have a visible disability. And believe me, I'm the first to not want Roxy lying on the floor of a restaurant because of my concerns that it may not be sanitary. I ask that you meet us halfway by giving us patience and understanding. My brothers and sisters who served and me aren't trying to bring discomfort to your surroundings. None of us would ever wish you to walk a day in our shoes; we don't advocate for that kind of understanding. We only ask that you hold the space for us to find our ability to walk in our own again without it feeling debilitating. Just as we trained to serve and protect for our country, we have trained to ensure our service dogs maintain your safety. Our vow is to always keep your well-being first in our priority. In order to do that, we need our service dogs so that we can continue believing. A belief that we have a purpose in living that includes a fur coat and pawed feet.

Dad, have I ever told you that though that Hollywood sign was cool and all, and Alaska was beautiful to see, the best views I have had is when driving the Florida coast beside you in the front seat? I am getting really excited, too, for graduation day. I think I'm going to be the best-dressed student walking the procession in May. And I'm so glad for how well you know me, Dad, no investing in a cap to match my gown. That cap would very quickly be left behind me on the ground! And to think I will get to do this not just once, but twice. Heck, Dad, maybe even three times if you decide PhD sounds nice. I like that thought—Dr. Roxy. It has a rather nice ring to it, don't you think?

Dad, I'm proud of you and your incredible bravery. I know some days threaten to take you to your knees. Yet, ingrained in you since the day you enlisted for the Marines, you have a mission to serve and protect others in need. Some moments of that day the need is one of your children when they are calling. Other days it is Mom, or as you like to call the love of your life, your wife, Jess. Twenty-four hours a day, of course, it's yours truly. Along with your brothers and sisters who are also fighting this PTSD enemy.

It is said that we may not always know the difference we make in someone else's life. Yet, by us fully showing up as ourselves, we may inspire a stranger passing by. Dad, I know you don't necessarily see the classmates watching you and me or some of the strangers in a store when we pass by their staring. Yet, I see their eyes as they look at me and you. Many of those eyes speak, "Thank you for all that you've done and all that you do."

One of the gifts of being a dog is I can hear hearts without words spoken—like how I can hear things you say when your eyes look at me. Or how I can hear the pain you are feeling sometimes when you sleep. So, Dad, trust me when I say there are many eyes looking at you in gratitude. Of course, their eyes will never begin to reflect as much love as I have for you. Two halves to make a whole, that is you and me. Where I begin and you end is stitched together in perfect harmony.

TOM AND ZOEY

*I am not the same having seen the moon
shine on the other side of the world*

—Mary Anne Radmacher

On this side of the world, Mulino, Oregon had been home. A small, hometown community of 1,200 neighbors I had known. If I was given only one word to describe my upbringing, fun would be the most fitting. Like the classic movies or a perfect dream, athletic, popular, well-liked by teachers—that was me. Molalla High School saw my coming of age. Then off to college I went with a plan to be like my father one day.

I would follow with certainty in their footsteps when adulthood would find me. I would build a similar foundation for my family. The sureness, the safety, the love around which I was raised. Yes, my children would know the same "someday." I would marry and I would have two sons so that they could know brotherhood like my own brother and me. And I would have a daughter—their sister—for both sons to protect and keep watch of the boys that come knocking. I would provide all that my family could want or need. My wife would be the glue that kept us all on track, from sunup until it was time to sleep.

I would walk steps similar to my father's, my grandfather, my brother, two uncles, and great-uncles as well. Yet, it would take until I was twenty before I felt compelled. My father had served in the United States Army during the Vietnam era and my grandfather a Purple Heart veteran fought in the Battle of Okinawa during World War II. One great-uncle fought in the Battle of the Bulge and another great-uncle flew thirty-five successful bombing missions while he served during World War II like my grandfather had, too. Another uncle had served in Vietnam, and my brother was currently in active duty. No longer resistant to the recruiter, I knew it was now my time to carry forward this part of the family legacy. I began basic training at the age of twenty.

My ultimate goal to follow in my father's footsteps as firefighter was held firmly in my clenched fist. First, my goal was to serve with the 82nd Airborne as my father did. First, Fort Benning, second Fort Sam Houston, and then one step closer to being in Airborne school. I then found myself assigned with HHC as I desired to be. With HHC, First 505th PIR (Parachute Infantry Regiment), division of the 82nd Airborne where I became infantry medic—*Dad, look, I'm one step closer to my dreams.*

Life has a way of helping us realize our dreams, yet sometimes the realization isn't matching exactly. I became a firefighter, but not of flames that are tackled with water to extinguish their destructive tendencies. The fires I would be putting out were of crisis moments saving lives and addressing physical injuries. I was destined to be put into the center of one of the hottest fires, metaphorically speaking. Destined for sure, given a knee injury.

It has taken time to understand that a *no* in 2001 was leading me to a larger purpose I was meant to fulfill during my deployment in 2003. Sometimes I still question how it is said we are always right where we are supposed to be. I was stationed at Fort Benning when another paratrooper landed on my knee. It was April 12th 2001, my 21st birthday. I remember it well for it was the day I graduated and during the ceremony my father pinned my wings on me. This very special moment shared with my father followed by knee displacement, two broken ribs, and knee surgery.

Fort Bragg, North Carolina would be my next home destined to be. A second knee injury during the Best Medic Competition required a second surgery. It was September 13, 2002, and as I recovered, my unit deployed without me. It still creates a catch in my even breathing that I was separated from my 82nd team. Loyalty runs deep, along with brotherhood bonding. Distance and accidents don't separate those feelings. I was reassigned to the 28th CSH, 44th Med Com, 18th ABN Corps not yet aware a whole new definition of what it means to be a team was waiting for me.

My time to serve was coming just a few short months away. Of course, I didn't know that until a funeral leave needed to be shortened to one day. I was on emergency leave to pay tribute to a great-grandmother when the call came. *Thomas, you are needed immediately back at Fort Bragg. Soon after, you will depart for Kuwait.*

I landed in Kuwait March 9, 2003. Now on the other side of the world away from lush green to sand as far as the eye could see, Camp Doha became home for a few weeks. Destiny by my side, though I couldn't yet see, I was being led to the greatest fire any of us had known. It is the fire that fuels the human spirit—the fire of the soul. Just as my father vowed every day for thirty-three years he would serve and protect families, so I would give my all to serve and protect for my country. I would whisper these same words when the signal came: *When I am called to duty, God; wherever flames may rage; give me the strength to save some life, whatever be its age.* As the Firefighter's Prayer further communicates, this too I would vow to pray: *Enable me to be alert; and hear the weakest shout; and quickly and efficiently to put the fire out.*

Before I would step beside the beating heart of these fires, I first had to build my armor of strength. Tested in my resilience to the missile interceptions overhead and held under chemical alert until an all clear that we were now safe. March 20, 2003 launched missiles flew over this base. I was in the warehouse at the time when we heard the sirens signal *air raid.* From this, it was deemed we were now at a Level 3— translation, wear chemical suits in 125 degree heat. These suits were chemical-protective clothing for our safe keep. Twenty-four seven our attire until *all clear* from the NBC (nuclear biologic chemical) team.

It isn't always easy to recognize where grace walks amidst the demolition that war brings. Life has a way of bringing gifts quite miraculously. Before leaving Camp Doha for our mobile surgical hospital setup, I volunteered to convoy as one of nineteen. Our mission was to get vehicles from Camp Arifjan back to Camp Doha quickly. Upon arriving at Camp Arifjan, I recognized a placard with the numbers one, eight, and three. That placard could only mean one thing, my certainty. *He is here, he is here somewhere, I know he must be!*

My legs felt like they were slow-pouring molasses as I tried to move quickly when I saw my blood brother's back. Then again, I don't think I've ever run that fast. Let me say, grabbing a soldier from behind is not necessarily a wise thing. It earned me a flip onto my back before my sibling recognized me. The desert was a little less dry that day as both of us shed tears. And I can still hear my mother's voice when her two sons called together easing her fears. I will always be grateful to the commanders who let me stay the night with his team. Talking, playing cards, and ingesting some of my big brother's bravery.

Each experience in life is the paving stone for the next step in our journey. I was taught a high degree of confidence in my military training. Yet, we also need each new experience to grow in our abilities. That five-day convoy from Camp Doha to Camp Dogwood would significantly teach me. In 2003, everyone was learning; not just me but our overall military.

We didn't have armor to wear, nor was it part of our vehicle designs. Canvas doors and wooden slats for the tailgates was what we had to hide behind. Civilians were hungry and thirsty, begging of anything we might be able to spare. *Look again, that civilian is holding something else as he stands there.* An outreached left hand could be holding a bomb in the right. Continuous threats everywhere for our lives. Five days of my life a blur convoying to our soon-to-be tent hospital in the middle of sand. In other ways, it was the longest five days of my life I have ever had.

We reached an old abandoned power station complex with multiple outbuildings. And, the flattest desert area as far as the eye could see. There was one oasis between five—seven thousand meters away. Engineers had arrived before us to dig the trenches around this hospital base. Trenches were necessary for two things. One for us to retreat in if necessary, and the other, to bury those no longer living.

When in high school, I thought I had learned how to make decisions quickly. That was the other side of the world, before I would learn a whole new meaning of "rapidly." Word quickly spread that there was a hospital in the area for patients in need. Before we were fully set up, we were treating the injured—some quite severely. We were welcomed, and we were not, equally. As we treated patients, we listened to mortars falling routinely. Marine LAVs (light armor vehicles) guarded our backs as we strived to be the backbone for those in need. Now a hospital tent city set up, saving lives while vigilantly alert for the lurking enemy.

Perhaps now as you read this you are having a memory flash. You may be thinking about Hawkeye, Trapper, Margaret O'Houlihan—characters from *Mash*. I, too, sometimes prefer to think of my experiences like this TV series. Except, one key difference from TV and reality—unlike *Mash*, we didn't know who was friend or enemy. There were no distinct lines between those who meant us harm and those dressed in civilian clothes. An enemy could be standing right next to you, and you wouldn't know. Sometimes it is easier to think of my memories watched and not lived firsthand. Most of the time, I am so very proud of the experiences I lived, serving beside and for my fellow man.

Our tent camp had two field medic landing zones for air ambulances, eight trauma beds, X-ray capabilities, an ICU, an ER, and a surgical "room" too. For our tent camp, think of an A-frame about eighty feet long, twenty feet wide, and eight sectional rooms. Our OR was a metal box—think shipping container modified. Much better than a tent to keep sand outside. Very tight corridors putting it mildly. Tight space for nonstop response to incoming patients with little reprieve. One doctor, two nurses, and two medics were the staff per shift, though the twelve-hour rotations were only a formality. We were a twenty-four seven operation, our seven-person team. We did our best to rotate, taking turns sleeping. A curse and yet a blessing was when a shamal would arrive. Translation—a forceful dust storm that would halt all missions for a short time. Though we didn't need the raging dust to threaten our makeshift hospital already coated in sand, we welcomed sleep as the gift this gale-force wind was holding in its hand.

I anticipate you've heard the expression "wearing many hats," and now I hear you chuckling. You know this expression quite well, then, as I see you counting. Sometimes it is hectic, isn't it, juggling the different roles? I empathize with you on how it can take its toll. I wore the hat of medic, and sometimes I had to put on other hats when we were extremely busy. I was nurse and I was physician assistant if need be. I didn't anticipate I would acquire the skill to perform hemothorax treatments, or the method of relieving excess blood out of a chest cavity. This was a lifesaving measure to restore the ability to breathe. I also didn't dream I would have the responsibility of putting to final rest civilians whose loved ones were not able to claim their bodies. I know a reality of war can mean unmarked graves; that I could have ensured proper burials for each one remains my wish today.

Each emergency event can replay in my memories with such frequency. In those moments, I can find my adrenaline racing as fast as if I were back in that medic seat. I still remember moments like the time a local prisoner of war camp had been mortar attacked putting eighteen individuals in traumatic need. I "broke the rules" that day with my CPR training; though I used both hands, they were not in unison for one heartbeat. My left hand was working to save one individual while my right hand was working to get the other person to breathe. That the blood of the soul pressing the chest under my left hand was covering the soul whose chest I was pressing under my right is a memory I cannot easily free from my mind's sight. Vigilant for the two souls directly in front of me, while also aware that behind these two individuals were more wounded incoming. *We don't have enough resources*, our urgent plea. *We need more resources, you, over there, help right here, now, hurry!* Soldiers not trained as medics were quickly learning how to insert an IV. The wind swirled the sand around the tent flaps as we clamored to restart a heartbeat.

I was handed another hat to wear, burning like that fire I mentioned above—the fire of an individual heartbeat. Some heartbeats were so very faint, a voice no longer able to speak. Yet, I could listen closely to the whisper of their soul communicating *help me have peace and dignity.* I still hold tightly to this hat I wore then, clenching it so tightly I'm convinced life will not come back into my white knuckles frozen in place. I am certain each and every one of their faces will be with me the rest of my days.

I anticipate if I asked you about a time you stood at a crossroads to decide left or right, you would share with me a time you were wrestling with what to decide. Have you ever had a time where you felt yourself squeezed between wrong or right? For me, what I think about each day is being sandwiched between death and life.

I stood next to a critically wounded soldier while a doctor performed a cardiac massage to resuscitate the soldier's now quiet heart. Death entered and took this soldier in its outstretched arms. A civilian also critically wounded was the next patient in need. At this point there was no clean surgical equipment due to the influx of mass casualties. In addition, the doctor was tending to other trauma injuries. Those multiple hats I mentioned previously—well, I wore another one when I assisted a doctor to perform hemothorax treatment by removing blood from a chest cavity. Our tools were a medic's Gerber knife, pliers, and iodine to sterilize these tools before using.

The doctor and I were a team working feverishly side by side, the actual time to perform this lifesaving measure quicker than I can describe. The doctor inserted a blade of one tool while I opened the patient's chest. Then with another multi-tool, the doctor broke ribs to allow hand access. Strength of my body was required to expose the pericardium for the doctor to begin the massage of the heart. Then, while the doctor prepped the pacer, my hand became the heart's massage. Together we completed the last step which was attach clips to the pericardium for the pacer to take over what we were doing manually. The patient was then rushed to surgery. With a doctor's guidance, I had just performed my first heart massage to keep someone alive. Miraculously—and I still can't quite believe it was at our hands—this civilian survived.

And here is a test a veteran faces every day as they journey with PTSD. To find the ability to focus on the lives saved and not continually see the ones who no longer breathe. I close my eyes and imagine this civilian with his family. I close my eyes tighter as tears roll down my cheeks. *Please know comrades and civilians who I couldn't return safely—alive—to your families, I was trying my best to do just that—that I couldn't, I'm so very sorry.*

There is a quote by A.D. Williams that talks about the bond between animals and humans: *When I look into the eyes of an animal I do not see an animal. I see a living being. I see a friend. I feel a soul.* Though I didn't know this quote then, this is how I felt tending to each person before their return to home. I couldn't necessarily erase the wounds of the living nor make whole those whose heart was now at rest. But I could take the time and extra measures to make sure they looked their best. Dignity for the solider and for the family. Some very small part I tried to play in easing the journey for loved ones about to step into profound grief.

With this same compassion, knowing that underneath the skin we each are the same, I would try to tend to civilians the same way. Sometimes we had to make choices to honor their souls differently than might be their belief. If we couldn't return their physical bodies, we would trust we were still acting respectfully. We tried our best to honor the religion of civilians by burying souls with their heads toward Mecca and before sundown. If we did not have a full body to link arms and legs to, we felt it better to cremate to protect from wild dogs. *Ashes to ashes and dust to dust* as cremation took place. The best we could do to bid someone their final rest with reverent grace.

I know I am sharing much that may be hard to read. I don't blame you if you are saying to yourself *when can I read about Zoey?* There are two reasons I share details about my first deployment as I have in my story. One is that when other veterans who struggle with PTSD read this, they will know that someone understands their pain kept under lock and key. No one wants to hear the ugliness of war we've experienced, or so we perceive. The second reason is I believe that to truly know one feeling, one must experience the opposite feeling. To know why Zoey has given me hope, understanding my hopelessness is beneficial so that you can truly appreciate how important she is to me. Maybe I have a third reason, too, in sharing these details of my story. That you can find compassion for veterans suffering from PTSD. Perhaps my story can bridge your empathy to our suffering that is not always visibly seen.

Let me shift gears a little and talk about some positive experiences near the end of my deployed time. Like mail, relocation to Baghdad, and a firework display grander than any Fourth of July.

If you ever wonder just how much mail means to a soldier on

assignment away from home? Let me tell you, to receive mail is like receiving gold. At one point during deployment roadside bombs limited supply lines creating significant rationing. Two bottles of water and one meal per day and no physical activity. I come by it honestly, the desire to help and serve humanity. One letter home and my medical team I was deployed with was immediately adopted by my family. Package after package, filled with such precious commodities like peanuts and beef jerky.

With one particular package, my father put himself in my shoes instead of the other way around. Magazines, toothpaste, toothbrush, and Listerine mouthwash upon first use I instantly spit out. A note from my father confirmed the contents of this different tasting mouth rinse were for a different type of swig. The note read simply *Focus on the mission. Keep your teeth clean. Enjoy the Listerine.* I am certain I am not alone from my team in still feeling that sweet pause in time; for a bit the war was farthest away from all our minds. We passed that bottle of whiskey around like it was better than a third bottle of water we might get to drink. Twenty minutes later a mortar attack delivered to us more wounded, and a rapid thrust back to reality.

In August 2003 we relocated our tent hospital to Baghdad to a building permanent and stationary. No more tent flaps, a mobile chest for an inpatient desk, or a shipping container for surgeries. Ibn Si'na Hospital, now known as the Green Zone, we reestablished. Medical maintenance teams refurbished broken equipment getting them operational once more. We even had barracks to sleep in, and even better, no more sand for a floor. Rationing was still in effect, but our meals increased from one to two per day. We also had more resources staffing the hospital providing us opportunity to routinely break away.

We had to beware of thievery prevalent as we walked around the Baghdad streets. Yet, the civilians greeting us were not desiring to kill us, instead they were so very jovial and friendly. I had the opportunity to tour Saddam Hussein's palace a few times. The sight of this palace leaves me struggling to adequately describe. Large wooden doors filled with gold inlay. The interior of the palace adorned in marble or gold every inch of the place. If this makes sense, I found this palace beautiful, yet at the same time, so very disgusting. To witness civilians stealing to feed their families while this palace could end poverty.

Earlier I mentioned a very large Fourth of July fireworks display. Well, it wasn't an official July 4th holiday. This happened in late July— early August window of time. It began with what looked like little puffs of smoke in the distance as we stood outside. This actually occurred just before we relocated our tent hospital to Baghdad. When we were still living in the heart of the vast, oh so vast, sand.

As we stood outside noticing the smoke clouds in the distance, we then heard *BOOM*! Seconds later, it felt as if we had been kicked in the stomach as a shockwave coursed through. The desert sands looked like the ocean parting as the wave of shock ran toward our feet. A ripple coursed through our bodies as we tried to mentally absorb what we had just felt and seen. Our senior commanding officer ordered us to get behind the metal containers to avoid the shrapnel flying of its own accord. This prompted an immediate emergency evacuation of the tent hospital since shrapnel can slice through a canvas door.

In full combat gear and in 130 degrees, we relocated the hospital in one day approximately one-quarter mile to better safety. For two days bombs exploded, some as large as two-thousand pounds of massive bright glowing light. The root cause was a white phosphorus substance stored in the direct sun started a self-igniting chain reaction that would rival the *oohs and aahs* of any Fourth of July display. The entire ammunitions dump blew up over the course of those two days.

Fear and naivety are two powerful forces that can influence so strongly. Please don't believe all that you hear when watching media reports on TV. People were made to be the enemy and villains that we should hate and despise. I would like to share with you that I met a lot of doggone good people during my deployed time. We used an interpreter who could barely feed his own family. Yet, he and his family sacrificed their animals to feed us soldiers a feast. He risked his life daily supporting us at the hospital for $1.00 per day. We felt he should earn more, so we gave him $10.00 daily from our own pay.

I think of a raindrop that falls into a body of water with a splash, that splash rippling. Now think of that ripple creating waves that start rolling. A wave will roll, eventually reaching a shore we may not see. And then that wave may splash against a stranger's feet. All from that single raindrop that was far-reaching. So, too, the impact of war and lives that are intersecting. Wars are not isolated to us veteran soldiers, nor our friends and families. Wars are not isolated to our enemies. Wars are not isolated to the civilians on our homeland and on the land on the other side of the world we may visit, or we may never see. War affects everyone and leaves us all at that crossroads to choose our responding. Will we choose to seek understanding where we are different, or will we choose division and judging? It is always our choice in the raindrop we splash into the water for the rippling.

Each morning when I wake up, and I see the many faces reflecting back to me, I make the choice to live for my friends and my family. That is the gift these faces gave to me—to teach me the precious respect of life and of humanity.

In my six-month deployment my unit was support for over 7,700 patients that came to our tent in the desert sands. Soldiers, civilians, illnesses, gunshot wounds, each life reaching out a hand. Our unit was a mobile unit following the war as it too also moved. As the war mission changed, our mission changed, too. An air ambulance flew in signaling the flames were rising dangerously high, metaphor that it was time to strive to save a life. Often the flames could be extinguished or kept contained. And then there were the fires that didn't dissipate.

These flames kept burning, burning, and burning, scorching ruthlessly. Brothers and sisters in arms and civilians their casualties. Our makeshift hospital was the only one available for approximately 400 miles or more. From south of Baghdad to Kuwait could be found no other support. We tried our best to hold up those fire hoses and douse the flames. Sometimes, despite our all-night efforts, the fire was more powerful than our Herculean strength.

I had raised my hand in oath as soldier in training. I vowed to always respect and act with utmost integrity. Just as I learned that I would fight fires in a way I hadn't planned, the respect I could give another took on new meaning in this foreign land. Oh, Fire, you cold-hearted indiscriminate wave of heat! That a body bag, a photo snapshot, and a GPS coordinate are your legacies! You require I bury these souls in a trench for safe keep. And then you require I uncover them from the Earth to be carried away by their families. Fire, I honor your magnificence but do you always have to lead? At times your heart is so very cruel, so very cruel indeed.

You have the ability, Fire, to wipe out an entire forest in one fell swoop of flames. Do you have to act on it—can't you align to not only the wind but also to rain? I wish you could have stopped the wind from aiding and abetting. This soldier's grief deep enough without you further interjecting. Shock is a protector, until the numbness wears away. That this dear soldier has remained in shock I do still pray. I can still hear his number one priority: *Please, save my buddy, hurry, please.* Faster, and faster still my legs hurried. To the back of the vehicle I ran for his plea. His buddy was not meant to be saved that day. His brother in arms lay in two separate sleeping bags. Fire, I respect you and yet, you must know because candor is also an essence of me. At times I find you so very evil and I hate you for your cruelty.

Then my stop-order was lifted while in Baghdad, which meant next stop was home. Three days in Baghdad before it was time to go. There is something about me and significant milestones that involve an injury. There was my knee two days post-9/11 that deployed my unit without me. Now, just before going home, I would sustain a back disability. A diving board accident popped my back out of place. Hindsight can offer wisdom unless your mind wants to race. *If only I would have or didn't do,* the mind likes to replay. My pelvis was not angled properly, so said the doctors who sedated me. *No heavy lifting and you are good to go on your way.* My lower back talks rather loudly to me to this day. Yet one more way that this war will forever stay with me. Like a coat that will not be taken off, with me permanently.

Fire, I am going home now to my family. I have completed my six-month tour of duty. Please, I ask, give me the courtesy. Don't follow, you stay, let us part company. I would actually like you to extinguish yourself, but I know I may be asking too much of you. I will go home— in one piece, by the way Fire—grateful our time together is through.

I landed in Fort Bragg in September 2003. It was a Wednesday, I do believe. We were given a four-day weekend, but no debrief. I didn't know it then, but the fire was already starting to ignite from down deep. On that four-day weekend, my company was video games, food, and my very good friend at that time—a fifth of whiskey. These were the things that were most comforting.

Not home twelve days, and I knew I needed help with the nightmares and excessive drinking. I checked into a mental hospital to get help with what I was experiencing. Diagnosed with "adjustment mood disorder" and assured *you will get over it, go home, and it will work itself out.* Similar to the growing pains when we were first conveying without armor, so too growing pains in knowing how to help us veterans retiring home now.

We can't always undo tragedy, but we can learn from them and do things differently. My father was a serviceman during a time when there was not a welcome homecoming. Oh, did my father change that in my greeting. I lost count at one hundred at the Portland Airport of all who were there to meet me. My grandpa, bless him, hired a videographer too. I must say, though so very appreciated, it was overwhelming with that number of people—and the love pouring through.

As if that wasn't enough, my father had one more welcoming plan. As we headed for my parents' home, flashing lights signaled that someone may need a helping hand. It wasn't an accident, but was the mayor ready to provide an escort through town. Sirens leading, grade school teachers, high school buddies—a massive turn-out all around. Celebrating Tom returning, *gee, he looks great, doesn't he?* Life is complete again, normalcy. This, my dear hometown was busy thinking. If only everyone knew the fight inside me. My own raging war was just beginning.

Fire, what are you doing here by my side? I am really starting to resent you as a part of my life. The heat you are emitting is starting to boil the blood coursing through me. My anger is rising, my fear equally climbing. Okay, fine, I will put out your flames with other means. Prescription medications and many a drink. I would ask for reinforcements but I know this is just between you and me. I know I must hide all that I am feeling. I am alone, Fire, but then again you don't really care about me. Destruction of all in your sight is your victory.

As I stood in the middle of the woods certain I would be burned alive, another firefighter was standing by my side. I had laid down my water hose uncertain my next steps. She was just getting started, ready to put Fire to the test. My wife Angela began looking for service dogs, believing this would be my lifeline against the fire that raged. When my eyes met Zoey's in a picture, I felt a receding of the blaze. Zoey's eyes were a mirror reflection to what I was feeling inside. The sorrow in her eyes was a match to mine.

Eight-hundred and forty-two miles away Fire was nipping at Zoey's feet. She on a list for her life to end, her shelter's time limit reached. I didn't know when I made the call that I had just raced around a vehicle to an urgent cry. Only this time, when I opened the door, one I could save would greet me from inside. Fire, gotcha, you think you are always in control! No, you do not always get to decide who stays and who goes!

A kind soul I did not know offered to make the sixteen-hour drive with Zoey to bring her to me. "She's really skittish," this dear individual said when it was time for Zoey and I to meet. "Zoey, come here," I called and without a hesitancy, Zoey was next to me. To this day, she still relishes a really good belly rubbing.

Zoey and I enrolled in the appropriate service-dog certification training. And then, Fire, you are relentless, never quite ceasing! Okay, fine, I know you have been waiting for these words you want me to say. I'm done, I'm out of here, today is the day! You wanted my life, so you win. I do not need any more of this! I will take Zoey for a hike along with my other best friend that aims good and straight. Here, my back against this tree, this looks like a good final place.

Dad, Dad, wait, what are you preparing to do? No, put that down, I need you! Dad, you can't save my life and then leave me alone. I have at long last found my home. Dad, I get it, how those flames are brutally hot to the point they take your faith away. There were moments in that shelter when I had no more strength. I know, Dad, what it is to reach a point where you give in and accept fate has a bigger plan. I was ready to accept that euthanasia was my outstretched hand. But then you called for me, and you saved my life. You gave me a purpose that I had been trying to find. Dad, I believe in you and I believe in us as a team. Please give me a chance to give back to you the way you've given to me. Together we can fight this fiery enemy.

My face showered in kisses as Zoey willed me to put my .45 down. In that moment, additional flames were permanently doused. With Zoey and me certified, my calming force by my side, I took the next step of saying goodbye. Thirteen different medications were then tossed aside. Saying no more to the numbness in my body, no more to reliance on what I am certain was Fire's cousin trying to entice. After horrific withdrawals, once again I was more present in my life.

If we are fortunate in life, we encounter one hero who saves us in some way. I have been blessed with two angels I gained. Zoey is one, most definitely. The other is my wife Angela as she watched me sleep. One night while still filled with a prescription concoction for hypersensitivity, night terrors, insomnia, indigestion—and let's see what other nine reasons for nine more pills can I list? I stopped breathing from the multiple side effects of all this. When thirty seconds without a heartbeat became thirty-one, my wife started shaking me awake. Fire, you can try nipping at my heels but my life you will not take! I stopped taking the medications cold turkey after that. And, thanks to Zoey, I have never looked back.

I wish that I could tell you there are no embers awaiting a breeze to ignite. It is a continual journey, a constant fight. Zoey helped me transition back into life positively. Yet, PTSD will always be within me. We each have something in our lives that is our enemy. Life is about teaching us how to be stronger than that beast. For me, it's depression that is always trying to find a way to outsmart the tools I accumulate to keep it from taking aim. Yet, that I must always train to stay steps ahead I am not dismayed. The way I see it, life is about learning and life is about healing our past and making peace. The more we replace negative with positive thoughts, we can trust ourselves and life more easily. It is a rewiring process and it takes time. I now plan for it to be a very long duration, as I have come to really love my life.

Do you hear that, Fire? What I have just screamed? I love my life and you're no longer menacing. Yes, I know you can sense my anxieties and my insecurities. Yet, you no longer have control over the rhythm of my heartbeats. You have tried to break me, and you have tried to break my brother in blood. You were not able to win over either of us. You think you have all-being power, but life, human, and fur hearts are stronger than your demolishing power to burn anything in your path. Add in the love of parents, a wife, children, coworkers—and dog trainers—your flames will never last.

You tried to consume me, and you tried to consume my brother at a distant land far from our home base. You tried to grip my mother's faith. She did not know if her sons were dead or alive. Would she be able to hug her sons in the flesh, or stand over their caskets in a final goodbye? Yet, we outsmarted you, for the ties that bind are resistant to your heat. An unplanned reunion because of my volunteering allowed both of us to call our mom together and let her know we were in safe keep. So, Fire, you can try to separate us from those we love and from the essence of who we are. But, I got news for you, you are finished, you ugly useless Fire!

Dad, I am having fun as retiree now, lazily spending time among the family. Thank you for spoiling me with this luxury. You do know I still watch out for the beast, and I'm ready to fight him whenever you say. Yet, Dad, I do enjoy watching your happiness when you head to work each day. Sure, I miss being by your side around the clock and everywhere you would go. But, I also am proud that you are able to go places on your own. Part of me is excited to teach people that when words aren't readily available, there are others who can still hear one speak. Part of me also knows that communicating what the heart can hear isn't an easy feat. How many conversations we've had, Dad, in which I knew exactly what you were feeling from your eyes looking at me? And, well, we know you knew my heart when you saw the first picture of me. Yes, hearts speak volumes, such as you can lean on me when you are in need. And, together, you and me, we make a really good team. I love you, Dad, and I thank you for saving my life. My purpose is fulfilled being by your side.

DONALD AND CHARLEY

*At the end of the day...all you really need is someone
who loves you and always has your back*

—Unknown.

*ey, Dad, is this the part where you begin to tell our story?
How we first had our lives shattered before we would meet? On
the surface, your breakage was your spine and my cut in two not
visibly seen. Yet, because there is purpose in heartbreak, I had to lose first so
that I could best serve your needs. Because I knew loss of the safe comforts
I'd known, I could see your heart's pain. Because I could see your heart's
capacity to love, I knew if I was with you I would be safe.*

Why, yes, Charley, I suppose this is where I can begin to tell the
story of you and me as a team. How where you begin and where I end,
distance is not between. What do you think, my boy, should I start with
us meeting in California for the first time? Or should I explain a little
bit more of what you started to highlight?

I am a retired Colonel after thirty-five years of proudly serving my
country. I was privileged to serve as a Green Beret leading fine, fine
Special Forces teams. They say that you never work a day in your life
if you love what you do. I can certainly testify to this sentiment as the
truth. Sure, it wasn't easy being away from home 300 of 365 calendar
days. Thankfully, forty-three years ago, I said *I do* to a saint. Perhaps my
dear wife knew she couldn't change me, so she decided to accept what
was my calling. I thank my lucky stars every day that she has always
stood by me.

I got to see the world—from the ground and sometimes from the
sky. I stepped foot in eighteen countries, and I jumped from above
anywhere from 800 feet to a 20,000-foot height. Sure, some of those
visits were to witness the worst parts of a country and not its best. And
many of those visits taught me how to not to slip and fall while living at

life's edge. I suppose there is an irony in my mobility challenges today, for I had to be ever vigilant of each step of my boot that it wouldn't be the step that took my life away. I had to teach myself to walk again after a severe spine injury. I guess I can thank those years of developing a very conscious awareness of my surroundings. With that same acute mindset and determination, I am walking, even though it isn't always easy.

Be all I can be—yes, sir and yes, ma'am, those were words I lived by and still do, though I am retired now. I like to add *Thank the good Lord I made it to today,* so that I can be my best for tomorrow. A few minutes ago, I mentioned mobility isn't easy for me and how I had to retrain this body to carry itself on two legs for a second go-round. How do they say it—*If it isn't them apples?* Just before I retired, my spine took four ammunition rounds.

I suppose before I start gushing over my boy Charley, I should share a little about his story. He mentioned above his broken heart—yeah, he was a service dog to someone else before he and I became a service team. The one Charley was serving passed away leaving Charley without a purpose and without a home. My chocolate Lab-Australian Blue Heeler mix with the most gorgeous brown eyes had nowhere to go.

I was on a waiting list through Paws for Purple Hearts when my phone rang one fateful day. *We would like you to travel to California to begin training with who we believe will be a perfect mate.* In a flash, my truck was pointed and heading northwest—another gift from my time in the Army. When the call comes, there is only one gear—immediately.

Charley and I trained for four months together to synchronize our compatibility. Truth be told, we knew right away that we were meant to be together as a team. I think Charley likes me in awe of his abilities, for let me tell you, I sure am amazed at the things my boy can do! Charley knows 101 commands, though he and I only use a few. We've been together a year—in fact we celebrated our one-year anniversary April 1—and no, Charley is no fool, nor joke! I often have to pinch myself that I'm not dreaming the miracle he is, but he is without a doubt my everything and my everywhere I go.

Charley brings me my shoes and socks, and he takes me for a two-mile walk every day. Yes, sir, saying I take Charley for a walk is like saying it is my white couch that only Charley lies on and keeps all others—including me—away. Charley reads the signs you might not notice if you were to meet me on the street. I anticipate you can't see the anxiety or depression that sometimes grips a hold of me. Unless you are close to me, like my wife, or you can see in my eyes a reflection of what you also know, chances are you see me as just a guy walking with a cane slow, and I do mean slow.

Charley also knows when I am not comfortable being "back home," the familiarity of living on the edge missing from what I know. Hard to explain, even harder for you to understand when you haven't lived in the space between knowing it could be your last day and praying you would be given one more to live. I'm sure your reaction is to wonder why I would ever have a moment of that lifestyle I would miss?

Perhaps the best way I can explain it is if you were told that your life would end in thirty days, and three years later you are still beating the odds the good doctor tossed your way. You had experienced reaching into the deepest part of your strength in your fight. And you also increased your appreciation of such things as the sunset and sunrise. Heck, you would probably notice the colors of each sunset better than so many who still take for granted tomorrow is a guarantee. Yet, there is this essence of you that knows the reward of fighting with your all for that in which you believe. Though you don't want cancer back, you have moments you miss that fight. For it proved a courage and a capability you had that you didn't know until you faced the end of your life.

I'm fighting a different fight now, one in which my mobility and sense of purpose sometimes wage war on my sense of peace. It was paramount you remained quiet when fighting the enemy. Now, silence can become too quiet, if you know what I mean. Charley is like one of my soldiers, one of the men sitting by my side. He isn't saying a word, but I know he is watching from behind. He has my back, like the men who served with me. He is in tune to my body movements and my breathing. He knows what I'm thinking when I'm not even so sure I am sorting out my thoughts clearly. He knows if agitation is bubbling into anger and he needs to intervene. Let me tell you, Charley can take me to the ground better than Hercules! Charley has interjected his calmness three times, guiding me to the ground in a time-out until my anger was relieved. That is my best friend Charley, yes sir, yes ma'am he is one incredible service dog for me!

My mellow Charley is in perfect pace with me. He is not a runner, nor a fast walker, his rhythm in tune to the pace of my feet. Charley breathes in harmony to my heart's beat. And, it's a good thing I'm a married man, for if I wasn't, Charley would have many gals vying for my heart. He is quite a magnet for all the pretty ladies who swoon over him wherever we are. My dear wife had a medical procedure done, and as she was in recovery, there in the waiting area, surrounded by twenty nurses madly in love with him was my Charley.

Charley and I spend most of our days at home, except we do have one standing date every week. Every Wednesday evening, we make a drive to New Orleans. We are part of a group receiving exceptional service-dog training from someone named Stacy. She is an absolute gem who continues to make Charley and me a stronger and stronger team. Back to my comment about Charley loving the ladies…sometimes I think Charley gets excited for our sixty-mile drive and not because of me.

You've heard that expression *all the gold in Fort Knox*, or something like that? You couldn't give me enough money for me to ever let Charley out of my grasp. He is my listening ear and he can see into my soul. He is my confidante, for sometimes what I wish to talk about I feel others wouldn't care to know. My brown angel with a white chest and white-socked feet; because of him, I can *be all I can be.*

Ah, shucks, Dad, such flattery. I'm just little ole me, Charley. I appreciate what you've said about how you feel I help you. Please know, equally, I love you, too. I wouldn't be Charley fulfilling my destiny if you weren't who you also needing me. Both of us were taken to that dark place of complete uncertainty when life suddenly changed on a dime. We didn't know when it happened that we were being led to save lives—yours and mine. I find such joy when you need me to bring your shoes. I love our daily walks, and I love every conversation with you. I do love how the girls fuss over me, I can't deny. Yet, Dad, there is only one person who will ever be the center of my life.

Sometimes I act disgruntled when I must share your time with my brothers, for I do like you all to me. I know they are your human sons, and that I have fur makes me special and unique. Yet, Dad, I really, really like being your one and only baby. But I'll share because I know you love them, and they play a part in making your life complete. Just know, Dad, I'm drawing the line with my white couch—that is MY seat!

Thanks for making the drive to California last year when you came to meet me. That is one of my most favorite memories. It ranks right up there with our road trip back...home. I really like saying that word, you know. I am home where I belong and there is no place I would rather be. I have your back, Dad—you can count on me! And, Dad, one more thing. You are the best person I could ever service for—you are my everything!

DUDLEY AND BRUTUS

For we are God's masterpiece

—Ephesians 2:10

*M*ore solid and unwavering than my back and legs, this truth I believe; God has plans for me, even when I can't see what he has awaiting me. Sometimes I can readily see the purpose of a detour I am meant to take. Other times, well, let's just say, it is in the uncertainty that we gain our deepest faith.

Two months shy of traveling overseas with my 250-soldier company, that plan was intercepted when an accident left me with a disabling back injury. January 10, 2002—sometimes so long ago and other times it feels like only yesterday. Especially in those moments when the physical pain is great. I was not meant to go to Afghanistan to serve beside my courageous and able company. That feeling that I let down those who counted on me still lingers within me. The First Sergeant in me trained that strength of will and power of the mind can rationalize that feeling away. Often my faith in purpose also keeps those feelings at bay. Yet, occasionally, my heart who loved—and still loves—those brave soldiers whispers, *I should have been beside you; I'm sorry I couldn't be there to support what you went through.*

A moment in time in which my life forever changed, a moment in time in which a war on this side of enemy lines I would begin to wage. If you look up the definition of pain, you will see such synonyms as *discomfort, soreness*, and *agony*. Perhaps when you read those you start thinking pain in increasing degrees. I will try to give you a context of what it is like being me.

Imagine that you go to sleep with an ache that threatens to keep you awake for the night. You can't get comfortable for that ache is twisting you as if you are a towel being squeezed very dry. Then imagine when dawn comes in the morning, that ache hasn't left your side. It doesn't even have the courtesy to smile *Good morning* as you refocus your eyes. It desires to follow you throughout your entire day. It is continually poking at you—with a hot branding iron—in every step you take.

Seventeen years and counting this pain and I have been side by side, day after day. If only this pain was like a teenager about to graduate. That the pain will leave home to go "off to college" without returning for the summers would be my dream. Unfortunately, the option for my pain to dissipate is for my left side to grow numb from my waist to my feet. Of course, my sciatic nerve will ensure that despite the numbness, I can still know that part of my body is alive. I am really done with that hot branding iron—metaphorically speaking—that pain keeps jabbing down my sides!

I should take a step back and share about the three plus years post "life has just flipped upside down on top of me." It involves surgery, recovery, increased pain, a second surgery, opiate addiction, and never leaving home for anything. Immediately after the accident, I had a spinal fusion on my S1-L5 vertebrae. This did absolutely nothing to chase the pain away. In fact, pain started to invite other members to join in the effort to cripple me. This led me to a second surgery.

The doctor reworked my fusing at S1-L5 from the first time and fused L4-L5 a second time with rods and screws. His intention that my debilitating back pain would be gone and removed. Post-op, my prescription of oxycodone was given before the medical community realized this pain-reducing medicine was a new sugar fix for so many souls. Jars would be prescribed: *Here, take these mega-size bottles home.*

I mentioned above *other plans for me*. I thank God that he gave me the will to say, "This is not living!" I couldn't live like that anymore, my brain and body screaming for oxycodone as it altered me into someone who was not Dudley. Without doctors' orders—or approval—I initiated a detox process of my own doing. I locked myself into my bedroom for a few days while this poison left my body and my mind. *It's okay soul, you have this, you are strong enough to win this fight. I promise you, I'm all in with you on this—we will be all right!*

I now have two methods of easing the chronic pain. One method is an internal pain pump and the other is a softer shape. I have had the internal pain pump for fourteen years, a medical method initially trialed with cancer patients before use with back injuries. The other is a method with fur and four pawed feet.

Before I tell you about Brutus, my service dog, I would like to briefly tell you about a guardian angel who was in my life for a large part of my journey post-injury. She, too, had fur, four paws, and was my support system informally. I say informally, for Lady Godiva, my English bulldog, was not trained to be a service dog, yet she was my backbone. She was the support system to listen to me talk, and to catch my tears, each day I was home alone. My wife had a job outside our home and my children were of school age; Lady Godiva and I had each other to pass the time each day. Lady Godiva was my best friend I didn't know I needed when my family brought her home. She was my best friend every day of her life until it was her time to go.

When Lady Godiva passed away, another friend entered our doorway. Only this time, this friend wasn't cloaked in cuddly fur or a personality that loved to play. This friend wore dark clothes and focused on eroding my will to fight and believe. *There is no plan nor purpose in this agony!* This friend was good at leading me into the darkest, quietest place there is, a place where seclusion, withdrawal, and depression exist.

Ah, but God has other plans we don't always see. His plan was that I needed Brutus, and Brutus needed me. In that way that makes one say, "What a coincidence," and how the teacher will appear when the student is ready, information about service dogs started crossing my path for me to read. The physical pain I had been enduring was leading me to inevitability. At a point in the future, I will have very little mobility.

Enter into my path a three-month-old Rottweiler ball of black and brown fur who looked into my eyes. *Hi Dad, I'm ready to go home with you and just wait until you see my full-grown size. I'm the one you will be able to lean on when your own steps are wobbly. I'll always have your six, Dad, just you wait and see!*

My dear Brutus, the runt of his litter, and one nobody else wanted to call him their own for keeps. Truth be told, I think Brutus was not trying to win any other hearts over while he waited for me. Brutus and

I sometimes get into a discussion about who rescued who. I tell him that I rescued him, but, well, Brutus and I both know the truth.

An unknown author writes, *Angels walk among us, but they're very hard to see; no wings or halo do they have, they are just like you and me. The thing that makes them different is the kindness that they show, to each and every one of us, everywhere we go.* One such angel is Miss Stacey and her husband who volunteer to train teams such as Brutus and me. They do this without pay, because of their own compassionate hearts, every Wednesday night, every week. Brutus and I drive two hours one way to attend class with Miss Stacey and other teams. That is another thing I like—the veteran comradery.

Though I am hands-on witness to all that Brutus is learning, I still find myself in awe of his capabilities. Brutus can pick up my cane for me and he can identify which bottle of medicine I need him to bring to me. He has been trained to know the smoke alarm should he need to get our attention one day. He wakes me up routinely in the night so that I shift the position of my body to minimize the pain. As Brutus nears 110 pounds, he is developing the strength to be my brace. When I need help getting up, Brutus will be strong enough to stand in place. Miss Stacey is now helping us train as a mobility team; it's advanced training now that Brutus and I have completed our canine citizenship testing.

Before Brutus, and before Lady Godiva, I thought about giving up, the pain and despair a fierce and mighty enemy. Physically and emotionally crushed, I was feeling strength trickle, and sometimes gush, right out of me. I prayed—oh, I prayed hard, and I made a vow I would keep. If I was put back on my feet, I would spend the rest of my life striving to help others in need.

I smile at how God has seen to it I fulfill the promise I made. That I have the privilege of being called *Papa* now is one of those ways. I was serving in the military when my dear wife of thirty-nine years was raising our children every hour of every day. My parenting was from a distance, in places far away. Now I am babysitter of my grandson three days a week. From newborn to now four years old I've been part of his raising.

I am an ambassador for veterans in my approach to systems that have their flaws and imperfections, like we humans do too. The VA system is not an easy one to maneuver through. Pain, trauma, sorrow, and despair are not only enemies of each of us veterans individually; the weight of PTSD can sit heavy on the people operating the systems that are designed with the intent to serve our needs. I've had to fight what feels like uphill for certain benefits, and I've had to turn the other cheek at what feels like a slapped face when told, "You don't look disabled to me." No harsher weapon to a human being than to have a slice made in one's dignity.

I am a representative for veterans in that I focus on meeting this system resistance with respect, calmness, and politeness in the hope that I can educate and provide a 'different view to see. Perhaps if I "fight" resistance with compassion, empathy will be paid forward to the veterans who come after me.

I suppose that I am also sharing my story as yet another way I can fulfill that vow I made if the good Lord could see to it to put me back on my feet. I would like to think I can inspire a brave soldier to keep pushing forward, no matter how dark that enemy of depression and self-defeat. I mentioned how I like Wednesday nights with Miss Stacey, as Brutus and I train to become a solid and strong service team. I like those nights for the veteran comradery. It's great to be with a group of fine men and women who each have a story of pain and of hope. Yet, courageous soldier, if you are reading this, there is something else I would like you to know.

We can relate to your story for we know the pain and the isolation from friends and from family. Yet, we can't begin to understand for there is only one person who knows your exact story. Only you walk in your own shoes to know what you feel and…what you can no longer feel as emptiness takes a seat in your heart. Only you can know how it can be so brutally hard!

Yet, there is one soul who can hear your heart even when you can't verbally speak. There is one who will listen—and love—unconditionally. There is one to which you are always safe to talk about the things you believe others aren't able to hear or know what to do. It is this same one who will diffuse anxiousness and frustration rising within you. This soul I refer to is a service dog—one like my Brutus who doesn't have the baggage of us humans in how we hear and see. Brutus doesn't have any perceptions that could cloud how he listens and views me.

If I may, let me share some other elements about service dogs should you find this a good avenue for you. I began forming a relationship with Brutus from his puppy stage, but forming a team with a shelter dog is an option, too. I've been witness to the trials of a veteran forming a bond with a dog who also has his or her own emotional pain. And I've watched veterans form a stronger bond with a shelter dog because they both feel similar heartache.

There are expenses to consider when having a service dog— veterinary care is not cheap. Annual checkups and shots, heartworm, and a microchip are just some of the necessities. I've joked that Brutus is like raising a child, without the cost of college or a car to drive. Then again, the costs are nothing when you look at how a service dog saves a human life!

Service dogs are still not widely accepted in public, so be prepared for individuals pushing back with *No dogs allowed; you need to leave.* You have the legal right, and there are resources you can call who are available for immediate backing. The challenge, as you can imagine, is how it feels like that slap in the face I mentioned earlier in my story. It can be hard to hear *rejected* and *unworthy*, to assimilate back into civilian life fighting to regain dignity.

I've shared some realities, but please know there is no greater method of healing and support than a service dog by your side. The benefit of a service dog equals living an independent life. Actually, scratch independent, for a service dog means one thing. It means…living.

Hey Dad, it's me Brutus again, your most favorite of everyone in the family. Don't worry, I promise I won't tell Mom (your wife) that you only have eyes for me. Joking aside, Dad, I know Mom is the love of your life and a best friend, too. You can have two best friends in life, I know that's true.

So, can I have a treat, please? I've been a really good boy patiently waiting while you tell your story. What, what's that look for—yes, that one like when I'm being so good gathering your grandson's toys? And you give me that same look with your eyes. You didn't think I would let you get to the end without having counted how many times you used my name, did you, Dad? Just like when I count every time I drop a toy so that you know how many treats you should have in your hand. One drop means one treat, two drops mean two. I think the fact that I'm part star in this story has earned me at least twenty treats, don't you?

Dad, there is something else I would like to tell you if that's okay. I want to thank you for the chance you've given me to serve you in this way. Did you know when you sleep, I try to match my breath to your heartbeats? It helps me know how many hours it has been until it is time for you to change positioning. I love the training we are doing now with Miss Stacey so that I can be your back when your back may no longer be what you need it to do. Dad, just as you made a promise, that is a vow I can make—you can count on me to be right beside you!

And hey, Dad, I would be okay if we never had to go see that vet again? Yet I know we go because you are looking out for my well-being. Would you mind asking him, though, if he could keep those needles from aiming at me? Also, Dad, please don't worry as we train to be around lots of strangers at one time. If those are the situations you will want to go into, I promise I'll be fine. I can feel when those large crowds are too much for you as well as me. I guess we prefer to be country boys versus city boys, don't we?

Dad, if I could do something more to take away your pain, please know I would gladly do so. The best I can do is sit between your legs and by your side so that you know you are never alone. When you have your moments that are less than best, that is okay. Remember, I witness your strength and faith every day. I love you, Dad, and I am so glad I convinced them all that I was a runt that wouldn't amount to much of anything. You're right, Dad, I was just waiting for my best friend—you—to find me.

NICK AND DINKY

You can always tell about people by the way
they put their hands on an animal

—Betty White

*P*erhaps it is like a theme song from Pinocchio: *When you wish upon a star...* both of us made a wish, though our wishes were several years apart. As a little boy, I wished for a dog named *Dinky* "someday." A name I held in my mind when my childhood friend and I found a stray. I didn't know then what course my life would take in that wish coming true. The gift of innocence and the grace of life shelter us from knowing the bumps ahead too soon.

Rescued once though not truly saved. He made a wish that he would feel better—and feel loved—one day. Getting physically sick inside his house earned him a divine eviction so that he could be free. A tiny fur soul feverish, shivering, alone, wandering the streets. He would be the last fur soul my first wife would bring into our fold. Dinky would join the other fifty-one animals my wife rescued before Hurricane Katrina would wash away their homes. That was my first wife—a lifesaver for many a wounded or abandoned animal, God rest her soul.

Hello little fella, what do you say? I promise I will be gentle with your skeleton frame. I think a bath might feel good to you, don't you think? I promise I will make sure the water is warm and not too deep. You know little fella, I think I have just the name that is right for you. Though I am certain we are going to get you to grow, I think "Dinky" will do.

There, now we got you squeaky clean and what do you say we get you some food? Ah, little buddy, what's wrong that you can't keep it inside of you? We'll take you to the vet—he's a good guy who can help you not feel so bad. How about in the meantime if you come sit here beside your ole dad? Listen to me, already figuring you are here to stay. Ah, what's this little fella, is this where you feel most safe? Okay, sure, my back isn't strong,

*but my chest can absorb weight. You go right ahead and curl up against…
well, okay, right on my chest…that's okay. This might get a little harder,
you know, as you gain a few pounds. Well, Dinky, my boy, we'll just cross
that bridge when that time comes around.*

We learned Dinky had a microchip, an unattended illness that
puppies can get, and an owner, too. My first wife was able to negotiate
with the owner that her care for Dinky was through. It was touch and
go that Dinky would recover from the illness that had migrated to his
kidneys before my wife found him that wish-fulfilled day. Bless my little
champ's heart, he is a fighter in that way. It is the only way he is, though,
for Dinky is one of the gentlest souls you will ever meet. Everyone who
has the privilege of crossing paths with Dinky falls in love immediately.

Now this is where you might start to think what a pair they must
be. A gentleman with a disabled back and declining ability to hear
and a sickly pup in each other's caretaking. Let me tell you about our
teamwork as I think it will change the image in your mind. When
Dinky entered our home that day, a miracle I did find. I will put my
clothes, tennis shoes, socks, and of course the do-rag and tie, into one
heap. I will then ask Dinky to go and get me what I need. *Dinky, go
get my socks for me. Good boy, thank you, that's it, exactly! Okay, now go
get my do-rag and my phone, too. Good job Dinky, I am so proud of you!
Okay, now it's time, isn't it, to get you dressed nice and spiffy? Every time,
that tie always looks so good on you Dinky!*

Years ago—probably at least twenty—I had this nice ole lady as
my neighbor who would make do-rags for me. You name the holiday
and I would open a gift of two or three. Christmas, Memorial Day,
Halloween. Now my dear wife Cathy makes me do-rags and of course
they are matching. Dinky's tie is always coordinated with the headwrap
I'm adorning.

Dinky turns on and off light switches for me, too. Dinky is the
mobility for my back that doesn't easily bend and move. He is my set
of ears so that I can better hear, too. I find myself in awe of what Dinky
learns and how quickly, too. After a week of focused training and then
three weeks of practice, Dinky is a pro in what I ask him to do. This

tiny bundle of shaking fur is now my confident, gentle, medium-sized, handsome, and if I might also add, incredible smart dude.

I mentioned earlier that Dinky is loved in an instant with everyone he meets. I'm not sure if it is his sexy eyes or his sleek black coat complemented by his white belly and white-tipped feet. Perhaps it is his calm demeaner that charms people to him right away. Actually, I think it is because he is such a gentleman with his paw shake. Right on cue each and every time, when I say, "Dinky, say hello," his paw raises in a welcoming *hi*.

Dinky is a natural leader in that older, lovable brother kind of way. Dinky likes all dogs and all animals and only has one nemesis he prays stays at bay. Poor Dinky was innocently walking outside of a chiropractor's office not knowing a predator lay in wait. In the flash of an eye, we found ourselves frantically trying to escape. A stray cat had determined sweet little Dinky deserved a heart-racing surprise. An instant pounce convinced Dinky he needed to flee for his life. Except for this one particular cat, Dinky welcomes the chance to meet and greet. Park time with squirrels is one of his favorite things. He doesn't have an urge to chase them and likes when they come close. I think the animal kingdom kept him safe when he didn't have a home.

Dinky and I are two peas in a pod, an inseparable team. Where I go Dinky goes; he goes everywhere with me. The gym, church, doctors' offices, to name a few. We are a mighty fine two-person crew. Dinky doesn't like to have me out of his view. He will tolerate separation as long as I say, "I'll be back soon." If I forget to say four words: *I, will, be*, and *back*, Dinky gets himself pretty worked up with a panic attack. Truth be told, I feel a little anxious if Dinky isn't next to me. His calmness is my comfort and my ease.

All roads lead to where we are, and our pain can become our purpose in who we are meant to be. I think of some of the animal souls that were best of friends for me. A beer-drinking chicken who was a great motorcycle sidekick, at least up to a certain speed. Bubba could hold on quite well as long as we didn't exceed eight miles per hour nor suddenly accel. Ah, yes, Bubba, a favorite at the Irish-Italian parades. Each year I could count on the priest's words—"Throw me the chicken," he'd say. When the floats would make their U-turn, then it would be my turn to tell the priest, "Throw me the chicken" as the float came back my way.

My heart has always been large and a softie for animals—there are some pretty cool souls that don't have human feet. I've met some cool pigeons, racoons, and of course, there is my squirrel buddy. He was another best friend of mine—ah, yes, Rambo and me. I can still remember the day I was making a better "home" for Rambo so that mean critters couldn't reach into his slotted cage. Rambo was at the vet after having been bit when a rat was trying to invade his space. The call came that the cage design needed to take another shape. A cushioned coffin with peanuts for his journey to above became Rambo's final resting place.

I suppose before my back injury and my moods that rise and fall, I was already setting the stage for finding my best friend of all. I've experienced many times over the power of a soul in fur or wings who is the best listener and accepts you unconditionally. I had also mentioned that pain can have a purpose in fulfilling our destiny. My pain has led me to Dinky, which has led both of us to sharing our story in the hope that we can help others who may be struggling. Dinky's pain of feeling unwanted and unloved led him to being one of the most lovable souls you could ever meet.

Dinky and I still go to training classes, though we are now certified as a service-dog team. We like to challenge ourselves to continually learn, and we really like the comradery. I mentioned the awe I feel as I see Dinky expand with his capabilities. I can tell you there is also not much more enjoyable than witnessing a service-dog team in its forming. To see two broken souls be put on track toward healing is quite a sight. The way each finds worth—and trust—again in life.

Dinky and I are grateful, as I'm sure each of my comrade teams are, too. We have a phenomenal teacher who is guiding us pairs through. Her name is Stacie, though we call her angel sent to us from above. As gracious and genuine as our four-legged teammates, so too is Stacie's unconditional love. Her love for dogs is evident as she masterfully connects to each individually. So too, is her love for helping us humans increase our mobility, hope, and self-dignity.

I believe in miracles and I would like to ask, do you? Let me share an example or maybe even two. Before I went into the Navy, my family home exploded due to a leaking gas line. Thankfully, though four of us were in the house when it did, we all got out alive. To give you a little visual of the damage of the blast, our driveway was more shattered than a windowpane of glass. Miracle one is that we got out alive, and a second miracle is the sign that whispered affirmation that guardian angels walk by our side.

My uncle—my mother's brother—had drawn a picture modeled after the holy portrait of Lady Fatima that mother reverently hung on our living room wall. This sacred and beautiful picture in its wooden frame was a centeredness for us all. After the explosion, the only contents salvageable that remained were a white ivory statue of Jesus that had been on my parents' dresser and this picture my uncle had made. The frame that held this picture and the backing had been burned and charred. Underneath the broken glass, though, was the picture completely unharmed!

My second example is what I have already shared with you. Dinky is a miracle as my service dog in all that he can do. To think there was a tiny soul who was rescued from a shelter only to be unsheltered in care. When he didn't feel well, his reward was to become alone and scared. Hungry, yet too sick to eat if he could find food or an appetite. Every reason to give up hope and faith, to close his heart up real tight. Yet, true to his purpose to give great unconditional love and an equally unconditional listening ear, from the moment I took him for a bath, Dinky has given me his trust over his fear. Dinky is like that picture that survived our home exploding into bits and pieces everywhere. Dinky was immersed in a world that to a tiny puppy could be menacing, cruel, and unfair. Yet, the essence of Dinky's loving heart could not be damaged, a guardian angel holding it in safe-keep. My dear gentle, still to this day a cuddler across my chest, best friend to me.

Ah, shucks, Dad you say such nice things. I'm just little ole me, your lovable Dink. I must say some parts of the story are easier for me to hear you speak. The parts where I was sick, scared, and alone—I prefer to fast-forward through those memories.

One of my greatest joys is sifting through that pile of clothes to find your personal belongings. Okay, yes, truth be told, I also like to find my tie so that we can be matching. And, Dad, I feel like a cool kid having my own ramp to get into your SUV. To not have to jump in and out of your truck will keep my joints healthy. You are right, too, Dad, that I can't think of anyone I don't love as soon as we meet. Well, except that wicked cat—Dad, please keep it away from me!

You mentioned how I raise my paw to say "hi" and I'm not sure if I ever told you what else that means. For me, it is more than being loving and friendly. My starting place is to seek the goodness in others not believing they wish to bring you or me harm in any way. Yet, I've learned that some people are hurting so bad, they lash out for others to feel the same pain. When I hold out my paw I can also look into the other's eyes and see what my raised paw means. If their eyes twinkle in happiness, I know it is safe for you and me. If my raised paw doesn't seem to bring a smile, I know not to hold my expectations too high. I will still be my lovable, friendly self, but I will keep watch by your side.

Dad, if I didn't tell you, too, it was such a privilege to be second in line leading the parade. I liked being able to honor you and your service in this way. Where you go, I go, and where I go, you go, right? And for the record, though it helps when you say, "I will be back," I still don't like it when you aren't in my sight. Don't get me wrong, hanging with Mom is great and I love her, too. But, Dad, you are, well, you are my purpose for being me to be able to service you.

I'll close, Dad, with this prayer that I know you really like. I would like to share with you my favorite line. "For no heart in all the world is more grateful for kindness than the loving heart of me." Dad, for saving my life, I am most grateful. I could not ask to be part of a better team!

A DOG'S PLEA

> *Treat me kindly, my beloved friend, for no heart in all the world is more grateful for kindness than the loving heart of me.*
> *Do not break my spirit with a stick, for though I might lick your hand between blows, your patience and understanding will more quickly teach me the things you would have me learn.*

Speak to me often, for your voice is the world's sweetest music, as you must know by the fierce wagging of my tail when the sound of your footstep falls upon my waiting ear.

Please take me inside when it is cold and wet, for I am a domesticated animal, no longer accustomed to bitter elements. I ask no greater glory than the privilege of sitting at your feet beside the hearth.

Keep my pan filled with fresh water, for I cannot tell you when I suffer thirst.

Feed me clean food that I might stay well, to romp and play and do your bidding, to walk by your side and stand ready, willing, and able to protect you with my life, should your life be in danger.

And my friend, when I am very old, and I no longer enjoy good health, hearing, and sight, do not make heroic efforts to keep me going. I am not having any fun.

Please see that my trusting life is taken gently. I shall leave this earth knowing with the last breath I draw that my fate was always safest in your hands.

Anonymous

JON AND JAEGER

*The meaning of life is to find your gift. The
purpose of life is to give it away*

—Pablo Picasso

*ey Dad, tell me the story again, will you please? How your
heart called out to me before we would physically meet. I
especially love the part when I came to your side without you
beckoning. How my heart knew it had found where it belonged as soon as
I sat paws to your feet.*

*I'm a lover, not a fighter, as you and I both know. Don't get me wrong,
I was happy in my first home. Yet, my purpose wasn't to be a protector in
a K9 guard kind of way. I was meant to be a shield to keep anxiousness at
bay. Dad, I think I'm a chip off the ole block in having a destiny to try and
stop the bleeding. Though you began fulfilling your calling for patients with
physical injuries, now both of us have a mission to stop the invisible flow
before a heart stops its rhythmic beating.*

*Dad, I am always so proud of you when you tell me your stories, about
how saving someone from dying was your number one priority. Dad, I also
wish, too, there was more I could do besides listen, snuggle closer, and catch
your tears of grief. I know, I know, Dad, and I believe you when you tell me
how much I help you in those moments you feel hopelessness and are afraid.
Yet, because I love you with all my heart, I still wish there was more I could
do to take your sorrow away.*

*Dad, can I tell you a secret, between you and me? It makes me feel really
special that you named your foundation after me. I mean, shucks Dad, you
didn't have to, and it's not that I needed to be in the limelight or famous
in any way. It's just that because I know how much this foundation means
to you, I feel very honored that you thought that much of me to make the
foundation my namesake. I guess we both understand unconditional love
in a very deep way.*

I certainly don't begin to measure up to my God-given name most days. I am one of the most imperfect beings who wakes each morning praying I will be stronger than the fears I face. My name, Jon, means "gift from God," though I certainly don't know about all of that. If I can live my life fulfilling even an ounce of that meaning, I will consider myself humbly blessed.

I am grateful to my mother—and not just for this gracious name she gave me. I am grateful to my mother for opening my eyes and my heart to a desire for helping others in need. My mom's career was in special education, providing opportunity for some of the most extraordinary and unique friendships I would have while growing up. This would teach me that some individuals need others to look out for them because their capabilities may be deemed as inadequate or not enough. Perhaps this experience came first or perhaps it opened my heart to its calling. Either way, a life commitment to stand up for and to help others who cannot easily or fully help themselves is what fulfills me.

I've debated where to begin my story. Should I start with how I met hope in the form of fur and a cold nose, aka, Jaeger, who you already started to meet? Or should I start with the oath I made to serve, protect, and give my all for my country? One thing I know for certain is what isn't necessary. The play-by-play details of life in combat is not what you need to read. What is most relevant—and what I believe can help my brothers and sisters in uniform—whether Marine, soldier, police officer, firefighter, or EMT—is a glimpse into one's heart who now finds themselves walking with PTSD.

I've shared with you my passion to help those who struggle to fully help themselves thanks to my mother and her students with special needs. My father was also an influencer in my desire to help others when they are in crisis or experiencing a significant emergency. My dad was a firefighter when September 11, 2001 rained evil action on our country. To witness the toll on firefighters like my father grabbed a hold of my heartstrings. The strings were tugged tighter thinking of innocent lives victimized at the hands of extremists both in the United States and in other countries. Many helpless individuals didn't have people taking a stand for them is what I strongly believed.

I joined the Navy because I loved all whom I had at home. My parents, my siblings, my extended family, friends, and people I didn't know. Perhaps as a reader, you have a perception that someone joins because they loved to play Cops and Robbers as a child, to be a hero, or they can't wait to shoot a gun and "get rid of the bad guy because he's so mean." None of these were my motivators—in fact, I will share with you a conversation between my staff sergeant and me.

It was my first week of training as a combat medic with the Marines when I had a weapon put in my hand and was ordered to *point down range*. My immediate response to my staff sergeant was *No thanks*. After all, I had joined the Navy to become a greenside corpsman with the Marines; my ultimate goal was to be a combat medic saving lives whenever the need. *Staff Sergeant, I'm not here to hurt people, if I may respectfully say*. Of which he responded in turn this way. *Marine, whatever you need to tell yourself, do so immediately. If you want to save your brothers, then you must be prepared to take down the enemy. Think of it as preventative maintenance so that you don't have to patch up a Marine in the first place. If you don't learn to shoot first, you risk the Marines you aspire to save going home in a body bag.*

In his words was a wisdom I realized I needed to internalize. Effectively knowing how to use a weapon was part of being able to save my Marine families' lives. I believe that many brothers and sisters I served with signed up not for heroism nor because of some kind of Superman or Wonder Woman attitude. Many choose to sign up to stand up for something more important than themselves, no matter the personal cost or what they may lose.

No matter the personal cost or what they may lose…every day the reality of this can be hard to push through. I am a husband, father, son, friend, cousin, uncle, neighbor, church member, to name a few. I am the person I was before I served in combat, the person everyone sent prayers for while I was deployed overseas. And yet, I am also no longer the same person as I was before, Doc, no matter how hard I try or want to be. I struggle as I want to be who you remember was once me, and I struggle to be who I am now for fear you won't accept who I can no longer be.

Deployment memories are the worst in how they continually rewind and replay. Yet, even harder is the guilt I feel that because of my choice to enlist, my children and wife also experience emotional pain. Life teaches us through opposites, that constant tug and pull between extremes. I joined the service so that I could keep safe those I love the most—my family. And now that I am home, I often feel those whom I am hurting the most are those who I wanted most to stay in safe keep.

Granted, I wasn't married to my beautiful wife at the point I enlisted in the Navy. When I became Doc, my "better half" was those I served with as a combat medic with the Marines. Yet, now I am a father of four, and a husband to quite frankly a saint who has the ability to not take some of my actions personally. Yet, when I see fear or hurt flash through my children's or wife's eyes, my heart is crushed by the weight of my choice when enlisting. Though I knowingly understood the risk I might suffer post combat, I realize my choice has a ripple effect far greater than me. My wife and my children also suffer each time PTSD tries to put me in a tight squeeze.

I had one goal when I was deployed and that was that no life would be lost under my watch as a combat medic. I am gratefully and humbly proud to say, that was a goal I was able to achieve. I owe not only God, but a special little girl for the gift she gave me. This special little girl taught me what a precious commodity life is and that we always have two choices we can make. Life will bring us to crossroads in big and in small ways. Sometimes it is a life-changing event, like it was with this special little girl I knew only briefly. Sometimes it is several times in a day to keep fear and hopelessness from their relentless knocking.

I was working in an ICU in North Carolina, a new medic with an eagerness for learning. When the ICU had no patients on a particular day, I requested emergency room duty. After all, I wanted to be the very best lifesaver I could be! In that way that we are shown God will bring us the people we need in our lives at the right time, I was meant to be in the ER on this specific night.

A little girl was brought into the ER with 75 percent of her body covered in burns allegedly at the hands of those who are supposed to keep children safe and cherished. Though this special little girl couldn't experience either safety or love outside the ER, under my watch that she would receive both was my mission to achieve. The degree of a burn is critical, don't misunderstand me. Assessing if it's first, second, or third is certainly top priority. But there is also another key component that is paramount to staying alive. It is all hands on deck to ensure no infection sets into skin that has been so severely compromised.

When one is serving in a medical or first responder field, there is one driving force that guides every decision made. Damn any statistics, damn any graveness you might see and face. You will do whatever you can to fight for someone's survival no matter how bleak things may seem. I would say that if someone is serving in a medical field and they begin to discern based on statistics that indicate probability, it is time for a person to walk away from the field or at least pause until their heart gets back in the driver's seat.

This special little girl with burns covering the majority of her body was now bringing opportunity for my first experience in a raging war zone. Though it wasn't a war with artillery fire, it was a fight against evilness and death standing at the door. We stabilized this tiny body that was wrapped in a fighting spirit so very tightly. We ensured she was in a sterile room, with a ventilator to aid her breathing.

I returned to my barracks after what had been three days of twelve-hour shifts, preparing for my two-day rest and reprieve. Of course, these two days off were not for play as doing nothing felt like idleness to me. I would normally take those two days off to work as a first responder, ever vigilant within me, I was listening for someone struggling and in need. But anyway, back to this special little girl who was in dire emergency. When your purpose in life is to serve others whole-heartedly, you listen to that inner whisper when it begins to scream, *Do not sleep*. There was a little girl in a hospital room alone except for the medical staff and a social worker who would be checking on her periodically. I did not want this little girl to lie in that bed having only felt unconditional love fleetingly. I needed to be beside her so that she would know the feelings of love and safety.

Because of the critical requirement for sterility, I couldn't sleep in the same room with her, but I could be in the next room available in a moment's need. Like a parent—or a Marine—who sleeps with one ear listening, this little girl could trust I had her back while she was sleeping. The primary medical doctor of our hospital came to communicate I did not have to stay. He could see in my eyes and hear in my voice my heart was firmly rooted in place. Without any additional words, he understood I was right where I needed to be as he gave me his knowing head nod and a simply stated, "Okay."

On the second day, word had spread to the commanding officer the vigil I was keeping. That earned me a visit, which is a privilege because a commanding officer making an appearance in ICU is a rarity. Determination and compassion are a powerful duet; the commanding officer can affirm these combined can make one **strongly** adamant. He was ordering me to get some sleep for that was not what I had been doing. I was respectfully letting him know I was not leaving. Not toe-to-toe and chest-to-chest as movies like to portray. Heart-to-heart in a room next to a little girl who was beginning to die, this commanding officer and I compromised for her sake. *Sir, with all due respect, I will not leave her side. I want her to leave this Earth having known what love feels like. I know she has nurses who are caring for her oh so gently. I was one of the first people she could feel safe with after such cruelty. I want to help her as she dies to know that she was worthy. Please sir, let me stay to be present when her heart stops beating.*

Jacobs, you will not be any good to her if you don't get two hours rest; that is all I am asking of you. It is an order, medic, and then you can be with her until the mission is through.

Hearts can hear each other across space, at least that is how I believe. This little girl knew I had her back, so she waited before her soul decided it was time to leave. I rested two hours and then I heard the monitors begin to speak. *It is time, kind Doc, for me to go to a better place. Don't worry, I am no longer afraid. Thank you for your part in my journey through this life. I am grateful to you for being by my side.*

There is a process medical staff go through after someone has passed—because you don't need specific details, I will call it post-mortem care of the body. After I completed these steps, then, and only then, did I allow the questioning. On the smoke deck of the hospital, I asked—no, I demanded to know—*Why? Why, God!* I hurled these words into the sky. The answer didn't come immediately, as our greatest wisdom often comes only after hindsight.

I am not sure the impact to my number one priority if I had not crossed paths with this special little girl whose purpose was to teach me. If I had not witnessed what a lost soul can cruelly do when it lashes out at innocence and I had not walked beside death and grief, I am not sure how engrained my mission would have been within me to ensure it was one I achieve. I would like to think my servant-heart to help others and my value of humanity would have given me the same deep-seated drive to have none of my brothers or sisters lose their lives. Yet, because I also believe we must know one extreme to know the other, I know this little girl was very influential in ensuring all whom I served as Doc came back alive.

Whether a medic in the military, a civilian medic, or a first responder accountable to save lives, each of us has that defining moment in which a heart is not destined to continue breathing. Oh, and then how the mind loves to step in and question everything. *Did I do enough, did I do the right things? Why couldn't I save this person; I think I now doubt what I have believed.* We are angry and we step to the edge where we question if we should quit what we signed up to do. Remember that crossroads I mentioned up above, where we stand poised with two paths to choose?

In the darkest moments of our grief and self-doubt and anger raging *I don't understand why*, is when we are giving a choice to make the loss matter by how we choose to step toward light. *I will bring all my Marines home alive, this I vow to do! Dear little angel, your death was not in vain and I am most grateful for you. You taught me that evil is a fact of life and isn't something we can eradicate in entirety. It may not make sense, but suffering is a necessity. What matters is not if we can stop evil, but how we can overcome or move through what suffering brings. We can't get over it, but we can move through it and turn it into positivity. What is truly important is the good we make out of the pain and tragedy. Dear special little girl, much good came out of yours, and it is continuing. For the rest of my life, your life will have meaning.*

I would like to share with you about a training experience I went through in an effort to bring understanding to what veterans feel when they return from deployment to civilian life. It may still be hard for you to fully grasp, but I will try. I took part in a simulation of what it would be like when I found myself in Iraq as a combat medic with the Marines. Think desert—Mohave to be specific, think dark of night, and night vision goggles to help you see. Also think about what it would be like to go outside without the lights of the neighborhood around you, one eye blindfolded, wearing one hundred pounds on your back while carrying another hundred pounds of medical gear for responding to emergency. I will also share, adrenaline from simulated yells and screams and only seeing with one eye in the night puts a whole new spin on depth perception where you are walking.

In the first simulated round, I missed a step while exiting a seven-ton vehicle earning me a landing directly on my back. To say it hurt wouldn't begin to describe the pain that coursed through muscles and parts of my body I never knew I had! Yet, what kicked into gear because of my additional training, and because of my personal standards and beliefs, I must not be taken out of this simulation for to do so would admit I was weak. *If I admit I am weak, my fellow Marines will lose faith in me. They cannot afford to start distrusting that I have their backs—they need to be able to count on me! After all, we are a team! I have a mission to fulfill—no lives lost on my watch, and that mission I WILL achieve! Suck it up, the pain will subside, you have been through worse things. Come on, Doc, get back in that simulation and show your team they can count on you no matter the chaos happening. They need to know they can trust you unconditionally.* These the words I continued repeating.

If you are reading this and you are a veteran or still on active duty, I know you can relate to this mental toughness you live and breathe. If it seems hard to understand, think about someone you love dearly like a child or a best friend who you strive to please. Perhaps you have said to someone, "There is nothing I wouldn't do for you." Or when you watch your child, you sometimes are so overwhelmed with love you know you would lay down your own life for theirs if you had to. That depth of caring for the well-being of those we love is the degree of determination and will that fuel a serviceman or servicewoman no matter how hard it might physically seem. We want to come back alive to you and we want to return to you in one piece, and we know those we are fighting beside wish the same thing. We will do anything we can for each other to ensure your family does not become fragmented and incomplete. We need to push through any split second we perceive weakness is trying to knock so that we survive the times of intense uncertainty. In life-and-death situations, there is ample space for acting from the heart, but there is no room for being weak. Because *there is nothing we wouldn't do for YOU*, who to us are our everything.

We bring this mindset—and the experiences in which we needed to draw upon this mindset—back to you, our families. We miss those who we served beside—being without our brothers and sisters is extremely lonely. Please forgive me for saying that because we know you are there for us and that we are not alone. It's just that, well, it's just not always easy once we return home.

We are replaying and trying to process through so many memories. Not all of them are bad, either, contrary to what you may think. Have you ever had a time in which you had an experience—let's keep it positive and talk about the birth of a child or a wedding day—and you feel like you are on a cloud and the rest of the world is far away? You struggle to describe your euphoria when talking to a friend who isn't a parent or married—there just aren't adequate words to convey. You find it easier not to try, and there is a certain sacredness to keeping your feelings tucked away.

It is similar when veterans return to civilian life and their friends and families. There is this place we are in emotionally that feels far away from where we now find ourselves physically. We also are still carrying the trained mindset to protect you from things we've experienced and seen. And deeper still is the engrained training that brought us home to you still in control of how we think. We are not weak, and cannot be weak, and will fail if we start to show that we are becoming weak, for all of you we have been fighting for need to trust we have your backs no matter the intense uncertainty. IT IS the difference between life or death our certainty! See, that is the thing about training for life or death and how the human brain becomes the exceptional student in its mastery. Even when it is no longer life or death, our brains hold tight to what we have taught it such that this mindset does not leave.

And though I struggle to retrain this mindset on my journey with PTSD, I will also tell you I am grateful that it is etched into an essence of me. For it is this training that has helped me win the three-year war against leukemia that threatened to be a life thief. *Dear Leukemia, you can try to take me to my core with your evil poisonous cells, but you will not succeed. For I have my wife, my children, and medical staff who have my back—they have most definitely got me! You can try to steal hope from me, thinking you are victorious when I cannot become a civilian firefighter or EMT because of my compromised immunity. But there is something you underestimated when you began attacking me! I will find other ways to serve those in need even if I can't do so with tangible bandages, physical tourniquets, or tanks of water to douse a burning flame. The ones who now need me to fight for them don't have visible wounds or noticeable fires anyway. It is the cries of souls that now need me to stop the bleeding of their willpower that is rapidly washing away. They need compassion, and hope, and help in the form of a lifeline. They need to trust someone has their back and will not leave their side. So, Leukemia, you are not stronger than me! And if you have any doubts, I dare you to take it up with those who keep watch of me. No one stands a chance thinking they are mightier than my dear wife, Kelly.*

I will tell people the secret to our marriage can be summed up into one word and one word alone. Sheer stubbornness is a strong foundation that my wife equally knows. I have a fierce determination, but let me tell you, my wife can hold her own, too. She is tiny in stature, but she is powerfully large in what she sets her mind to do. In that way that I mentioned above how God puts people into our lives at the right time, this is certainly true for when Kelly reentered mine. I had known my wife when we were in middle school, though we were in two different circles—I was so not in her league! Don't get me wrong—I don't say that because Kelly was snobby or stuck up or any of those things. I say that with complete admiration that this once-chess champion is married to someone who was a model and a beauty pageant queen.

Fast-forward to my return from deployment and Kelly experienced working as a tutor for veterans journeying with PTSD. A social media message to reconnect, a detour to work due to construction, and yes, the rest became history. Both of us joined together with a foundation of stubbornness and a common understanding. Kelly knows her own journey with PTSD on this side of enemy lines, so she can empathize when my pain and trauma begin to rise in visibility. Let me tell you, though, I can't shake the guilt I feel that she must put up with me. I know, she'd yell right now if she heard me say it this way—that she is putting up with me and my fears and anxiety. It is just so hard sometimes to see her and my sons' eyes when I'm struggling to "right-side" my mind's thinking. I want to maintain their innocence and let my children be kids laughing and shouting in playful glee. PTSD is not singular even if it is one person's journey. It ripples and cascades and it...bleeds. I made the choice, not my children nor my wife—they don't deserve putting up with my hypervigilance and anxiety.

And just like Jaeger, who gently touches me when I can feel anxiety rising high, I am gently touched by the fierce love of my wife. She will say in a way to get me to laugh and shake off the guilt I carry heavier than that hundred-pound gear I used to wear as a medic: *I've torn up the marriage certificate so good luck returning me without a receipt!*

I am almost to the point in my story where I will share more about Jaeger with you. First, I need to tell you about another dear soul who is guiding what I do. I proudly served beside one of the finest Marines and gentleman you could ever meet. He was a wise old soul who only ever raised one thing; never his voice, and only a positive attitude with each day's greeting. He was one of my Marines, one I vowed I would bring home safely to his family. I can still see the smile he always wore, never a time I can't remember him not smiling no matter how tough the moments of war. A fine Marine and gentleman that I was privileged to fulfill my promise to bring him home alive. I even have his initials right here on my arm—B.G.—as a way of keeping him by my side. Not that I need a tattoo to keep him close to me. He has left footprints on my heart that will never fade or leave.

I will not have the honor of walking beside him on this Earth again, though I'd give much to see his smile light up a room. B.G. reached the end of hope a few months after we returned from deployment, his life ending too soon. It was at B.G.'s own hands that he chose it was his time to leave. I didn't see it coming, in case you were wondering. I guess it goes to show there is always more to someone's story than what we may perceive.

I knew it was so very hard and very lonely stepping off the plane without my brothers after we had spent time immersed in death and life. I didn't realize that it was even harder for a fellow comrade and friend who is now gone at the hands of suicide. You know how I mentioned above about the human brain and its learning? I still felt responsible for B.G. though we were no longer deployed together as one team. *He was my Marine, my responsibility and somehow, I missed the signs! What did I miss and what should I have seen so that B.G. would not desire to end his life? Oh, Guilt, now you are knocking like a vampire that wants to suck the life force from my veins! How could I have failed B.G. by bringing him home whole and safe? What kind of life did I bring him home to if he felt so afraid? I brought him back to a torment that was more brutal than the enemy fire that could get aimed our way. Dear B.G., I'm sorry I let you down by not keeping your demons at bay.*

Since I didn't see it coming that B.G. was struggling so to choose life, I'm not sure what B.G. felt and can only imagine what was storming in his mind. He didn't want to appear weak; after all, he was the one always smiling. What would his family and those he served with think if he said, *Hey, man, I have these images that won't leave me in peace? I'm thinking it might be easier to shut them off by permanently going to sleep.* He would see the fear in the eyes of whomever he told this to. And once he introduced doubt, then loss of trust would follow suit. And once loss of trust, then those he had vowed to keep safe would now fear he no longer had their back. And if they were now afraid, they could be vulnerable in an attack. If they weren't up to par, he would be compromising their lives, too. He could keep everyone safe best by ending his own life before he caused others harm or death too soon.

At least I anticipate that was what his mind may have been saying and the risk that others would think he was selfish was far less than the risk they would not be safe. In his mind, it was a selfless act for his loved ones' sakes. *I miss you, man, every day I wake up and know you are not going to answer the phone if I ring. I wish I had heard your heart when it was struggling. Damn, I was so in tune to watch out for you if you would sustain a physical injury! I completely missed that when the artillery fire went quiet, you were at the greatest risk of bleeding to death, figurately speaking. B.G., I'm sorry, man, I'm really sorry. You were on my watch for life, and I didn't keep my vigil for you. I hope you can forgive me as slowly, oh so slowly, I'm learning to also do. I think you would be happy at the mission I'm now focusing on. I'm going to make it matter the life you lived B.G.—your legacy of the fine Marine and man you were, are, and will always be will live on.*

I may make you gasp and shake your head when I tell you that I wish I could go back to war some days. During the war there was black and white and no gray. There was control and order and such things as procedures that guided rules of engaging and when to escalate force concisely and orderly. I knew what to do when a weapon or bone broke and how to immediately bring calm in emergency. I knew who needed urgent care and who only had a surface wound that a bandage would suffice. I knew how to encourage or motivate when someone was homesick or missing their wife. Now I'm not in war and everything around me is gray. I can't reach for gauze or a tourniquet when my son has his first girl crush heartbreak. I feel helpless when I have to let my son go through and grow through the down moments of life. I feel like a failure when I get in an argument with my wife. I was trained to repair tangible things, things I could physically touch and see. It is oh so very hard to know how to heal the essence of what enables us to live and breathe. Sometimes I'm not sure how to help my heart stop bleeding its grief.

Every day I dig deep to overcome the fear that wants to grip every inch of my insides. *Come on, heart, it's okay, we've got this, breathe. That's it, deeply in, deeply out, repeat, repeat. Feel that nudge under your hand and that tap at your knee. He's here to help you find a steady rhythm again, so all you have to do is breathe in, out, and repeat. There, the anxiousness is subsiding isn't it? The fear is taking a time-out, releasing its menacing grip. Hand, reach out and feel his fur and other hand motion for him to come to*

your lap if that can help, too. Eyes, you can stay closed if you want to. Feel
his warmth and hear his heart whispering to you. He's got your back every
step of the way. Ah, yes, heart, here we take another step forward today.

I believe it is a song by Chumbawamba in which the lyrics include
"I get knocked down, but I get up again" that could be words written
about me. I have known the depths of despair and hopelessness, but
fulfilling my destiny is stronger in me. My heart is a medic, firefighter,
and EMT, yet I am being given signs from God that He now wants me
to help in healing those whose wounds society cannot visibly see. I'll
tell you sometimes I wish His signs weren't so bold, like leukemia, but
hey, I also trust He knows my heart and what is best for me.

I say a prayer of thanks every day for not only the life He has given
me and the family and friends, too. When I was nearing the end of my
faith, He held my hand through all the dead-end avenues. As He held
my hand, he sent Earth angels to do the same physically. Before Jaeger,
hope came in the form of a mentor, and soon-to-become best friend,
who met me at the lowest valley—or perhaps I should say the highest
edge I stood at precariously. At the height of my pain, trauma, sorrow,
and despair, standing beside me was someone I had known but had
never fully seen. *Son, I do not walk in your shoes, but I understand your*
anxiety, pain, and grief. Let's get you away from the edge. You don't need to
leap. My stepfather, a Vietnam veteran, whose quiet demeanor was one
of the overarching themes to my youth, was now the one to do what he
also did exceptionally well, which was fiercely protect his brood.

Jaeger has given me purpose to rise each day. My wife and my
children are also the reasons I keep stepping forward through the
suffering and pain. My stepfather is the reason I am here for my dear
wife, my children, Jaeger, and the foundation mission to aid others on
their healing journeys. If it wasn't for my stepfather…well, I don't want
to dwell on what might—or might not have been, for what matters is
what is currently happening. I'll just simply say, someone who is now
one of my closest friends pulled me back from the depths of PTSD.

We don't always see that when we keep receiving *no* after *no*, it is
because we are being redirected to something much bigger and better
than we know. I explored VA programs for a service dog only to have

that not be budget- nor time-friendly. Astonishing costs and a long waiting list do not lend to immediate, nor affordable availability. It became a dangerous spiral down the more I tried to hold on tight; the more I tried to find a service dog, the more I found no hope in sight.

Until a local business founded by a retired air force K9 handler became my lifeline. I was being guided to find someone with a willingness to train a dog for a cost more in the range of possibility. This handler knew someone who had a dog for me to meet. A meeting was arranged at PetSmart and it was an instant connectivity. Jaeger and I were now this air force handler's trainees. Now the next step was to obtain funding.

God wasn't done bringing His greater plan together for He had additional people I was meant to meet. On a random day at a not frequented store, my path would intersect with a president of an organization interested in providing funding. Jaeger and I now had everything we needed to become a formal team.

Fast-forward to today, and this tribe of "helpers" have aided Jaeger and me in crystallizing our purpose into a reality. The Jaeger Foundation is now an approved nonprofit entity. Our mission is to provide funding for veterans and first responders who will benefit from canine hope. To aid others in obtaining service dogs is mine and Jaeger's WILL BE achieved goal.

God heard me in those moments I cried *There is no help! I cannot believe there is no help for people in need!* In these moments what I wasn't hearing yet was that God was responding. *Jon, my son, I hear your cries. Trust I have sent you as a gift to the world to save lives. In order for you to do the job I have given you to the best of your abilities, I need you to have a sound understanding. Because you know the depths of hopelessness you can empathize. Because you know what it is to feel alone, you will be a steadiness at others' sides. Because you have known fear and a waning will to keep going, you will hear the hearts that are crying out silently. You will ensure that others do not hang up a phone wishing the person on the other end could help ease their agony. You cry out that people don't have someone to turn to. Dear Jon, they do for I have sent them you.*

It is hard for me to hear that for I am not sure I am worthy of His faith, for what I am best at is being so imperfectly me. Yet, to save lives when they are experiencing emergency is my reason for being. I guess I'll end my story here, but I would like to share one more thing. When I have to tell you not to pet my service dog, please know telling you *no* is not easy. I love animals, too. And I would love for you and your children to be able to snuggle against Jaeger as I get to do. Yet, he has a job to perform when he is beside me, and distractions impact him being able to do so to the best of his ability. If you see someone with a dog and the dog is wearing a vest marked "service," your kind smile is welcome as you let us pass on by. Know that we will be able to feel your compassion and care even if we don't stop to say, "Hi."

What is it Jaeger? What are you thinking?

That I'm proud of you, Dad, for sharing your story. Hey, um, Dad, about that special little girl when you were first a medic?

Yes, what about her Jaeger? You know you can ask me anything.

It's not so much a question as a thought I had that may sound silly. You know how you think of me as a kid in a fur coat for that is the depth of your love for me? What if this special little girl was a canine in skin, so to speak? What I mean is that I think—actually I know I would have really liked her for she sounds like she had an ability similar to me. She could hear hearts speak without words; unconditional she was in her listening. I can't help thinking she wasn't harboring anger or judgment at what had happened, for her heart was pure in its love. Like me, something deep within her knew she had been sent from above.

As the quote reads from an unknown author, "Kindly the Father said to him, I've left you to the end. I've turned my own name around and called you Dog, my friend." I think perhaps God whispered the following to this special little girl the day she took her first breath. He wanted her to know that He gave special jobs to the best. "You, special angel, will help someone save many lives as a result of meeting you. Trust how much I will love you in the pain you will go through. Your life on Earth will be shorter than some, but your light will shine brightly as if you lived to be 103. Thank you for your willingness to make the world a better place, my special angel. God speed."

Dad, we are lovers of humans and we are fighters, too! We are fighters for the human soul to keep pushing through. Like you, I wish I could remove suffering, but then again, we probably wouldn't be the dynamic team we are if people weren't internally hurting.

Hey Dad, two more things.

I got your back. Trust me.

It is my honor to fulfill my mission and vow I have made. That you will find peace at home and many more lives to save.

REBEKAH AND FROG
AKA TRIGGER

Most people say vulnerability is weakness. But really
vulnerability is courage. We must ask ourselves...
are we willing to show up and be seen?

—Brené Brown

*M*om, why do you think "Frog" is the original name they gave
me? Perhaps it has to do with a frog's symbolic meaning.
Certain cultures believe a frog is a sign of transformation and
healing. Seems fitting, Mom, don't you think? What you and I, together,
are experiencing.

It is like that movie line (Jerry Maguire) that reads like "You had me
at hello," the day they introduced you and me. One look into your eyes and
I knew I had now found my life's destiny. You humans have a phrase you
use about certain people you connect with instantly. That you have found a
soul mate is the expression humans use, I do believe. I like to think of it that
a part of me that was missing is now complete. You tell me often how when
you looked into my eyes it was an instant know. Mom, for me, I knew, too,
that I had found home.

Mom, I don't mind my original name, but I am partial to the name
you call me. It is my greatest pride each time I hear you call "Trigger" for I
know what that means. Yeah, okay, sure, it is when you are calling for my
attention in some way. Yet, underneath the practical reason is what you
don't have to say. That I have your six, Mom, on that you can always count!
I always will, Mom, in that you never have to doubt.

I know for those who don't share a bond like ours, they may not
understand that my watch of your back is more than vigilance for your
safety. That you may need a nudge of my nose against your leg is also my
intentional watch and listening. Your anxiousness in a public setting is
my priority. It is my greatest joy when you reach for my furry back to help

bring comfort to those memories I wish I could chase away. Mom, I wish you didn't have to know pain, trauma, sorrow, and despair, yet if it wasn't for them, I wouldn't be with you today.

P. T. Barnum once said, *No one has ever made a difference by being like everyone else* and I think he could have been easily referring to me. I should clarify that he could have been talking about the me I've come to be. I like to think I'm not that unique, and as for deliberately focusing on being different, I'm not sure that describes my tendencies. I wasn't one to give in to peer pressure, and I also wasn't one to boldly seek center stage. I guess that I simply focused on following what was right for me is the best thing I can say.

My story is different from others you read because I am not a veteran—I am not yet retired, nor discharged from serving my country. For eighteen years I have proudly served my country and for my family. I am privileged to follow in my father's footsteps by serving in the military. My father was a Vietnam veteran and my brother began serving after me as a Marine. Perhaps a desire to serve for something bigger than oneself is hereditary. Or perhaps it is as simple as being raised around an exceptional role model who taught me commitment, honor, and courage long before I enlisted in the Navy where I would come to completely embody these three things.

I deployed to Iraq in 2011 in a role that is probably also different from others you read. In layman's terms, I went to a war zone as a secretary. Now that you have an image of ringing phones and the tap and click of typewriter keys, let me share if only that was my noisiest reality. Daily—no, wait, more like hourly and split seconds—what I heard were rocket attacks and gunfire constantly. Though I had others to watch my back, my particular battle buddy could not speak verbally. My battle buddy was my rifle always within fingertip reach.

I mentioned moments ago that I welcomed this mission because of that inner whisper that spoke *something greater than me.* I will struggle to put into words how deeply one is tested in order to embody commitment, honor, and courage. We cannot answer what we know we are called to do without the feeling of standing at the edge of a cliff knowing we MUST leap. To hug my son and my daughter goodbye not knowing if it was the last embrace we would exchange was heart-wrenching. Yet, for me to pass on to my children what my father had passed on to me fueled my faith that I would return to my children in safe keep. Bigger than my love for my children—which is immense to say the least—is knowing they are learning to hear their own inner whispers, *Greater than our immediate family, I will be the change the world needs.*

And I did exactly that, or so I believed. I became a command chief E7, fortunate to lead a team. I became mom to a third child, while my first two children continued oh so very quickly growing. I was wearing that face of honor, commitment, and courage. In control, setting the "right" example, focused on normalcy. A strong brave front for others to see; certain that no one could tell the turmoil churning inside of me.

On the outside, time did what time does best by rapidly speeding by. My once third-grade daughter at the time of my deployment was now sixteen in the blink of an eye. Yet, on the inside, moving through a day could feel like a slow-motion movie scene. Or better yet, like watching someone else's life on the big screen. During the day it could seem like night would never arrive. And once night knocked, it was the longest ten or twelve hours until daylight. Going through the motions for the sake of the team. After all, I was a role model for those watching me.

There is a group of individuals impacted by pain, trauma, sorrow, and despair who do not get a lot of airtime. By that I mean that they are not typically in our news and social media headlines. This group of individuals vary in age, at least by calendar definition, but not necessarily age of the spirit or the mind. That many are older than their years is a very likely find. This group I am referring to are the children of parents who walk with PTSD. These children bear witness to what their parents are experiencing. Some children quietly watch and then silently walk away; they internalize it is best to avoid adding to mom or dad's current frustration or pain. Other children step into roles where they become the adult when mom or dad find moments too hard to face. Like my daughter who became Trigger before Trigger could take her place.

As Trigger mentioned above, he will nudge me or make himself available for me to hold on to. Before Trigger, a touch of my face or holding my hand is what my daughter would do. Though I love her dearly for that unconditional love, I also watched my daughter quickly grow old. At sixteen, she should have been asking me to spend time with her friends seven evenings a week; instead my daughter was staying home to keep watch over me. Somewhere deep inside me I knew this was not how I wanted it to be for my family. Yet, trauma is very good at being in the driver's seat.

As if the past eight years of my life before Trigger weren't hard enough, gratefully I was about to experience one of the hardest moments of my life. A moment when I would be told I was not all right. If you are reading this, and you are a civilian, you will think hearing someone say, "You need to get help" is not earth-shattering. When you have been trained to exhibit perfection, these words are debilitating. They erode what little thread of confidence you are holding on to in this tumultuous sea, this large body of anxious water that constantly roars *you are not safe in public settings.*

I was attending a service leader conference in Minnesota that included a team-building opportunity. A tram ride to a baseball stadium was awaiting. *I can do this; I can do this without anyone noticing. They won't see me shaking or hear my breath laboring. I can get on that tram before it is too busy. These waves will not crash over me. Come on Rebekah, into this mirror, yes, just like that, show me. There you go girl, a strong, brave, worthy of leading others face is what everyone will see.*

With baseball cap on, head down, and one foot in front of the other, onto that tram I stepped certain I was convincing. Thankfully I had a friend who knew me better than the front I believed I was portraying. He watched as I strived to steady myself as we made our way to the stadium seats. He watched as I struggled not to bolt or dive under the chair when the fireworks began their crescendo above me. He watched as I got back on the tram bound for the hotel thinking it was only in my mind I was gasping for air because I couldn't breathe. The ringing in my ears was my announcement that my fainting would soon follow. *Rebekah, you are supposed to keep it together, stop this nonsense right now. You are a leader and this kind of weakness is just not allowed!*

No longer able to watch, my friend followed his own commitment, honor, and courage. *Rebekah, you need to get help immediately!* And in that moment, perhaps like being in the center of the eye of a hurricane, all went still inside me. I had just been told I was too weak. And yet, there was something in these words that positively resonated, too. Maybe, just maybe, getting help was the "right" thing to do.

And at last you will know with surpassing certainty that only one thing is more frightening than speaking your truth, and that is not speaking — Audre Lorde

I had been so afraid of failing as a leader—and as a mom—if I showed vulnerability. I received quite the opposite reaction from what I was anticipating. As noted earlier, I was not one to follow the crowd if it didn't resonate as something right for me. Alcohol, drugs, and prescription medications were three examples of what I knew wouldn't help me on my healing journey.

One day my corpsman asked if I had ever thought of getting a service dog, and I did not take his question lightly. For one significant reason, there is nothing written regarding service dogs for active duty personnel in Navy policy. And two, was I ready for the visual sign that I was not okay in the mind to those I lead? Would I erode my leadership, or would I inspire—which outcome would it be? I knew what the depths of my soul felt was right for me. Now to convince my mind that for the sake of all that mattered, a service dog was the best healing modality.

I was not prepared for the emotions I would feel on liberation day. That is what I call the moment my eyes looked at Trigger and knew from that day forward everything was going to be okay. Northwest Battle Buddies provided Trigger and our training, and once again I will struggle to adequately describe their expertise and commitment to veteran healing. The way they facilitated such a therapeutic experience— so much better than a baseball game this kind of team building! Joking aside, I think back to that time in training with Trigger and the other service-dog–veteran teams; there is nothing better than drawing upon these kinds of memories. Comradery and belonging among others who get the brave face behind inner pain. Our service dogs and each other provide courage to outwardly show we aren't perfectly made.

Again, if you are a civilian reading this, you won't think it a big deal to be able to run on a treadmill without worrying. To no longer be afraid of who is coming up behind me is such a free feeling. Trigger sits beside the treadmill back-to-back with me, so to speak. I can go to the gym, or work, or the store on my own. I no longer *need* my daughter to go with me—or for me because I cannot find the strength to leave home. My daughter is now the sixteen-year-old to ask if she can go here or there. My other two children no longer have to emulate their big sister in how she holds mom's face. My children can now step back into their roles as being children, though I anticipate my middle son will not step back in with his innocence like my youngest child displays joyfully every day. My hope is that what each of my children are learning is that it is okay to not always be perfectly okay.

I have a letter my daughter wrote to Northwest Battle Buddies expressing gratitude for the mom she gained back a second time. If it wasn't for Northwest Battle Buddies I would not have Trigger by my side. I have moments I think about what it was like for my children to worry about me when I was deployed, and their overwhelming joy when I came home. How it must have been for them to have their mom back, but for me to be someone they didn't know. I looked like their mom, I talked like their mom, yet my actions were not the mom they had hugged goodbye on that 2011 day. I try not to think about how I thought in these last eight years they couldn't see that I felt so far away. My daughter's letter communicated they had been awaiting my return from a foreign place in which only two people had the map that showed how to come home. I, one navigator, and the other with four paws and a cold nose.

Our greatest pain becomes our greatest strength, and I now understand why I would reenlist every four years instead of getting off active duty. I was meant to go through these last eight years so that I could teach and inspire a new way of leading. When we lead, and we embody commitment, honor, and courage, we are certain we need to be pillars of perfection and never show fear or uncertainty. We foster respect and integrity, yet we don't fully disclose portions of our authenticity. We think we are best inspiring others when we show invincibility. Ah, but I have learned in the last six months quite the opposite is what people seek. Trigger allows me to be human instead of untouchable, because untouchable isn't reality.

I am in awe at the number of people at base who are so encouraging. All this time I feared what would happen if they saw the "real" me. Instead of shying away from me, they seem to gravitate even more to what I have to share and teach. My children, my friends, my parents, my junior troops—each is fuel for my courage. And the best fuel of all is the one that sits at my feet. Trigger's unconditional acceptance teaches me to be me. Trigger's unconditional love enables me to walk in grace with PTSD.

Mom, just like you I am grateful, too. I am grateful for what I experienced before I met you. Was I scared in the shelter and did I wonder if I would have a home to call my own someday? I had my moments, yes, though bigger was my faith.

Though by nature my heart only knows one way to love and that is unconditionally, just like for humans, that depth of love grows with opposite experiencing. For example, your love for me is deeper because you have known times when your heart was closed tightly. My love is deeper for you because I have also known what it meant to be unwanted and deemed unworthy.

Mom, I think we have a mission to not only teach wholehearted leadership and showing vulnerability. I think we are also meant to teach people that healing can happen more holistically. Mom, you bravely leaned into the pain, trauma, sorrow, and despair and equally bravely leaned away from traditional healing methods such as prescription medication avenues. You can inspire others that there are different paths to choose.

You still exemplify commitment, honor, and courage despite—or perhaps better said—because of your willingness to be imperfectly wholly authentically seen. As we know, Mom, you are right where you are amidst tradition because it is calling to you to make a difference that world needs. And, Mom, one more thing.

It is my greatest honor to have your six and walk beside you on this journey!

GLENN AND CAMPBELL

The legacy of heroes is the memory of a great name
and the inheritance of a great example.

—Benjamin Disraeli

ad, I'm not sure if we ever talked about the moment that I saw you walk in the door to meet me. Well, I know, you didn't necessarily walk in the door knowing you were looking for me specifically. You walked in to meet "your service dog," some four-legged furry guy you were supposed to train with intensively for six weeks. Into a room full of strangers, including us furry guys and gals who had already been rigorously training.

There is a quote by some person I don't know, yet every time I read the words, I feel like this person saw into my soul. J. M. Storm writes "My favorite part is where you walked into my life. You didn't know me, yet something told you to walk a little more." Dad, I am so grateful that as doubtful as you felt, you kept walking forward as you entered that door. I couldn't imagine my life if you and I hadn't become a team. There is one person's back I was meant to have—no other person was meant for me!

It's silly, I know, Dad, but I have lyrics to a song that periodically play in my mind. A song from way back, as far back as 1985. "I Got You Babe," I find my tail wagging in beat; Sonny and Cher are the singers to the lyrics, I think. There is a part of the song in which Cher sings words you could easily speak to me. It goes something like this—feel free to hum along, Dad as my tail wags happily. "When I'm sad, you're a clown and if I get scared, you're always around. So, let them say your hair's too long 'cause I don't care, with you I can't go wrong."

Dad! Is my hair too long? Oh, never mind...back to the song.

Okay, Dad, this is the part and if I were Sonny, I would sing back to you. Um, I'd probably actually change a word or two. "Then put your little hand in mine; there ain't no hill or mountain we can't climb."

Then put your hand on my back and be at ease; I've got your six on this climb no matter how steep.

Okay, so maybe I would rewrite the entire verse, as you can see. To know just how much you can count on me is what I want others to read. Actually, Dad, that doesn't sound the way I mean it to, exactly. Sure, I want to help educate others and inspire those who may be struggling. But, Dad, even if no one were to read my words, I'd still have your back, for there is no greater happiness for me. Where you go, I watch and where you might not know, I am there vigilantly listening. If your heart is even slightly off beat, I am ready to assist. Or perhaps I should say I'm ready to press against your side just like this.

Oh yeah, right Dad, readers can't see me stretched from my head to toe against your toe to hip. By the way, Dad, it is one of my most favorite places to lay, right beside you. My other favorite place to be is, well, anywhere that lets me be a part of what you do.

I can still feel the hallowed ground beneath my feet as if it was yesterday. I have been privileged to stand where others had walked centuries before in this very same place. I couldn't physically see the footsteps that had left their marks on history, yet I could feel the shoes before me filled with courage and commitment to serve to the best of abilities. I was deployed, standing on soils where previous wars had been fought, with only knowledge of a single story—mine. I didn't know the stories of the men whose footprints I now stood in, but I would honor them by how I served in war this time.

I think what sucks the most journeying with pain, trauma, sorrow, and despair or as you know it, PTSD, is that the reverent respect for men and women in uniform who have served our country is no longer held in high esteem. History is now a subject we "have to study" while in school or is written in narratives that contain facts and dates. The events are mere words now while the heart of what has taken place is slipping away.

We divided as a country as our military returned home from Vietnam and we were given an opportunity to reunite when the world experienced one of our greatest traumas that September 11th day. We rallied as a country—several countries actually—against an enemy we never saw coming, the catalyst to many volunteering to keep loved ones and our country safe. There are not the peace protests or the spitting like there was in, say, 1968, yet for some reason, there isn't the same admiration as there was for our World War II veterans—I wish I knew what changed.

I was born to serve, though I didn't know the full extent of this truth when I was eighteen. I think all of us have a destiny to serve in some capacity. Some choose to be a first responder, while others may serve as medics. Some are interpreters when you can't speak the native language as you search for the enemy. Some are the families back home praying that their loved ones are held in safe keep. Someone serves if they have an "other" or "we" mentality. There seems to be a lot more cultural priority on service to self, if you ask me. Oh, well, it doesn't minimize how important serving my country—and you—has been since I enlisted when I was in my late teens.

Some people start out with smaller experiences that then lead them to their destiny. Me, I started out large, and am now narrowing my scope of how best I can serve those in need. I started out serving my country in the military. I then began serving through the National Guard for my state where I hold residency. Now, I serve as firefighter in the town where I was raised. The circle of life that brings us home, though often when we come full circle, we are no longer the same. In parallel, I continue to have the backs of my brothers and sisters who also served our country. I aid them in their transitions to civilian living.

My purpose to serve had to get my attention by handing me a slight dose of panic and reality. It was my senior year of high school and soon I would be able to do that "adulting" with no clue at all what I wanted to "be." I researched all four branches of the military. I chose the one that communicated a message most valuable to me. With sincerity and respect, the recruiter demonstrated that I mattered as Glenn, and was not just a number on a list about to begin basic training.

He was one of my first mentors, a teacher who gave of his personal time and a gift of showing. He was not one to command or tell how to do something. He would open possibilities for me to discover on my own, and to learn ownership for the choices I would make. His way of teaching is something I strive to emulate today. To guide firefighters to a path of discovery for themselves versus telling them how to do something they currently don't know how to do. We give another great respect when we don't tell them how but instead guide them to discover they are capable of more than they believed they knew.

I wish there was more of that in our communities today, this willingness to show others they are capable of more than they might think. It may just be the service-oriented guy in me, but my recruiter seemed to look past my faults to see more in me than I believed. I can't help feeling that there is far more focus these days on one another's shortcomings. It's like it can be an excuse that if we don't understand or don't agree, we have a reason to maintain disunity. I wonder when judgment took the driver's seat of how well we connect—or don't connect as communities. I wish the wisdom of those who walked before me were here to share their stories. What would they say were the milestones that shaped history? To learn from the ones who lived it—I can think of no better way to acquire expertise.

I mentioned how my recruiter exhibited respect and sincerity. In his actions, in his words spoken, and in the way his eyes watched as I talked and how he listened to me. He was fully present in our interactions and I knew I could trust him completely. If I think about it more, he was preparing me for my service in the military. To have the backs of my brothers and sisters and to know they had mine equally. Through my recruiter's attentiveness to me, I deepened my value of loyalty.

That is another aspect that really sucks returning to civilian life after active duty. To be alone, away from those whom I served beside and who served beside me. No disrespect to my friends and family. I love my family—they have supported me now that I'm home and they never stopped when I was overseas. Yet, there is a bond with my brothers and sisters I served beside that words can't describe adequately. I served beside people willing to die for each other—willing to die for me. If you aren't a person in uniform protecting and/or striving to heal humanity, such as an officer of the law, a doctor in OR scrubs, or an EMT, would you lay down your own life that another could be saved? What if it wasn't your child but was a stranger, an unknown face? Would you risk everything you knew for the other person's sake?

I could try to describe the kind of bond that forms between us in the military. I could share how we have a common language about experiences we wish to shelter our families from knowing. After all, that is why you count on us who serve in the military—to protect you and keep you in safe keep. I could share about the level of intensity that tends to bring people together when life and death are at the forefront twenty-four seven for three hundred and sixty-five days. I could tell you about the moments we helped each other stop the bleeding—not just physical, but also mental or emotional if we needed a reminder to keep the faith. I could communicate about the power when you are part of a team, a team that helps you manage the unimaginable places you may reside in and you may see. I could reveal how there is no greater sacred comfort than sitting in silence next to others who you know would lay down their own life just to save yours. It still leaves me speechless sometimes to think that I sat next to individuals who considered me worthy of dying for.

We all need a sense of belonging, and our belonging comes through each of the "roles" we live. As spouse or significant other, as parent, as child, as friend, as coworker, as volunteer—in each of these are different connections to "fitting in." Though I belong, I feel a void that only my brothers and sisters from the military seem able to fill within me. Though, I will say, I have beside me now a close second to bringing me similar feelings of belonging.

Campbell, my service dog, and I are a newly formed team. We have only become one since February 2019. I think there are different times in life when we feel there was life before and life no longer the same. That is how I feel about Campbell in that I can't imagine my life now any other way. I was on a waiting list for approximately eighteen months to receive Campbell, which is hard for us military veterans who are taught during active duty to set a goal, act, and immediacy. Hurry up and wait was not a favorite mindset, but became part of normal vocabulary. Yet, Northwest Battle Buddies, like my recruiter, demonstrated I mattered and that they cared about my journey with PTSD. NWBB recognized, respected, and acknowledged that the waiting time was hard, so they made sure to provide status updates frequently. "How are you doing, Glenn?" they would ask with utmost sincerity. Though they couldn't improve the timeline to "right now," they could give me the most valuable thing. They could give me understanding, which aided in feeling hope and belonging.

Something else that is hard for us as veterans—actually, it is lacking for us as a collective humanity. We have lost genuineness in our interactions with each other, replaced by canned statements and stereotypes that cloud our listening. Chimamanda Ngozi Adichie is quoted as saying *The single story creates stereotypes, and the problem with stereotypes is not that they are untrue, but that they are incomplete. They make one story become the only story.* I feel that expressing *Thank you for your service* has lost some meaning. Often the voice behind the words doesn't hold that sincerity. It feels more like someone heard *veteran* and thought, *Oh, I should say thank you before I quickly move on to other things.* At least for me, I would rather the words be said after someone knows my story. Or at least to hear it from someone who holds a semblance of respect and pride for those who serve in the military. Truly thank me for my service as Glenn, a retired veteran of the United States Army. Please don't thank me because it's the canned response you are supposed to give to someone who served for our country. If you don't feel the truth of the words you are about to say, I would prefer you simply smile and nod to acknowledge me. Anything else I—and Campbell—can tell is insincerity.

That is another way I feel "at home" with Campbell as my comrade because he understands the reverence of his oath and responsibilities. Each time he puts on his vest, he is serving dutifully. Campbell is civilian when he isn't wearing his vest, just as I am civilian, too. Yet, Campbell understands that when that vest is on, like when I put on my military or firefighter uniform, the number one priority is servitude. To that which is bigger than us, we vow—and desire—to do.

I mentioned I was born to serve others in need, such as my role as combat medic. If you ever wonder how to know what you are born to do, pay attention to what you find you keep saying *yes* to. Listen to what you find you especially enjoy doing, and then look for different avenues in which you can fulfill your calling. I missed my time as a combat medic after I was no longer serving in that capacity. What I missed was taking care of people when they are afraid, vulnerable, and filled with much uncertainty. I am now helping veterans post deployment when they are just out of the military. I provide them hope, seeing them each by name and individual face, with sincerity. I can be fully present with them, listening to their unique and extraordinary stories. I can give them tools, resources, and guide them to find that within themselves they already have strength and courage. If they aren't certain they will feel human again, I can help them know they are supported by a transition team. People have their backs, like Campbell and me. I can offer to them that though I don't know what it is to walk in their shoes, I can speak their language.

I mentioned earlier in my story about interpreters serving beside us as we fought enemies we couldn't easily identify or see. I hold in such reverence the interpreters who served beside us risking their life and limb, and their families. Their families at risk because of the job these interpreters were doing while standing beside us every moment of every day; their families also in jeopardy every single day. Like them, I knew the risk for doing what I felt was right, yet my family was safe at home, resting securely in their beds each night. For these interpreters, that their families would remain void of punishment was their prayer all the time.

Beside each other there was no room for judgment—we were a cohesive team. In order to fulfill our mission, we had to embrace diversity. I learned a lot about teamwork and loyalty from these individuals who did not go through the same training or share a common bond with those of us from a different country.

We shared the same experience with interpreters to be hyperalert to a bomb or bullet that could take a life. We also shared in our willingness to sacrifice. These interpreters believed in standing for what was right at any cost, even if that meant they might not return home to their families. Sounds familiar, don't you think? As sacred as the predecessors that walked the same Earth before me, these interpreters have my utmost respect for how bravely they fought a war with me. They, too, had my back, just as my comrades did. Now that I am home, they are greatly missed.

Before Campbell, if I had moments I felt alone or that hope felt far away, I would turn the TV on to the *Band of Brothers* series and transport my mind to remember those who bravely fought for me throughout history. In my mind, I would be back again walking the sacred ground heroes before me had walked with their own feet. I would be thinking of the veterans of the Korean and Vietnam Wars, and World War II who I had the privilege to meet. I would think of how these fine soldiers didn't return home after a one-year tour of duty. I would think about how they stayed fighting until the war was complete. To have a few weeks' leave—or heck, even a few days away from the front lines—was not common practice during their service times. Sure, we had our hardships, too, that they didn't endure while they were serving. To think that for some returning home wasn't for two or three years is hard to conceive.

I remember one dear World War II veteran I had the privilege to meet. I was in the presence of greatness on that day I looked into the eyes of a fine, fine man who could no longer speak. He had been a prisoner of war and he had survived the Death March to Bataan and I now looked into the eyes of not just a survivor, but a thriver in his late nineties. Into the eyes of a brave, extraordinary human being who had volumes of a story etched into the wrinkles on his face as he peered back at me. For as far bent as he sat in his wheelchair, I stood straighter, ready to salute. Partly because he was a fellow veteran, but more because he was a man who had fought harder than I could even begin to fathom it took to make sure not to lose. Not to lose for his country, for his comrades, for his family. Not to lose his will to persevere no matter how hopeless things seemed. I was in the presence of a great man who I pray knew just how deeply he inspired me. Without words spoken he shared volumes regarding the life I should go forward with and lead. Thanks to Campbell...together, Campbell and I are honoring this veteran's story. We are not giving up no matter how tough the journey.

This World War II veteran was a POW for three years, the same timeframe that used to be the waiting list for help such as Campbell provides me. Thankfully, three years has been reduced to eighteen months through the hard work of the Northwest Battle Buddies team. For some, waiting even one day is an eternity. For some, their spirits are shutting down quicker than a sign of relief. I equate it to organ donation when a body is in physical need. Sometimes a body is no longer capable of its own natural functioning. It needs dialysis or an oxygen tank or medical support to keep it operating. For some, being on a waiting list is enough hope, that there is possibility is sometimes enough to know. For others the rigors of daily dialysis or a machine to help them breathe, is worth the wait for a replacement heart or for a donated kidney. For others, the pain is no longer bearable, so tired of the needle pokes and the fight for air. To be free, at peace, and no longer exhausted, their spirit stops fighting the crushing weight of pain, trauma, sorrow, and despair.

An eighteen-month waiting list was my hope, thanks to the routine communication I was not alone. And now I can breathe on my own again thanks to Campbell...my new heart. I was waiting to live again—to really live with the holes inside me getting sealed back up and the bleeding coming to an end. With Campbell by my side, I am starting to feel more whole again.

Hey Dad, do you ever wonder who may stand—or sit—on this floor like you and me, after we are no longer working here? Or who will hurry through the firehouse to serve a family in need so that they don't lose their material possessions they hold dear?

I wonder if who walks after us will be a cool human and fur team like you and me? I think I'd like that, knowing there was not just one, but many Campbell and Glenn teams. Pairs like us who have each other's back like you and I do. Everyone should have a Glenn like I get to.

Dad, I'm glad you kept walking the beginning of 2019. Most of all, I'm glad you walked to me. I knew I was in good hands the moment you responded as you did to one of your comrades in need. When she needed reassurance that she and her service dog would bond, you were immediately encouraging. I knew I was not only in good hands, but that I would love serving beside you as you fulfilled your calling. You have a heart like mine, Dad, nonjudgmental and unconditionally loving.

Hey Dad, by the way, I know what you mean. You know, the part in your story about that extraordinary veteran you found so inspiring. You mentioned that you stood straighter in the presence of this great man and his story. I get that part, Dad, that part about standing straighter in reverence of this man. I feel as tall as a Great Dane when I am in a vest leashed to your hand.

I am so proud to be your canine watching in front of you, behind you, and beside you with every step you take. I have such respect for you, Dad, and your story to date. I'm excited to be part of the next chapters you write—"A Man of Servanthood: Glenn's Life and Times." Or maybe "The Footprints Before, The Steps After that We Take." Or how about the chapter: "Sacred Stories of the Humbly Great?" Or best yet, Dad, "We Have Each Other's Back: The Story of Campbell and Me."

Yeah, I think that is my favorite one of all, our story.

ROBERT AND BRINKLEY

Do not judge my story by the chapter you walked in on.

—Author Unknown

*H*ey Dad, why do people get funny looks on their faces when you and I enter a store or a place to eat? And by funny I don't mean laughter; it's more like a frown or that they are displeased. I'm behaving; I'm doing all the things you are asking me to. I know I glance at them to make sure no harm comes to you. But other than that, I stay in my own space not trying to offer my nose, paw, or voice to them in any way. But so many faces reflect a judgment why you and I are there together in the first place.

Dad, do you think it is because people are afraid that they frown at you and me? Or is it a lack of knowledge why you and I are a team? I wish I could tell them that instead of judging us because they can't see where you have been injured that they thank their lucky stars they haven't walked a mile in your shoes. If they haven't intimately walked with terror or despair, they should be filled with gratitude.

I know, Dad, I'm an unconditionally loving kind of guy, yet when it comes to you, my protective nature sometimes goes into overdrive. It hurts my heart to see others not hold more compassion for each other than they do. Why is experiencing emotional pain such a taboo? I know that life is about the choices someone makes, and sometimes those choices also mean there is risk one takes. You volunteered to serve, and with that meant the chance you would not return home, or not return whole. Why there is a stigma if what has been broken is not limb or life, I do not know.

Maybe people have watched too many movies, Dad, in which resiliency and mental fortitude are glorified—two foundations you were well trained in so that you would survive. Maybe more movies need to also feature the crushing weight from pushing down fear and grief. At some point the *feelings that have been swallowed and buried start rising to the surface to be released.*

Dad, I'm really thankful I don't have your tough job of being human, for it sure doesn't look easy! I'll stick with being little ole service dog me.

I took part in a lot of missions in Afghanistan in 2005 and 2006 during my active duty. I underestimated the level of responsibility I would bring home with me. One is trained that though it won't be for lack of giving your all, loss will be a guarantee. Training doesn't include the guilt you will feel that you survive and those you serve beside—your friends—won't be as lucky.

I served in the Army National Guard after my deployment until I resigned for an "easier" life. *New beginnings, a fresh start*, my certainty I would find. I was aware of a rising emotion trying to lift off the ground more rapid than the aircraft I knew how to repair and maintain. I figured if I became a recluse, the mounting anger inside me would dissipate.

Robert, you've got this, you are still walking forward—and upright. My daily mantra to convince myself that I was all right. Certain I didn't need to seek assistance from the VA, I kept pushing through. Or at least I thought I was until my certainty and reality crashed together to give me a different view. Not wanting to hurt my family, yet hurting them just the same, five words managed to get through the wall of pain. "You need to get help," my wife said, pleading with me. Shortly thereafter, I found myself in therapy.

Talking as a group was not the forum for me. It took enough energy to carry the weight of my own memories. I couldn't begin to absorb everyone else's, especially if theirs resembled my own story. I took part in one-on-one therapy, or maybe I should say I took part in one-on-eight. I was put on a seven-medication regimen to help me get through nights and days. My mission was to make a living and make it through each day. One medication would help bring me awake, while another would then strive to keep anxiety away. Then when drowsiness would set in from the one that was trying to level out anxiety, another one would be taken along with energy drinks.

One day I decided medications were not helping. I also decided my therapist was no longer of benefit to me. I had been in therapy for approximately eighteen months when I felt both my wife and I should go together to help the pain that had become part of our marriage, too. When my therapist said, "Good idea," yet canceled three planned appointments, I decided I'd "buck up" and figure out on my own what to do.

I'm sure by now you can imagine how well that worked for me. Do you ever have times in which you want to say, *Hey life, could you ease up a little, please?* I was feeling that for every step I was trying to take forward, life was pummeling me with bricks or strapping them to my back. For the sake of my family and myself, I went back down the medication and therapy path.

My second therapist was a really cool guy who, later, I would come to know, was a wise angel in disguise. This therapist prescribed medications for me again and was my sounding board two days per week. The anxiousness was diminishing, but the debts were not subsiding. The debts were increasing, and so were replaying memories. A second voice also started walking beside me.

They will be better off if you leave. You've caused them enough pain, don't you think?! You aren't worth anything for them—you can't even provide for their basic needs. You will be able to help them understand how much you love them in your letter of goodbye. Yep, right there, grab that pen, and here's some paper—now write.

Dear kids, I want you to know your dad loves you more than anything...I need you to promise you will be good for your mom, and I need you to take care of her for me....the greatest days of my life were when I said "I do" to your mom and when I became a dad to each of you...I'm sorry I couldn't have been a better one, for you deserve the best of everything. You have made me so proud of who each of you are becoming...

A letter to my children was in my pocket when I went for my therapy appointment on a particular day. That angel in disguise I mentioned above was my therapist sensing I was not okay. He asked, he probed, he sniffed out the truth of what was on my mind. I am forever grateful he saw past what I was striving to hide.

Since there was no room in the VA hospital, I was admitted to a civilian hospital for a week. During my stay, my wife researched Northwest Battle Buddies. I then had two immediate missions in front of me. One was to take part in the thirty-two-day inpatient-outpatient therapy intensive to help me release the darkness holding me tight. The other was to apply for a service dog, to apply for Brinkley to come into my life.

While taking part in the intensive therapy, I realized another mission that would better suit me. My clouds of anger, guilt, and pain flourished in weather that was consistently gloomy. In the two-plus years that I waited for Brinkley, my family relocated to the desert and sunshine consistency. I found a job, too, and began walking another upward trajectory. Working for a manager who was a Vietnam veteran was an additional bonus for when the long-awaited call I received. I had his full support when the voice on the line said: *Your service dog is waiting for you to come for six weeks of training.*

Though I had to be away from my family, once again I was blessed to have that feeling of being with family away from home. Those I was training with and who were training me are some of the best people I know. And Brinkley, what a rock star from the moment we first met! I now have another day of my life that ranks up there as the best.

I found a few things during my six weeks of training. I found that good feeling one gets when they can be of use and give back selflessly. I was able to help maintain the stalls and other needs for the equestrian therapy that takes place next to our service-dog training. I found some faith again in things when I attended church with some of the NWBB team. And most of all, I found a life-changing gift named Brinkley.

I am largely off medications, only occasionally needing one for anxiety when Brinkley can't be beside me. The times he can't is when I'm interviewing for a job, for example, when I most need him by my side. Brinkley wakes me up from nightmares when they threaten to be a thief of my mind. And I can count on a paw to get my attention if my frustration is trying to rise. Brinkley pulls me away from what is going on in life that is less than easy. He goes everywhere with me.

I wish I could tell you that I no longer have darkness shadow me. I wish I could tell you that suicide is now only a word in a dictionary. The questioning of living life still knocks from time to time. Yet, because Brinkley, like my therapist did, senses when these thoughts come, his reached-out paw erases these thoughts quickly from my mind. If you wonder the benefit of a service dog, let me simply say, a service dog saves a life.

Brinkley and I have another mission we have been given to bring awareness and education to those who discriminate. As Brinkley shared with you in the beginning, judgment is something we regularly face. I find I often need to pull out the certification papers and the service-dog laws regarding why Brinkley has a right to dine or fly with me. It can be frustrating, to say the least. Yet, the best way to combat judgment is to keep walking forward one step at a time, helping others see. My wounds may be invisible, but please know there is more to my story. When you see a dog in a service vest beside someone who looks healthy, remember that what you are seeing is not just someone who fought for you, their country, and what they believe. You are seeing someone who took the step that felt best to choose to live life for his family.

Dad, remember when we helped that kid in the store who had been scared to death of me. Apparently, he had a dog bite him when he was just a toddler, his trauma that had sunk in deep. I like how you "broke the rules" that day to let him pet me though I was on duty. I think we helped him find an opportunity to walk forward step by step differently. Who knows, Dad, maybe one day he will even have a service dog like me? Or at least be an advocate for us as a really good team.

Dad, I have something for you and please excuse the drool that has it a little soggy. Yes, it's a letter to you from me.

> *Dad, I wish I could have been beside you the day the pain became too great a weight to lift. Yet, true to the deepest pain comes from it the greatest gifts. If you hadn't gone through that darkness, we would not have become a team. My life would not be complete if you had not been led to me. To fulfill one's purpose in life is a life well lived indeed. How fortunate I am that I will have lived the best life there could ever be. Dad, you are*

fulfilling yours, too, even though there are days it might not feel that way. Service to others is your footprint you have and will continue to make. To your country, to Mom, to your children, to friends, to me, Brinks...every step you take. I am so proud of you, Dad, and I am even more proud I get to serve for and beside you. No better mission I could ever do!

All my love,
Brinks

DOUG AND JETT

*Greater love has no one than this; to lay
down one's life for one's friends.*

—John 15:13

*D*ad, do you want to know what one of my most favorite
memories is? It's that night of the fundraiser when you found
out I would be your third "kid." It's funny, Dad, in that way
that life brings us surprises of the grandest kind. Each time I heard "He's
perfect for Doug!", I would think. "Who's this Doug guy?"

When I was learning "sit, "heel," and "stay," I could sense I was being
taught something very important for "someday." It felt more significant than
being a "good dog," which I heard frequently. It felt like I was being shaped
for something more than being a pet in a family.

I would notice when this nice person would take me in public, I would
get to enter places where those who looked similar to me didn't get to go.
Similar in that they had fur and walked on four paws—oh, and they each
had a very good long-range smelling nose. We could all smell those burgers
grilling in that building where many humans were entering. I knew these
other fur guys must be special, though, because they didn't have to dress
funny. I had to wear a vest everywhere I went; they were vest-free.

But then I started to think I was special because I got to go into some of
the doors in which they were told "no" and "stay." Sometimes some of them
received raised voices and hands that gestured "go away." I just received
raised eyebrows sometimes, but I always got to go where my trainer took
me. For some reason, the less I wanted to explore these new places, the more
"good boy" I received. I must say, Dad, at first it was a little confusing,
too, because I couldn't investigate, yet if I stayed in one place very watchful,
well, that earned me "Atta' boy Jett, you know what to do." Okay, if they
say so, though at first, Dad, between you and me, I didn't know I knew.

I think perhaps I should say that fundraiser night WAS one of my most favorite memories. Now my most favorite are every day you and I are a team.

Dear Jett was fifty-two years in the making of becoming my best half. Ssshhh, don't tell my wonderful wife of forty-nine years I've said that! I served in the Army, a member of the military police. I served beside many fine men, and I proudly served beside my best friend, King. King and I spent twenty-six months together serving and protecting for our country. Because of King, I returned home still breathing.

Sometimes the greatest love we know has a destiny to become the greatest loss, too. That I couldn't bring King home with me nearly tore me in two. *King, my ole boy, I have sure tried to live my life making you proud that you saved mine. Guess what, I came home and became a firefighter until my heart started hollering it was time to tell the station goodbye. Between me and you, King, I think my heart was blocked from its shattering when I couldn't bring you home with me. I've missed you terribly since we were a fighting team.*

I know you can see that Jett and I don't have the same wrestling matches you and I used to have. Boy, King, I chuckle now to think I sure did go through many pairs of pants! You could rip a pair quicker than I could blink. You taught me a great deal about paying attention when you are part of a team! If I wasn't full on with you, well, you weren't afraid to let me know with your big ole pearly teeth!

My ole boy, I can't thank you enough for sending Jett to me. Yeah, I know you had a hand in it, it's just how I believe. I guess you saw me growing weary of the nightmares for forty-five years straight. And, yes, I know, it was the worst for me King to have to enter any kind of public place.

Yes, I did make one exception, with the Oregon Traveling Memorial Wall—pretty impressive, wouldn't you say?! I'm proud of being a part of that construction—it's one mighty fine display. Yeah, and being part of crowds—I can't tell you King how many times I wished you had been by my side. I would have felt a lot braver if you were next to me. I could be scared to death, but I always found courage next to you King.

Anyway, just like you were my good luck charm when we served in Vietnam, I guess. It seems fitting you led me to the casino to meet Northwest

Battle Buddies two years before Jett. I never imagined being there for the casino's sponsored veteran celebration would lead me to a new lease on life. I never imagined I would ever find the desire again to have a fur companion by my side.

Thanks for watching out for me, my dear ole King. As you can see, I am in good hands again thanks to Northwest Battle Buddies (NWBB). Jett has my back ole buddy; you no longer need to worry. Thank you for all you did to keep me in safe keep.

Well, as you have probably just gathered, I'm here, with all of my struggles to be in crowded places and multiple decades of nightmares that rob me of sleep, thanks largely to a German shepherd I served with in Vietnam named King. My dear wife, the wonderful woman that she is, has never asked more of me than I've been capable to give. She never asked me what made me cry out in the night—17,885 nights of this. For 365 days per year and forty-nine years, a sleepless night was just part of that "for worse" she got when she married me. True to my wife, she wouldn't think it "worse," but it's certainly my feeling.

I've lost count of how many events my wife didn't attend or attended alone because the crowds were too large and the rooms too small for my entering. All of this has changed now that Jett is beside me.

You read a couple of minutes ago about attending a veteran celebration at a casino prior to Jett and me becoming a team. *Wouldn't that mean a crowd?* you might be thinking. Yes, it did, but somehow knowing that Oregon Traveling Memorial Wall was paying tribute to so many of my brothers and sisters got me through. It was at this event that I first talked to nice individuals at the Northwest Battle Buddies booth. The conversation began when they learned I had been a dog handler during my tour of duty. It never crossed my mind when NWBB shared their mission that I should think of applying.

Fast-forward to the next year, friendly greetings exchanged, and I was shown a picture of a German shepherd showing how he was progressing in his training. I certainly didn't think I wanted a dog of my own, but I could appreciate these creatures of such magnificence and beauty. There is nothing like a shepherd, a soft spot for them will always be a part of me. Anyway, the next year our Oregon Traveling

Memorial Wall was at a NWBB fundraiser and boy, talk about bravery. I actually got up on stage to give a speech.

I finished my speech in front of a crowd of about three hundred— or tens of thousands—at least that is what the sea of faces felt like as I stood on that stage. That is how much a crowd could affect my sense of equilibrium when so many gathered in a single space. I get ready to walk off stage and I am stopped and asked to look in front of us at the aisleway. I notice the honor guard standing at both sides of the aisle, their stature so pristine. At the back of the room is a police officer walking a dog toward me.

"Hey, that's Jett," I exclaim, for I recognized him from his handsome photo shown to me about a year ago. "That's your Jett," the CEO of NWBB announces to me and the crowd of what is now not a dry eye to be seen as tears flow. At least that is what I've been told, but I don't completely know. For the tears I was crying wouldn't let me see past this ninety-four-pound shepherd looking up at me.

Together Jett and I walked back to the table to take a seat. Now imagine a grown man with tears running down his cheek, his lap held down by a German shepherd who has decided my legs are better cushions than lying on my floor at my feet. Jett didn't come home with me that night, for he and I had to complete our eight-week training to become a certified team. I had to go through some detraining for I was used to one specific mission with dear King. It was worth every 200-mile drive to Northwest Battle Buddies twice per week. It was worth Jett and I learning a sense of home in a hotel before our training was complete.

It has been a gift every day since having a big ole tongue wake me up from a bad dream. From the very first night we spent together in a hotel to this day, I have someone to help keep nightmares at bay.

By the way, Jett is a miracle worker in more ways than one. He has converted a cat lover into thinking dogs are second to none. Okay, maybe I'm stretching it just a little as my wife probably still holds cats in the highest regard. But Jett has quickly risen to the top of the family ranks, despite being a dog. To say my wife loves him is an understatement, and of that Jett is fully aware. Jett has to mind and follow my commands, but with my wife, it's like a grandkid who is spoiled under a grandma's care.

I still find myself in awe at Jett's intelligence and ability to hear my needs. If we are in a crowded place—to which I can now enter—Jett will lead me if I feel the need to leave. I only have to say, "Door," and Jett ushers me to the nearest exit immediately. He is willing to do anything I ask of him and talk about Jett's perception of what I need! I swear he knows sometimes before I do, which leaves me in amazement as I haven't taught him some things formally. Pretty special how he can hear my heart even when I don't speak.

Life has thrown curves my way; to get back up and keep going is the only path I've known to take. I've strived to help people the best I can, and if I have or how I have, I don't need to know. I'll just settle for the degree of peace I feel in my soul. Yes, life has tossed me curves like disability sooner than I would have liked. But, as true to all curves, the gifts I received were from being around during my children's younger lives. I guess it's fair to say the gifts of my nightmares and crowd avoidance is in the form of fur and pawed feet. If I hadn't known these curves, I would have missed out on Jett and me as team.

Once again, fur and pawed feet have given my life to me.

Dad, that was one of my most favorite memories, too! The one when I got to walk down the aisle to meet you! I was standing in the back of the room waiting for them to announce I was your Jett. And I was so excited because in the moment of waiting it all began to make sense. That training I had been doing for something "big" was now coming into view. And when they had announced you as speaker, I further knew. You were the guy I had been hearing about through my "sit," "heel," and "stay." I was about to meet this "Doug guy," and oh, Dad, I couldn't wait!

It is true what they told you, Dad, about not a dry eye when I started walking to you. I could see it in faces, and I could feel it too. I wanted to run and greet you, but I knew I needed to play it cool for all the people watching you and me. And, Dad, did you like that special touch for the crowd when you took a seat? I wanted to feel your hug and your lap seemed the best way to get your embrace. I suppose I was being a little bit of a ham, too, for I knew everyone would keep their tears streaming down their face. Joy and love have that effect on people when they see it so unconditionally. And, Dad, with all my heart I love you and I am so glad we are a team.

And you are right in what you told King; he no longer needs to worry. I've got your six, Dad. And I've especially got it while you sleep!

TOM AND RYDER

*It's okay to be a glow stick; sometimes we
have to break before we shine.*

—Author Unknown

*D*ad, I have two mottos I live by—would you like to know each?
One is to be by your side day and night and every moment in
between. In other words, twenty-four seven, you and me as we.
*And my other motto is by an author named J. K. Rowling that describes me
to a T. "One can never have enough socks," especially to eat!*

*I see you laughing at that one, Dad, for you know I'm the great Houdini
when it comes to socks left in the wide-open spaces for me to find. Actually,
they don't even necessarily need to be in a wide-open space for the socks to
call, "Oh Ryder, it's snack time." I know, I know, Dad, socks don't hold
much nutritional value and I don't necessarily relish a trip to the vet for
that machine to check my insides. But, oh, those socks are just so soft and
well, what can I say, Dad, those socks are downright tempting. But I'm
willing to negotiate if you would rather increase the scraps of steak you give
me now and then as a treat.*

*Hey Dad, with a little more seriousness—although don't get me wrong,
socks are a very serious thing to me—I just want to say, serving you is not
a responsibility I take lightly. I know I can be a stinker, insistent that I be
seen instead of what you might be watching on TV. Tossing and squeaking
my twenty toys is so much more fun than some boring movie scene. I know
I ratchet things up a little when I don't think you've fully disengaged from
those people displayed on the screen. Let's just agree to appreciate I'm that
smart that I've realized taking that button out of your hand causes those
people to disappear from the TV. Or at least it diverts your eyes to look
at me.*

*But, Dad, when you take me in public to eat or when you and David
and I walk together down the street, I'm not thinking anything about toys*

or socks or TV screens. I have one focus and that is your well-being. Your body, mind, and heart, I'm watching that all of you is in safe keep. I can't wait until you tell that part of your story about the traveling. To think, Dad, there was a time in your life when stepping outside home was not a possibility. I mean, I suppose it was, except for how it made you physically sick and filled you with air-stopping anxiety. Okay, I'm jumping ahead, so I'll just sit here by your side while you tell people your story.

I served in the Army during the Gulf War, returned home, and deployed for combat missions four more times. After the Gulf, Saudi Arabia, Kuwait, and Iraq, I returned home and immediately immersed myself into day-to-day life. A single father, a full-time job, entrepreneur, and baseball empire in my spare time. All was well on this treadmill of living, or so I believed. I couldn't see that what I was doing was pushing down and away my increasing anxiety.

They say life can change on a dime, or swiftly in the blink of an eye. They also say that people who cross our path are teachers we are meant to meet. I don't know about you, but I only like to be a student willingly. When I was starting to feel myself speeding downhill rather quickly, I made an appointment to get a Gulf War syndrome evaluation at my wife's very strong urging.

My path intersected with the nicest guy who understood my stories. He, too, was a veteran of the Gulf War who understood things I was feeling. I don't remember if our appointment was for less time, but all I know is sixty minutes later I had just experienced a sense of being home. In a way I couldn't talk with my family, here was a guy listening who just seemed to "know." He "got it," if you know what I mean. Someone to listen without judgment at things I was experiencing.

I left his office, got into my vehicle, and did something I had never done in my life before that day. I cried, and I cried, and I was crying so hard I couldn't drive away. For two hours, I sat in that parking lot, tears not stopping. Fear unlike any I had known before—and I had my fair share of fear while serving in the Army—I sat in that car unmoving as I felt myself rapidly falling.

Exit tears, enter flashbacks and nightmares as part of my nightly routine. I started to act out events that had happened in my life previously. The aftermath was significantly scaring my family. If only they knew how scared I was inside that I didn't feel I was in control of, well, quite frankly, anything. Certain I was going to land at the bottom of that hill in a heap, and when I did, there would be no more air left in me to breathe. I was scared to go to sleep, and the less sleep I got, the scarier I was to be around for I was less than nice. *On second thought, perhaps landing at that bottom of the hill no longer able to breathe would be fine.*

This wasn't my life for one month, or one year, or even two. For nearly five years this was the journey I went through. I had this mask I wore every day. Translation, I became very good at wearing a happy face. I thought a happy face could disguise my reclusiveness, that becoming a hermit was normalcy. There wasn't any harm in having my wife think I was just slightly crazy. Or at least that was my internal convincing.

Hurry up, hill, closer, come closer, I'm now ready. Just let me finish making sure I've provided for my family. I'll then be ready to hit the bottom of your steep incline. Just so we are on the same page, when I hit the bottom I'm planning that puts an end to this life.

Yes, you just read it right. I reached the lowest point of my life. Here is where I will share what was also my reality at the time. Let me first say, my intention is not to make this a story about blaming. I am sharing to highlight just how beneficial a service dog is to a veteran on their journey with PTSD.

I was taking not just one, or two, or even three medications meant to help my highs and lows not be so extreme. I was taking several, all playing together to give me the feeling I was completely crazy. If these medicines were supposed to aid me in wanting to be around people or ease my anxiety, well, I can tell you it was the complete opposite—I was scared to death to do anything. I didn't trust myself to leave my house, and I didn't trust myself at home around my family. *Oh yes, hill, I'm on my way. Oh, at the bottom will be my sweet reprieve.*

This is where I should pause and reach out my hand to my dear wife. She is hearing about the depths of my despair for the first time. I know she was witnessing it every day and probably aware more than I knew. Yet, to voice it out loud that I thought of leaving this Earth isn't something I've been able to do. I am a lucky man that my wife has a wisdom that allows her to see more than meets the eye. I'm not sure how I got so lucky to have someone so willing to stand by my side.

I'm grateful for her insistence not just when it led me to my tears at the start of my downhill careening. It is because of my wife's insistence I apply for Ryder that soon you will hear about the date she and I had recently. If it wasn't for my wife knowing I needed to release deeply buried pain, trauma, and sorrow when she said, "Go get an evaluation, please," I'm not sure where I'd be today, but I'm certain it wouldn't be enjoying this thing called living.

Now, before I tell you about enjoying life—and that date with my wife, I need to tell you my first thought when my wife mentioned Northwest Battle Buddies. Absolutely without a doubt positively crazy! *A dog isn't going to help me want to leave this house again without vomiting. If you can't get me to leave this house what makes you think a dog will do any better at getting me to leave? Do what you want, but I don't see how a service dog is for me.*

Fast-forward two years, for that was the waiting time. And when the call came, let me tell you, that was the longest drive! For someone who couldn't go to doctors' appointments anymore because of how physically nauseous leaving the house would make me, driving two hours to meet the CEO of Northwest Battle Buddies was the lenthiest journey! To then meet another fine woman who looked past what she initially could see to know better than I did what was best for me.

The initial training with Ryder involved us going out in public, which as you can imagine put Ryder and me smack center stage. Because I had promised my wife that I'd give this a try, I held out hope getting physically sick in these public places would go away. To be the focus of strangers wasn't something I had experienced in, well, what felt like forever and a day. Thankfully it was only two or three times before the nausea stayed at bay.

Ryder and I had a different start from our classmates in that I couldn't pet him for the first two weeks. Ryder was high-spirited when he wasn't working. If I tried to pet him, Ryder would turn on his rambunctiousness for he didn't yet know how to receive affection with poise and ease. When his classmates were sitting on laps, he was learning how to lay at my feet. Boy, did that earn me looks like *what the heck is your problem that I can't sit where it is more comfy?!*

Approximately three or four weeks into our training, I could take Ryder home for a night. On that night, I had yet another one of those crazy dreams that leave me breathless from fright. Or I should say I started to dream, but didn't get to finish, thankfully. This eighty-pound rambunctious dog snoring in his deep sleep woke up instantly to wake me. In that moment, Ryder and I became a unified team.

Before Ryder, my wife and I would go out to eat three nights a week. To the same place, at the same time, to sit at the same table was our routine. That is if there wasn't something amiss in one of these parameters, because if there was, we wouldn't go out to eat. Now, with Ryder, if the time is different or if our option is different seating, I can still dine out with little to no anxiety. Ryder is on watch so that I don't have to be.

I no longer need to take the two "night" pills that were supposed to help me get more than the one or two hours of sleep I was getting. And now I no longer need to take the two "counter" pills to these pills each morning. I don't fear going to sleep anymore, for I know I have someone to wake me from nightmares and crazy dreams. My one-to-two hours of sleep a night is now eight consistently.

Now, here is the other best part of how Ryder has changed my life. I travel now, yes, you heard that right! Ryder and I, along with my son David, headed down the road where it wanted to lead. We didn't have a specific destination we set out to reach. We stayed at a different hotel just about every night, visiting Colorado, California, the Midwest, and Virginia, too. We stopped in New Orleans, and Kansas City where Ryder got to see his first professional football game in a stadium full of people, mind you. We ordered room service like royalty. Freedom, it took on a whole new meaning. That eleven weeks might just be some of the very best weeks of my life. Ah, let me say that again, **of my life**! *Hey hill, yeah, it's me up here near the peak. I'm no longer careening downward* *rapidly. In fact, I rather like the view up here, so here is where I will be staying. I mean we, Ryder and me.*

And hey, dear officer who stopped David, Ryder, and me in Idaho on a beautiful sunny oh so free, day. First, let me apologize for a little extra push on that pedal that caused your radar to send you a red flag. I also want to thank you not just for the warning to ease up without your autograph as my receipt. I want to thank you for your graciousness in seeing past my son David's outstretched hand and Ryder's protective watch that wouldn't let me get my license and insurance proof to you quickly. I know my son looks every bit the grown man that he is in size. I know it was concerning that he kept reaching for your pocket, but see, he isn't a grown-up of the mind. And Ryder, well, when he feels my rising anxiety, he knows only one thing. Engulf Dad in a full body embrace until his heartrate can ease. He was just doing his job, officer, and I thank you for seeing us three characters were just three harmless boys relishing the feeling of free. You are a fine serviceman to your country, and I am privileged my path intersected with you that day. Godspeed sir, and may you always stay safe.

Ryder and I fly, as well as drive. And as for that special date with my wife. Imagine two humans and a dog dressed up to see Steven Tyler in a show. We've also visited Hollywood and San Francisco, and now we need to decide where is our next place to go.

So, the best this once nonbeliever can say to you is that I am so grateful to Northwest Battle Buddies for giving life back to me. I was lost, I had given up, hope was elusive and out of reach. The medications were making it worse, not better, and it was starting to feel like an eternity of misery. I was a prisoner within home and in my pain with no hope that there was a key to set me free. I do not walk in anyone else's shoes to know what it is for them when they feel the depths of despair, but I understand how one can feel so helpless and that the help they turn to seems not to care. I was a patient name on a file, prescribed medications to "help," until my wife found a better healing methodology. I became Tom, a veteran, who no longer needs any medications except one who has fur, four paws, and a heart filled with unconditional love and acceptance of me.

That was a great eleven weeks, wasn't it, Dad, just the road, you, and me? I'm not sure which I enjoyed more—our day adventures or when it was time to eat. That room service was pretty cool, Dad, yet seeing new sites every day was fun, too. When can we go again, Dad, just the road, me and you?

There is a quote similar to one shared by a lovable bear named Winnie the Pooh. Actually, I think his creator wrote it for him, but anyhoo. "As soon as I saw you, I knew you would be an adventure of a lifetime" and I think, Dad, that is why I was so full of energy. I had this sense that I would be more than the one to keep watch over you in your sleep or have your back when in a restaurant to eat. I didn't necessarily know that it would mean exploring new states and getting to watch a football game. But I sensed there was a freedom we were both about to gain.

Dad, I know I am a little selfish about you when it comes to Mom and my sister, too. I know, I know, I can get a little bratty around them, but it doesn't mean I don't love them as you do. It's just that, well, they don't need me. What I mean by that is I feel I fulfill my purpose when I am serving. To be there for you, Dad, to be your reason you are excited to greet each day. To be there for you, Dad, because you now love to leave the walls of home and go play. And to help you keep watch of David, for I know he has needs, too. I'm able to be who Ryder is meant to be when I can keep watch of both of you.

So, hey Dad, do you hear that whispering? I think that is the road calling us to come see the states we haven't yet seen. Then again, if we don't leave right away that is okay by me. As long as I'm by your side I'm right where I wish to be. I love you, Dad, oh and one more thing. I'm so glad you converted into being a believer that I'm someone you need. My life wouldn't be complete unless I was part of your team.

JEFF AND ABLE

I'm going to make everything around me
beautiful—that will be my life.

—Elsie de Wolfe

*D*ad, do you think maybe we could just fast-forward to AA in
your story? I mean, after all, that is the best part, don't you
think?

AA, Able, what exactly is AA?

*Oh, come on, Dad, I know you know because everyone else tells you,
too. You know, when they say to you, "We don't know what you did with
that Jeff guy we knew."*

*Yeah, Able, that's true, I do hear it said many times that I am not the
same now that you are by my side. That there was this Before Able and then
after you is me happy in life.*

*See, Dad? I knew you knew what I meant when I said AA. Before me
and then After Able—get it—AA!*

Able is right that there is before Able, but after my time overseas.
And there are these past two years in which I feel like the Jeff I once used
to be. I volunteered for the service because I had a fine set of footprints
that had walked before me. My father, rest his soul, had also served in
the military. I fought the odds, so to speak, to be able to go. I think it's
fair to say there are just some things that are meant to be, you know.

I was sixteen years old when I knew my first disability. My fingers
on one hand and I went our separate ways earning me a prognosis that
I wouldn't have hand mobility. Tell me "I can't," and I will show you
Watch me! That tennis ball being crunched in my hand didn't stand a
chance against my determination to follow in my father's footsteps to
serve my country. I got up to 85 percent use of my hand, which earned
me the opportunity to raise it in the vow *I, Jeff, do solemnly swear that*

I will support and defend the Constitution of the United States against all enemies.

I was deployed during Desert Shield-Desert Storm, a short war but a war of great bloodshed. Though we are trained, and trained well, some things just don't leave your head. And then what stays seems to have this way of either sinking down into you or trying to boil to the surface when you are least ready. I know the expression "short fuse" has been around longer, but I could have easily coined that phrase as my own authoring. I sure got angry pretty easily. Jeff, prewar, wasn't an angry guy, but once I returned home, anger came so naturally.

You probably hear this from others veterans about this bond we have—how you are never alone without someone who has your back. Yet, at the same time you are lonely, missing your family terribly, so anxious to get home to them—and in one breathing piece. Those of us fortunate to return home, even if we have a broken-up shoulder and knee like me, find this civilian world we served for not necessarily inviting. It can feel like the nonmilitary organizations we try to work for are working against us and we are still in that shelter-and-protect mode when it comes to our families. To fully let our families see our struggling is not in our wiring. We come home no longer alone among those who love us, and we feel extremely lonely. It's such a weird tug and pull between two opposite extremes.

Before Able there was Hagrid, a white boxer not formally trained, though he certainly kept watch of me. Hagrid's only certification was to be my best friend upon returning home from overseas. They say that when we let go—or must let go—room is made for something else to come our way. I sure didn't want to lose Hagrid, and by no means could he be replaced. Hagrid was one of a kind in his own right. It took losing him to recognize I needed something more in my life.

Don't get me wrong when I say I needed someone to help take care of me. My family is a great support system that would provide anything they could that I need. Yet, all of us humans, no matter how hard we try or our best intentions, still bring a level of judgment to our interactions, even if subconsciously. We became very vested in our relationships in a way that we cannot easily separate from feeling things very personally.

We put expectations on ourselves to meet a standard that isn't always easily reached. Then we add on top of those additional expectations that others have of us, or so we perceive. Add in each of us holding our own internal fears of what the others might think. I think you get the idea how complicated it can become in a way a dog doesn't bring these nuances to the team.

A dog brings three unconditional things—acceptance, love, and listening. Add in a dog's ability to keep watch over me and wake me up from nightmares as I sleep. These things equate to having someone who can provide for me in a way that is impossible to be done by my family. Able is second best next to my wonderful wife, for she will always be my first priority. It might be only a millimeter distance between them, but she's certainly first best in my life. Joking aside, I think you understand what I can't always find the right words to describe.

See, that's the thing about Able—actually, that's the thing about service dogs and how they serve us vets. They have this ability to help us in such a way that we find it hard to explain why their mode of healing is the best. One way would be in how they are similar in their service to us, as we are for and with our brothers and sisters of the military. A service dog gives us something to think about bigger than ourselves and someone to hold in safe keep. I think "service" is the key word, for our family is also who we strive to keep from harm's outreach. But our families didn't have a rigorous training to serve and protect, nor do they dress in uniform to take care of me. Able did train to serve and protect, and each time he wears his vest, he is on a mission to take care of whatever I need.

Able and I have a relationship that can't be priced in its value he brings. How could I even begin to put a price tag on having someone wake me up when a nightmare is gripping me? And let me tell you, Able takes that responsibility very seriously. If his nose on my hip doesn't stir me, he's not opposed to sitting on me. Able, who was supposed to be eighty-five pounds, but he never heard that—or decided he would overachieve—is a determined one-hundred-pound-plus giant teddy bear when he needs to be. I would take his heavy weight on my chest any day and every night if it meant I could avoid those dreams. *That's okay, Able, you keep right on ratcheting up your tactics to alert me if I'm in a deep sleep!*

How could I price the value of his assistance in tight places when I feel my rising anxiety? I'm someone who, despite my knees screaming loudly, *What are you doing?* would take the stairs to avoid the elevators shrinking in on me. Now, my knees along with my entire body, are grateful that Able makes elevators a breeze.

How could I put a price tag on being able to go in public places again or go camping with my family? I can go out to eat again at a local eatery knowing Able is keeping watch for me. Prior to Able, to go out for a Wednesday lunch with my wife felt like the longest chore I had to complete. I could barely leave the house, the effort to do so was excruciating. And then now that there is Able, as typical when becoming a new parent and everyone oohs and aahs over the baby. I don't think my wife and I are even seen anymore when we take our seats. *Hello Able, Hi Able, so good to see you Able, Hey Able, how are you?* I am not sure the last time I didn't hear my name as an afterthought: *Oh, hey Jeff, I didn't even see you.*

We had to upgrade our camper to a twenty-seven-foot RV to accommodate our expanded family. Expanded as in an "eighty-five-pound" golden retriever who prefers plenty of room to stretch out comfortably. Speaking of, there is some negotiation that needs to take place between my wife and Able quite frequently. For some reason they both have the same idea they own the passenger seat of the RV. If my wife gets out of the seat, she returns to find Able has made it his for the rest of the ride. And let me tell you, there is not much convincing otherwise.

How could I begin to define the value on something I had lost and couldn't seem to find? That which has been found is being happy in living my life. Living being the optimal word now that it is…AA. I am no longer just trying to survive from day to day. You are reading a story about **living** with a service dog and what it means to smile again and no longer hurry time away. You are reading about someone who finds such joy in Able's twitching nose when he knows it's time to play.

The world experienced what it meant to isolate and remove oneself from the crowd under a mandated quarantine. Heck, I had been in a self-imposed quarantine for a very long time. This time it was different for me, though, in one significant way. This time fun and laughter were part of my in-house stay. Having a best friend by your side works that way!

How could I begin to adequately price something that helps me never think of suicide? I couldn't even begin to think of leaving him behind. To have a service dog like Able should be the medication any soldier is prescribed who has gone out and had trauma of some kind. I'm not sure I understand why more people aren't finding this the best solution instead of traditional therapies. This shouldn't be a best-kept secret or still doubted in its capability to significantly aid healing. Take it from someone who never thought he would feel like smiling and joking again who has now found life worth **living**.

It was midsummer when I met Able for the first time—July 9th specifically. My wife and I met the CEO of Northwest Battle Buddies who then introduced us to the dogs to determine who would be my pairing. As I watched the dogs, I instantly knew Able was who I wanted to be joined with as a team. I turned to look for my wife, but she was nowhere to be seen. She had left the office where she saw me smiling and talking to Able, telling him we were going home today. She was outside the office crying, so one of the dear trainers named Michele, went to see if my wife was okay.

Her tears were because she saw that immediate of a change. Right then and there I was no longer the same. She was seeing the husband she knew before deployment took me overseas. She was seeing a spark in my eyes again that had long ago gone in retreat. If I had all of the money in the world, it would still not be enough to pay back Northwest Battle Buddies for giving me not only the gift of Able, but for giving me back what I thought was part of the blank check I had written when I vowed at any cost for my country. I was given my life back, and my wife was given the Jeff she first married.

We completed our training in August and I don't think my jaws had ever hurt as much as they did from those six weeks. Far greater than the aches in my shoulder and knees was the soreness in my cheeks. Smiling so much can do that, you know. A pure happiness from the depths of my soul.

The first time I was able to take Able home for an evening was when I learned he wouldn't just lie at the foot of the bed with his back to me while he kept watch of my sleep. It was sometime between 1:30 a.m. to 2:00 a.m. when I felt a thump on my chest suddenly. *Wake up, Dad, you are having a bad dream.* If I didn't already love Able dearly, that moment was the deal-sealer for me.

I don't remember exactly now, but I'm pretty sure I was smiling when I drifted back to sleep.

Dad, did I ever tell you that I knew you wanted me to be your team, and just how excited that made me? If you have ever wondered why I ran to you and jumped in your lap so quickly. Well, it was because I was so happy your heart had picked me!

*By the way, Dad, I want it to be that way, too. Like your niece and her ratty-haired teddy bear from you. I love thinking about how she has never let that teddy bear leave her side. Twenty-eight years ago, it became hers when she was born into this life. Through moving away from home and then starting her own family, that ratty-haired teddy bear has seen her through her entire life journey. So yes, Dad, I want to be that teddy bear still by your side twenty-eight years from now. That is what it means to me to be **your** service dog.*

And hey Dad, one more thing. Can you ask Mom to just go ahead and give me the passenger seat?

PHIL AND RAVEN

*The wolf in my heart will never let you see the lamb
in my soul…but sometimes you see it in my eyes*

—Author Unknown

*ad, one thing I love most about your story is how you found
not just one soul mate but two. First you found Mom, and
then I was led to you. Or maybe it was that you were led to
me. Either way, what matters most is you and I are a team.*

*I'm really glad you are happiest where we have these wide-open spaces
to hike any day of the week. I'm also glad that you recognized you don't
do well when there is sun deficiency. I would much rather be living in our
quiet hometown surrounded by Nature's beauty. Dad, I think I would have
been a lot like you feeling pretty blue if it was relentlessly cloudy and rainy.
I know I would also have enjoyed it much less if cement and asphalt were
the only footpaths to take. I would have been with you, though, so I would
have mustered the bravery to be happy in a less-secluded place. But where
we are, Dad, well, it's home to me in every way!*

*Dad, when we are taking our walk on the trail, I can feel your sense of
peace. It's just you, me, and the sky above us and the surrounding mountains
in all their majesty. Dad, each time we are on a footpath, I feel like Nature
is cheering. I am not sure if Nature is cheering for us or because Nature can
feel how we are both so happy. When the trees stir up their gentle breeze. I
think it is the echo of our heartbeats.*

Let me start my story in 2009 when I was stationed in DC. They say
that each moment we live leads us to the next moment purposefully. I
guess you could say there is some truth in that, given my first assignment
as a Marine. I was a young pup, so to speak, with a very important
responsibility. Let's see, 350. Yep, that is the total I do believe. The total
number of funerals at Arlington in which I was in uniform stoically,

ensuring the family had the best possible last impression as the one they loved was laid to forever rest in peace.

It was also during this time of having been selected for this duty that I had the privilege of burying men I had trained with—friends of mine. I buried most of the men in my unit during this time. Yep, those moments that lead us to the next moment purposefully. Like learning how to separate your emotions that might wish to attach to what you are experiencing. Some things, for the sake of doing them to the best of your ability for others—and for surviving—means you let numbness create a shield to keep you from shattering. I learned to let death detach from grief so that I could clearly see. To do exactly that is what my brothers and sisters expected of me. Lives depended on detachment being my exceptional ability.

After my two-year duty at Arlington in DC, I was offered a choice to go home or to deploy overseas. I chose Afghanistan as a dedicated marksman, and now you may be saying, *Ah, now I see how Arlington was that purposeful moment in Phil's life. To immerse in death so that death would not win the fight.*

Well, I can tell you that the moments that lead us to the next doesn't necessarily mean that when we get to the next, we find it smooth sailing. I deployed to Afghanistan July 19, 2011, to find myself serving during a battle that history will define as the bloodiest to take place. It was my first day of deployment, standing next to intel, both of us trying to find in our two languages how we could communicate. In an instant, death was knocking for this guy, and death, as it can sometimes be, was taking its sweet, slow time.

Life teaches us in opposites, and boy, sometimes the lesson plans involve extremes. Here I was trying to help this guy while simultaneously responding to fire with fire to save my fellow Marines and me. I was putting my best foot forward in bravery while equally terrified at what was happening. I'm sure Arlington had prepared me, but it sure didn't prepare me to hear death coming. In Arlington, death had already arrived, silently. Well, except for the families whose tears could be heard as they grieved. On day one in Afghanistan, I was witness to how death calls instantly. I will just leave it at this by saying sometimes death is very vocal before it is complete.

And it was this moment of day one that led me to the successful missions that were awaiting me. Two days later, on day three, my unit was celebrating my abilities. I had kept death from knocking on the doors of my unit without terror arm wrestling the actions I needed to take. I thought I'd feel more in those moments in which I ensured death was rendered silent, but I had already learned detachment would keep everyone safe. Though the actions would still mean someone would mourn, it would not be for those I was serving with to return to Arlington for their final resting place.

Day three quickly became three months, where moments lived would become purposeful for…my path to cross with Northwest Battle Buddies. If it had been more like a jam-packed action movie, days one and three would be enough scenes to watch for you to understand the value of why Raven means the world to me. Yet, I still had a job to complete to the best of my abilities. I had an enemy to fight so that my unit would continue breathing. I had an enemy to fight that was not always easily seen. Let me just say, it isn't easy when you realize you can't trust people who look like civilians walking down a street.

You have probably heard the term "hypervigilant" and have an image of what that means. Let me try to put in context for you the kind of awareness you had to keep every single split second you breathed. A civilian kneeling, counting a basket filled with ears of corn was not someone going to or coming from the market trying to assess his offering. To have the knowledge that corn is counted by the bushel and not individually ensured in a split second, I was able to save my buddies. Narrowly, yes, but they weren't on their way to Arlington thanks to one of my fellow Marines and me.

Being hypervigilant meant listening to the deafening silence, which is not two words you would put together, would you? Silence is supposed to be soothing and put you in a peaceful mood. Silence during deployment meant a grip in your stomach as your intuition said, *This quiet is shouting.* To be able to hear above pin-drop stillness was yet another insurance we had to potentially return home alive. To be alert to this kind of quiet was the difference between being in a position to draw first or to reach for your weapon for what would most likely be the very last time.

Hypervigilant is learning to retrain your mind if it holds a fondness when seeing a gathering among family. Several seemingly related individuals of various ages don't necessarily equal home sweet home and a feast. It could mean that you are witnessing men and women in disguise, or if not all of them fighters, all are still willing to lay down their lives to die. And then sometimes, it simply meant it was a family gathered together, striving to survive. The kicker was trying to discern which was what which time. I can still see the eyes of one girl as she stared unblinking at me. Her family scared and crying, and there she sat unflinchingly. Emotions running high and still she sat motionless with her eyes glued to me. It was as if she could see into or right through me. Who knows, maybe she had a premonition of what would come to be. That a couple of months later in this very same village another one of my buddies would earn his place in Arlington in peace. Hypervigilant doesn't always mean you get to keep your friends from dying. Sometimes it just means you got lucky for another second or day or if you are one of the really lucky ones, your full deployment overseas. Then again, I'm not sure I always think it is so lucky.

I sometimes think it should have been me instead of Jacob whose family had to decide *to pull the plug if you are certain there is no brain activity.*

Thankfully, I know how to detach, right? Take your ten minutes of grief and get your head back into the fight. Swallow any guilt that ten inches in another direction and it would have been me instead of Jacob that a family said goodbye to. Swallow any pain or sorrow that I really—man, I really—liked that dude!

Oh, yeah, real heroic, yeah, sure, whatever you wish to think. This is a load of—well, you know what I was about to say to express how I felt about our homecoming. Celebration galore with tables filled to the brim with anything we could want to eat. *Great job, man; hey, way to go; man, you are a hero; glad you made it back to us in one piece.* All these handshakes, and slaps on the back, and so many just a grinning away.

Yeah, bartender, another Jack and Coke, and easy on the Coke, my routine for the next four days.

I didn't know stress in a war zone like I now felt as a civilian upon returning home. My brother didn't know what to think when we hopped in his truck to go buy ourselves motorcycles so we could "hit the open road"—you know, be wild and free. Yeah, heck of a plan that was when he saw me curl up like a small child in a fetal position in the passenger seat. The gravity box of the truck had banged when we hit a bump. It was more than an association of memories that made me curl up.

It was my cue that I needed to turn to my expertise of detaching. Only this time, I needed to detach from living. I'm not talking suicide here, though one could argue my methods were leading me to an early grave. No, I'm talking about stimulants to get my heart pumping in intense ways. Things like driving 187 miles per hour on a motorcycle and cocaine.

I retired from service four months after returning home, though the first month home was a blur for me. Suffice it to say that first month involved only one thing. How drunk could I get and how long could I avoid sobriety. I was engaging in a lot of dangerous behavior, though I couldn't see it at the time. After all, I'm a hero, and I was trained to separate death from life. And who needs to sleep and eat anyway, *I'm absolutely fine,* was my internal lie.

I came home a married man, and then I no longer was, thankfully. Hey, divorce isn't always a bad thing. When two people don't bring out the best in each other, it's time to let go. They say that we find a yes through experiencing the noes. And I sure did find my "yes," eventually. I had to isolate myself from everyone for a significant amount of time before I would be ready. But when I was, well, as Raven already told you, I found a soul mate to complete me.

Anyway, back to being divorced and recognizing one certainty. I couldn't be around anyone anymore who knew me. It was time to get away, and Europe seemed the right destiny. I wandered aimlessly and mindlessly, but let me tell you, not in that Zen kind of way that was free and liberating. Feeling isolated and like your mind is dying is anything short of free. But at least I wasn't around those who were searching for who I used to be.

In 2016, I returned to the United States and made West my home, working for a gun store. I found my appetite again—yeah, I sure did— I'm fortunate I could even fit through a door. An average 170-pound guy growing into a big boy of 316. And since I was earning a decent salary, well, *Hey bartender, pour me another drink. Ah, never mind, I'll just head on home. I can drink a fifth just as easily alone.*

That worked well, until it didn't, as you can imagine pretty easily. Those walls are brutal when you hit them at a high rate of speed. No man, not literally, but falling back into that bottle was certainly accelerating me toward an end zone. Of course, whiskey goes best with coke, as we know. And I don't mean the cola kind. Part of my daily routine was to arrive to work drunk and high. Yes, I was detaching quite well from living, moving quickly toward a destiny with the next "young pup" at Arlington in DC. Maybe I'd be able to enable the soldier there to add me to his tally sheet. Perhaps I can make it 351 for him and he could beat my record of the most laid to rest on my watch. Then again, I'd still have him beat if you counted the friends that I was fighting beside and then they were gone.

I hit that wall when I held up my hand and couldn't even count to two. Not two reasons I shouldn't plan my life was through. I woke up, I declared, "Today is the day," and I reflected on how it would feel to at long last detach and be free. Well, as you gathered I didn't, because I'm here telling you my story.

I sat there bearing the heavy load of my deployment and saw the weight set in the corner beckoning me. *Hey buddy, you just sitting there carrying the weight of your misery. Why don't you come over here and see what you can lift and bench press before you create your ending?* I lifted, and I lifted, and I lifted until I was exhausted beyond belief. I did it again the next day, and the next, and suddenly I had only one priority. I couldn't work the job I had sixty hours a week and have time to lift these weights equally. Something had to give, and you know what, this time it wasn't going to be me.

I took a year off from working to spend a year working on building up my body. The drinking went down in direct proportion to the physical strength I started building. The weight went down, and my mind's stableness increased. I wasn't "all better" by any means, but I was no longer detached from living.

I then met the woman who would become my wife and who could see things I wasn't looking into the mirror to see. She gently, safely, and unconditionally guided me to understand I had problems that needed addressing. She was a saint—or at least a very trusting soul willing to not immediately think the worst of the man she was starting to really like. I think any other woman might have been concerned when the man they were dating never slept at night. And it wasn't like she could get out of bed and find me staring into space in another room of the house. Not that she would have been comforted by that, but it might have been easier than me being nowhere around. I would go to the gym, and not just for an hour, or even two. Hours—and I'm talking hours—I would be consumed.

Raven mentioned this when she started out our story, but to further explain her comment about clouds and rain. Seasonal depression is real, let me tell you; if I am without sun and the warmth to go outdoors, I nearly go insane. My wife helped me realize this, too, when we were on vacation where we now live permanently. Four days into our vacation my mind was not churning with no reprieve. I was not anxious and therefore, my wife was calm, too. See, that is the other reason I went to Europe back when to isolate myself from those I knew. When you are depressed and anxious and so many other things, those you care about and who are trying to care for you begin to take on that energy secondarily. I had been putting a strain on my wife that quickly disappeared when we stood in the open space where we were vacationing. Nine months later, this place became home. Step one to a reconnection to the peace in my soul.

I tried CBD and was also on various prescription medications when I started watching YouTube videos of veterans who had service dogs helping them on their PTSD journeys. Each of our stories are different, so I wasn't necessarily comparing. Yet, I could sure tell these guys knew what it was to walk a footstep in my shoes. A service dog was for me, I just knew.

Yeah, about those moments that connect to where we now are, and let me tell you, sometimes those moments are ruthless in their history. Some moments have a way of becoming more like a haunting. I filled out an application to qualify for a service dog, and when I had to answer a question about my drinking, the approval would not be signed. The VA needed my answer to be zero and not an occasional drinker from time to time. That I was no longer best friends with Jack Daniels that is—fell on ears that didn't believe I had progressed in my story. I received an A, all right, but not A for approving. I received two words: *application denied.* I then tried again a second time. The answer returned the same. My hope was rapidly dwindling away.

I had been so hopeful for that signature to start the nineteen-month waiting clock. Now it seemed my waiting time for a dog would be somewhere between never and not. To say I was disappointed was an understatement; distraught would be more accurate to describe my state. I was screaming and crying, to the point I didn't even realize tears were streaming down my face. Rage started to rise from somewhere where I had been bottling it up and holding it in what I thought was a secure place. Could they not understand I was exhausted mentally? Could they not understand it was proving harder to hold on believing things would get easier for me?

As I was leaving the VA, an employee handed me a brochure for Northwest Battle Buddies. "Give this person a call," this individual told me. "They can help you, I do believe." I left a message and anxiously awaited hoping for a return call yet that day. Ten days later when I hadn't heard back, *I'm never going to get a dog,* my exhausted mind unendingly replayed. And then I got a call with apologies. *I was out of town and not able to respond to voice mails immediately. Let's get together to discuss and if it is okay with you, I'll bring my service dog, too.*

Phil, this is Sierra and Sierra, this is Phil who thinks he would like to be part of his own service-dog team? It's okay, Sierra, you can let him pet you even though you are on duty. One doesn't always realize how low they feel until they feel the opposite extreme. It felt so good to touch Sierra and to witness her guarding her veteran so lovingly. It's not that I needed convincing, but after that I was completely on board with finding my own "Sierra" as soon as I possibly could. In that moment, I felt if it could happen as quickly as "yesterday," that would have been good!

The application process took place July 20th, and I found myself in training as early as October 13th. Sometimes you just know when things are absolutely meant to be. Yet, I'll also be honest and say the thought of going to training was terrifying. I hadn't been to the West Coast before and just the thought of it crippled me with anxiety. Yet, in that dance between opposites, I knew the urge to go was stronger in me than missing the opportunity.

And speaking of miss, I was going to need to be away from my wife for five weeks. The thought of not being beside my soul mate was excruciating. We'd never been apart since my wife bravely saw in me that I was capable of more than what I believed. True to her unconditional love, she knew going would be the best thing for me. And oh, I did want Raven, though I didn't know Raven until after I arrived. That I would receive a golden retriever, or Labrador, I was certain in my mind. The CEO of Northwest Battle Buddies let me know otherwise. *Tomorrow you will meet Raven, a German shepherd who has been selected for you.* My heart only wanted her more as soon as I heard that news. A German shepherd felt like a more fitting breed for me and my personality. There is something about their stealth and fighting spirit that resonates for me.

A reduction in anxiety and the ability to go out in public to eat because Raven is next to me. To have a best friend who doesn't judge and who loves to go on hikes with me. I do look forward to the day when I don't have to explain Raven's mission and why she is, in fact, allowed where others are questioning her entry. Thankfully, most know Raven where we live, so now we can enter and exit businesses and restaurants without explaining. It gets old, you know, having to always explain about a key member of your team. And it gets even older seeing a flicker across others' eyes wondering, *What is his story?*

I would love to tell you Raven has made every day perfect since she and I became a certified team. Some days aren't as good, but let me be clear, it is not because of what Raven is or isn't doing. I don't think one can ever really let go of the traumas and losses experienced, no matter how masterful at detachment one gets to be. I'm grateful that at least now I can set my experiences down and step away from them periodically. Now that I have Raven by my side, I'm slowly starting to take that next step toward acceptance, which is a really hard thing to do. In order to accept, you need to revisit things you've locked and buried inside of you. If you want to put things to rest in peace, you must allow the memories to surface so they can be released.

At least now I don't cry out of the blue for what feels like no reason, or without warning. Now that I have Raven I don't long for a detachment from living. I don't need the stimulants that once helped me through. I no longer feel like I'm hurting those I love, or at any moment would be able to. My support system is small, at my choice, and that is okay. It has been a long journey to reach a point I feel safe. I've got my two soul mates who love me, and I have the sun and the wide-open space to immerse in every day.

Those moments that are purposeful to lead us to where we are meant to be. Perhaps it was the moment I turned to YouTube or the moment a brochure was handed to me. Or maybe it goes back a little further to a set of weights or back even further to day one overseas, when I was scared to death, yet that I was not ready to rest in final peace was stronger in me. Or maybe it goes all the way back to DC, when I learned there is a sacredness to life amidst the grief. Yeah, I know, it's a combination of all these things, probably. All I know is that I am grateful that where I am meant to be includes a German shepherd named Raven who is the best thing (along with my wife) that has ever happened for me.

Dad, share one more time just how much I was meant to be by your side on these trails we love to roam. How you went from never getting me to acceptance with a two-year wait to then only four months—and six weeks of training—so that I could come home. As much as I wish you hadn't experienced the rejection, I'm glad you had just a temporary "no." Only because it bought some time for me to be born and for Shannon to meet and then train me. If you hadn't had that "no," Dad, it just might have been a golden retriever on these trails instead of my pawed feet.

Dad, you talk about those moments that are purposeful to lead us to right where we are meant to be. I'm grateful for the moment in which Shannon selected me for training. When I entered this life, I felt I was destined to guard and protect, and that the soul was waiting for me. When I looked into Shannon's eyes, I knew she wasn't the one, but she would be the one to help me find who was calling my heart. You know, Dad, like those heart necklaces that are split into two parts. They symbolize two halves that when joined make one heart complete. I knew I was not fully whole until I found the second half of my heart's beat. And then you walked in the door at Northwest Battle Buddies. Our first two weeks of training were challenging because I would not stop moving, I know. It's just that Dad, I was so excited because at long last, I had found the one to make me whole.

FELIX AND STRYKER

Scared is what you're feeling; brave is what you're doing.

—Emma Donoghue

*P*lease don't tell Shannon this next part, for I don't want her to feel bad about the times I shared with her and her training team. Between you and me, Dad, the best years of my life have been these past two since you and I became "we." Don't get me wrong thinking that I disliked my training. Like you, Dad, I took what I was meant to learn very seriously. It's just that though I knew I was being trained to fulfill a special purpose, the reality of fulfilling it is far better than the practicing. The moment I met you and every day since has been the best of my life for me.

I think some people perceive if they hear "veteran" and "PTSD," it means something that took place in combat while deployed in a war zone. That it was because of a significant event in a war environment or because of the length of time someone was exposed. For me, my journey with pain, trauma, sorrow, and despair began during training. It began when my mind was stamped with the conviction I could not trust anyone not in uniform if I wanted to come home to my family.

As Stryker shared with you, I took my training seriously. My wife and my children, and my brothers and sisters, meant everything to me. *Do not trust anyone if they are not in uniform for, they could be the signal to the one who will end your life. Be vigilant to the movement of hands, of body language, of that toddler who you believe is innocently standing by. You may not believe it, son, that someone would use their child to harm you. If you want to come home to your own children, you need to embody this truth. Engrave it in your brain and never let it fade away. Your life depends on you seeing everything this way.*

It only took three or four months for this engraving in my mind.

When I got in-country, and began going on missions, it became an internal tattoo for life. I wasn't slated to go on missions when I first arrived. I was designated to stay on base and help improve the surroundings. Then my skill as truck driver became known to fill a battalion need. Each security briefing before a mission reinforced *be ever watchful* of everybody. Every briefing included a report of where we could expect gunfire or IEDs. Or I should say, where it was known, which left some of our route in uncertainty. *Be ever mindful of everyone not in uniform and everything that is different on the routes you are driving.*

I sometimes wonder what it would be like to look at something without second-guessing. I am not sure I will ever completely know that feeling. Thanks to Stryker, I have moments I breathe a little easier because he is a second set of eyes. Yet, being leery of my surroundings is still the lens for mine.

It doesn't take long for that permanent etching. When you are looking death in the eye, self-preservation is your security. I was scared to death on the first few missions, realizing that it was real I might not come back alive. One of two choices became mine. I could let my training kick in to be hypervigilant of everything I took in in sight. Or I could forego my training and my life.

Despite the harshness of the journey with PTSD and TBI (traumatic brain injury), despite every crippling anxious moment, burst of atypical anger, and fear of public settings, I would not trade one minute of wholly embracing my training. I would not give up for a moment that I am here to grow to old age with my wife and watch my children growing.

After my eleven-month deployment I came home to a three-day-out process that was as simple as this. *Welcome home, you are different now, and so is your family. They've been living life without you, so there will be necessary adjusting. And hey, good luck and thanks for serving.*

Yes, pretty basic don't you think? We aren't taught how to turn off our hardwiring. We aren't taught how to reintegrate back into civilian life and into trusting. We come home safely, feeling we are vulnerable and exposed in harm's way. We feel safest if we isolate. Of course, I had a family that needed me to be involved with them and to provide for them by working, too. To hide what I was feeling was the only isolation I could do.

I am blessed to be married to someone who unconditionally stands by me, with a pocketful of tough love she isn't afraid to use if need be. One significant panic attack while working was a catalyst to her stating, "You need to seek help for what you are experiencing." The more I turned off my parent-mode mindset—also part of our training so that empathy would not compromise our vigilant observing—the more my wife reached her certainty. *Get help now or the children and I will leave.*

As hard as those words were to hear, it was the best love given to me. It brought me into a reality that helped me start working on turning off my hardwiring. Unfortunately, or maybe I should say fortunately, for it is the "noes" that lead us to the "yes," the counselors I met with were not helpful in the way that was best for me. Of the half dozen I met with over time, each wanted to prescribe medicines to help my PTSD. That was not an option in my mind. *There must be some other form of help you can find!*

I asked this question when service dogs as a healing modality was just beginning. One counselor gave me a list of options for considering. How is it said, "Third time's the charm?" If only the reality had an element of charm for each "no" was extremely hard. It was a home run at four for me when Northwest Battle Buddies said, "You are a perfect fit for a service dog and we will be honored to pair you with the perfect buddy." These words I had so longed to hear! At long last, hope was near. That began the longest two years of my life, for that was the waiting time based on availability and those in line ahead of me.

I am not only grateful to NWBB for the training of Stryker, I am grateful to my family. I should have said it was the longest two years of all our lives—thank you to my wife and children for standing by me.

And then the call came—that blessed call to excite, scare, and rescue me. *Felix, we need you to be in Washington for six weeks. Your training will begin July 6th, and Stryker is ready for you two to meet.* Leave job for that six-week duration, check. Find a place to stay while in Washington, check. Take a very deep breath and ask myself if I'm sure I want to do this, check—I think so, okay, check.

I was nervous to meet the NWBB team and Stryker, my hardwire training in the driver's seat. Keep my emotions contained, stay reserved, be watchful of the surrounding space. One gentleman had arrived six hours in advance of our start time, he was so excited to meet his service dog that day. Me, well, I was on time, at least I can say.

The first week of training was not easy. That I was taken out of my comfort zone, most definitely. I was now gaining a teammate that was being encouraged to go to bed with me and lay on the couch, too, to be beside me. I grew up being taught dogs were meant to be outdoors, and certainly not on furniture or where we sleep!

We also were taken to the mall, a place I did not find comfort in visiting. In fact, I couldn't tell you at that point the last time I had gone shopping. Malls have far more people and walls than exit doors, and safe retreat. Malls have people not in uniform who I then must discern who is friendly and who is enemy. Being in a mall with a service dog means being the center of attention, which is also not my thing. Being invisible, inconspicuous, unnoticeable—somewhere else—was my priority. Walking around with a golden retriever in a vest with an American flag on it calls me into a limelight and I would rather not shine under its glare. *Ah, but what is this soothing feeling of wavy hair? Hey there, Stryker, I'm feeling a little better petting you as you stand beside me. Hey thanks, buddy, I'm finding my anxiousness is easing.*

It isn't easy to embrace invisible wounds, especially when I think of my brothers and sisters who have "true" disabilities. Or at least that was my mindset for a long time—that I still had my limbs and was not blown up in any way, so I did not have injuries. "I'm fine, I'm fine, I AM FINE," I kept repeating. I suppose for a brief time I thought I was convincing. Thanks be, again to my wife, who guided me to fully face reality. I am not fine, and I have wounds that run deep. I have wounds that will never be cured or disappear, always to be a part of me. Those who journey with PTSD always will; the effects of pain, trauma, sorrow, and despair don't completely go away. But with a teammate like Stryker to walk with us, we can keep the effects at bay.

After Stryker and I graduated, I established goals we could achieve. We started going to the grocery store on our own, and then we went to a restaurant to eat. We went to the movie theater together and now he is my workmate. For at least most of the jobs where I know he will stay safe. See, that is another great thing about having Stryker by my side. I have someone's back to watch again, just as I know he has mine. During deployment there was always someone with you; you did not go anywhere without being at least a two-person team. That is what I have again with Stryker beside me.

We have each had to take a stand for the other when we've felt the other was in harm's way. Strangers don't always like being told they can't pet Stryker, no matter what I say. And Stryker did not like a person who got physically angry with me, making it known with his growl that the person should back away. Much more often, though Stryker is loved, and we are both respected when he is in uniform, including never being rejected when we enter a public space. He is loved at our church, at my work—basically anyplace.

Does Stryker get time off? people wonder; does he get to play? Oh absolutely, and if you don't believe me you should see the circles in our yard from his stick finding and occasional bird chase. If he isn't in uniform, he might even show you his most prized possession affectionately known as "yucky yak squeaky," his most favorite thing. Well, actually, maybe his most favorite next to his ultimate favorite thing to do, which is eat.

I have not had a panic attack since Stryker and I became a team. Do I still feel anxious at times? Absolutely! But to feel like my throat is closing as the anxiousness rises to choke the last breath out of me is no longer my reality. I was fortunate to not know the grip of nightmares, but I have known the stranglehold of anger and at times, rage. These side effects of PTSD and TBI have also greatly subsided now that I have Stryker as my "prescription to take." You might find it amusing to see Stryker bark at a change in our yard, like a new pile of wood delivered by my dad. For me, it is a comfort I can't describe that Stryker is hypervigilant of any change we've had.

As I mentioned, it is a lifelong journey I know I will be traveling with PTSD. Yet, I cannot think of any better partner to walk this path with than Stryker, my battle buddy.

Dad, you mentioned my "yucky yak squeaky!" I love that it made your story! Um, but hey Dad, there is one thing you didn't get quite right. Yes, "yucky yak squeaky" is one of my favorite things, and that I love eating, okay, fine. But, Dad, eating isn't my ultimate, nor is "yucky yak squeaky." My favorite is being by your side watching out for you and our family.

See, I know, Dad, that you were trained to keep watch over your family. When you were deployed, your brothers and sisters were who you made sure were in safe keep. Now that you are home, its Mom and the kids that you are ever watchful of. Though you are my number one focus, I also help you watch over them because they matter to you so.

Where you go, I go and who you love, I love too. That is what buddies do, Dad, right? They are as one in all that they do.

Hey Dad, one more thing, and I hope this will come out the way I mean it to. I'm really lucky when you feel anxious and reach out for me to help you through. That didn't sound like I want you to have anxiousness, did it, because that isn't what I meant to say? It's that I love being needed like that, and that petting feels great!

Dad, I know I may never be able to completely take PTSD away from you. But just know, I've got your back, Dad, in everything you do.

And hey Dad, thanks for having mine, too!

ARMANDO AND ROCKY

Every man has his secret sorrows which the world knows not;
and often times we call a man cold when he is only sad.

—Henry Wadsworth Longfellow

*H*ey Dad, I know that when you tell people my name, the first thing they probably think of is that big, strong, tough, macho fighter in the movies. Don't get me wrong. I'm okay with them thinking that about me. Yet, as we both know, that is only part of what makes me your battle buddy. I'm a soft-hearted, gentle, sweet guy, too. You know, Dad, like you.

Why do you think it is, Dad, that people judge based on stereotypes instead of getting to know each other individually? It's like me as German shepherd and you as soldier must only mean specific things. I am a guard who knows how to attack. You are a soldier who is too invincible to ever crack. Be cautious of me for my ferocious tendencies, and certainly be equally leery of a veteran diagnosed with PTSD. We both get kudos for our bravery, both of us willing to enter where danger is in the driver's seat.

Yet, Dad, why don't people want to know that my heart aches when yours is hurting? Why do people feel so uncomfortable acknowledging sorrow and grief? I remember when you first brought me home as a puppy. I was scared to suddenly find myself without my siblings and my mom next to me. I knew I loved you, Dad—that was right from the moment you came to take me home. Yet, in your house I also felt very uncertain and alone. You would let me whimper and cry while you also reassured me it would be okay. You were patient with my fears as you helped me learn I was safe.

Human beings don't seem to do that, Dad, do they? And it seems that if you are a soldier or veteran, it is mandatory to keep tears and fears hidden away. I understand that for the sake of your safety—and your life—turning off feelings that could be distracting is a critical necessity. Yet, once you are no longer deployed, why does it seem that you must keep that button *turned off to help everyone around you feel at ease? Or maybe I should say, turn the button on, but make sure you only speak about certain things. To be transparent seems too big of a risk for both the audience and the person who wishes to speak.*

You know, Dad, I think I prefer being me. Even though it can be hard being a German shepherd sometimes, being unconditional in my love is a breeze.

I enlisted in the Army in 2003 with a goal in mind. I wanted to experience "more" for my life. I grew up in California and I was ready to leave. After all, there was a world "out there" for me to go see. I was eighteen, ambitious, eager, and…innocent in my decision-making. That I would be deployed several times into war zones was not what I was expecting.

In 2004, I was deployed for the first time to Fallujah—Ramadi and then Fallujah, Iraq at the invincible, "this is so cool mindset" ages of eighteen and nineteen. My mentality was that I was now part of an unstoppable gang—doing good gangster things. Capone, Pretty Boy Floyd, Bonnie's Clyde—that was my feeling. It was this mentality that helped me overlook that what I was experiencing was bad and full of traumatic imagery. *Button turn off, there is no room for emotional or mental fatigue.*

Just as I didn't foresee when I joined the Army that I would deploy several times before retiring, I also didn't foresee that my one-year tour in Iraq would be the preparation I would need. Baghdad would prepare me during my second tour of duty. Both were the foundation for the Battle of Kamdesh in Afghanistan in 2009. Fifty-two of us fought for all we were worth against four hundred, resulting in eight of our own losing their lives. But before I jump to tour three, I need to first tell you about the returns home in between.

Actually, before that, I need to tell you one more thing. Something about that first tour that greatly influenced the leaves in between. I had a best friend while serving in Ramadi who had just made sergeant during our time overseas. He was a guy I admired, not only for his leadership, but also for his love of his family. A father to a little girl, and you know what that means. A daughter who has the ability to wrap a dad around her finger tightly, and instantly. This daughter was nineteen months old when he became sergeant, a daughter he saw in person for only three weeks of her young life. Such is the vow we all make when we join the military – sacrifice.

I can already sense as you read this what you are feeling. Your stomach is starting to knot at what you believe you are about to read. My best friend was leading his first mission, his team in a truck crossing a bridge. A grenade ended their crossing, and his life, along with most of his platoon, except for one member who lived.

My tour up to that point had been an experience of a mission on the offense. In an instant, with these first causalities of my brothers, my time was now one of defense. Suddenly, being a gangster like Capone wasn't so exciting. *Button, off, and quickly. Focus, don't think what about if that had been me. And most of all, whatever you do, DO NOT grieve.*

I returned home to Fort Carson, Colorado to make my reentry. This equaled one opportunity to me—party! I was a grown-up now, no longer home, and I had just fought a war heroically. *Bragging rights, bragging rights, look at me. How cool am I that I can underage drink; stay off button and let's have some fun, shall we? One shot, two shots, three shots—oh no you won't see me yet, floor! Vodka, Crown Royal, liquor galore.*

Sometimes we receive a knock at the door, and though we may answer it, we aren't always ready to usher in who is knocking. This was me, January 1, 2005—translation, New Year's Eve. Certain I was coherent enough to drive from the bar back to base, I turned off the button calculating that a full bottle and then some of Grey Goose followed by a bottle of Crown Royal was over the legal limit for driving. After all, I was a tough guy, invincible, I had come home in one piece. *And besides, masculine men don't cry out loud when they are hurting. Remember button, remain off, and let me do the talking.*

I made sure to leave the bar in a brawl without me taking a swing. Drinking and fistfighting weren't my kind of scene. Until the military police and civilian cop pulled me over for drinking. I resisted the arrest at first, determined to enter the gate so that I could go to sleep. I got to go to sleep all right, in a cell at the station of the military police. In the tip of a glass, or I should say, in the bottle emptying, I made one decision that would significantly impact my career in the Army.

At this point of the DUI, I was three years in and had barely spent time as specialist, a ranking you work hard to receive. *Grey Goose and Crown Royal score two, me, score zero, instantly. Remember, button, stay off, and I will find a way to get us through this thing. Hey look, over there, they are grabbing the handle of something. Button, I think we just might get through this without them noticing. We were just having a good time on New Year's Eve. Shhhh, Grey Goose and Crown Royal, you don't know anything! I'm not turning to you for any traumatic or painful memories. Button, look, that handle is a broom, and I think I hear the swish, swish, swishing. Sweeping it under the rug, they are doing. Ah, thank you for New Year's Eve. Our perfect exclamation point for our drinking.*

Yes, sir, I am sorry sir, I know I messed up significantly. A cut in pay for three months, sir, okay, I thank you for such generosity. Forty-five days confined on base and enrollment in a substance abuse program, yes sir, I appreciate your care for my well-being. Again, sir, I am sorry for my stupidity.

There button, we did it without them suspecting. We kept the off switch on the anguish we are experiencing emotionally and mentally. Everyone sees what they want to see, and my leaders have chosen to see me as remorseful, and my drinking too much a one-time thing. They aren't choosing to see that I am a mess inside, quickly unraveling. Button, it is our secret between you and me.

I was supposed to enroll in a substance abuse program for nine to twelve weeks, three times per week. As noted above, everyone sees what they want to see. The nurse who interviewed me chose to hear my convincing story. When she asked why I was enrolled, I responded, "Command directed it for too much to drink on New Year's Eve." It made perfect sense to her to also see it as a one-time thing. Her signature approved me not needing to go back after that first meeting. *Button, we are good to go without any more probing. I guess it's off to Baghdad we go for our second tour of duty.*

I was deployed to Baghdad for twelve months, which was extended to sixteen months, but hey, that was less than others serving beside me. I survived thanks to the button I had become quite good at keeping turned to off while in the war zone. Or at least I thought I was keeping it turned off until I returned home.

Turns out when the button is in the off position it is still observing and experiencing what is happening. Even though it is off, it is still absorbing and stuffing. And funny thing about that button in the off position and memories of the past that don't fade away. Though the button is in the off position, it isn't able to erase. What stays pushed down deep begins to grow warm and heat up like lava in a volcano. That is how it felt once I was stateside again, though at the time I didn't fully know that I was trying to avoid a sudden eruptive flow.

This time instead of Grey Goose and Crown Royal consuming me, anger and rage were in the lead. Now I was twenty-three or twenty-four years old, single, and thinking it was time to get on with the next stage of my life. It was time I settle down, maybe buy a house, and find a wife.

Yet, instead of maintaining a positive relationship with a girlfriend, I seemed to be successful in causing reason for us to part. I thought I was turning the button on; I guess I should have told that to my heart. If I was allowed only one word to describe me from 2006 until about 2011, the word would be "mean." I wasn't physically hurtful, but my words could slice and punch quite painfully. It would be great if when we are in emotional pain we wouldn't lash out at others, yet it doesn't seem to work that way. I guess it is considered a cry for help, though I think the recipients of the lashings would have something different to say.

I hurt many, I know, including one of my other best friends who had to have a heart-to-heart with me. My mom, with her worried eyes and a mother's knowing, cautioned, "Watch yourself, Armando," as she noticed me changing. It struck me, yet, I overrode it with my certainty that what I was going through was normalcy. After all, what I was going through was the same thing as my battle buddies.

It is a tough place to be when stuck in the middle between opposing sides. It is even tougher when the opposing sides are the voices in your mind. When my best friend—the sergeant—had died only having seen his daughter three weeks of her one year plus nine months, I had vowed

I didn't want that kind of life. Yet, once back home, growing lonelier, I found I admired that the sergeant had known that kind of love, no matter the short time.

On one hand, I longed to make it matter that his life had ended tragically. That I didn't waste a day of living would honor his memory. On the other, I felt guilt that I was among the living. In addition, I missed my best friend and I wished he was beside me. I wished my best friend was texting me pictures of his daughter as she turned three, six, and thirteen.

On one hand, I longed to let down my guard of masculinity. I longed to turn on the button and show vulnerability. Yet on the other, I felt the depression and anger needed to be kept behind closed doors and out of view. The wrong pizza delivery equaled punching a hole in the wall or throwing the phone across the room. I didn't inflict injury on people, objects were the only victims of my rage. *Is this switch not working? Button, turn off now, please, oh please, give me a break!*

And now we are at the third tour of duty. The Battle of Kamdesh—fifty-two of us against four hundred enemies. October 2009, three months after I deployed for Afghanistan. Fighting for our lives, nonstop combat hand to hand. I had two primary roles during this ambushing: call for airstrikes and retrieve. What, I should say who, I needed to retrieve were our fallen heroes—more of my best friends like Sergeant in 2003. I needed to go and retrieve their bodies so that they would not be kidnapped by the enemy. I needed to do all that I could to retain their dignities and ensure they could return home to their families.

And then I got to stay nine more months on this tour before returning home. *Button, off, we only have sixteen more weeks to go. Stay clear in our judgment for we don't know if or when there could be another ambushing. Men to your left and to your right are counting on your clear and objective thinking. There is no room for fear nor grieving.*

I came home overwhelmed with one overarching feeling. I was extremely lost and not certain what my next step should be. Hindsight is 20/20 to realize feeling lost started in Colorado on New Year's Eve.

The fog started to lift when I attended an honorary event at the White House/Pentagon for our squad leader who was receiving a medal of honor because of his leadership that October day. It was for the Battle of Kamdesh, declared to the most decorated battle of that war, and our platoon was invited to celebrate.

I hadn't seen the guys in my platoon once we got out—another one of those opposites I mentioned earlier in my story. On one hand, staying surrounded by those you served beside would seem to be a comfort, and on the other, it was a constant reminder of unwanted memories. Although it was good to see the guys again, it wasn't easy. Some didn't look like themselves—high on substances to alter their mental states. Others looked like mirror images of me—a commonality in our stories of anger and pain. These guys knew me without me even needing to speak. They, too, had overwhelming waves of emotions, fighting the button to stay off continually. The third group had been to counseling and seemed to have themselves collected and functioning. They didn't appear to be lost like I was feeling. They were who I wanted to be.

In 2012, I started seeing a counselor, and I started to move from lost to found, or maybe I should say finding. I think it will be a journey of my life to reach wholeness, but I now feel like that third group of guys who seemed to be more at peace. I found my wife, and we have a family. And I get to see my children every day, what Sergeant would want for me.

In 2017, I retired from the service after an eighth tour of duty. Korea, noncombat this time, thankfully. Eight tours, with five noncombat, and then there are the other three. Life changing, I think of B.D. and A.D. As in before deployment, and after, in which I had to redefine an entire new sense of normalcy. Though I had started feeling whole again in 2012, I found myself temporarily lost again when retiring. I had known military life since 2003. Now what was I to do fully disabled, mostly skillful at one thing. Turning off that button so that the pain would not consume me. *Button, now what do we do on this side of enemy lines where we have a family? A family that is counting on us being wholly present, like attending school events in public settings. They are counting on us not only to provide and keep them safe. They are counting on us to go on dates and to laugh and play.*

One of the side effects of PTSD is not belonging. Actually, it's not a side effect, but a primary reality. In a "normal" world, people see butterflies and rainbows and my first sight is thunderstorms and borderline hurricanes or tsunamis. Even harder is that PTSD doesn't mean pain, trauma, sorrow, or despair to society. PTSD has a negative stigma equal to "going postal" or having violent tendencies. Mention that you feel anger you can't explain and immediately people put up a red flag. I usually notice the eyes are the first thing that people turn away.

And now for another life-changing event for me. The day I found a puppy who would come to be known as Rocky. German shepherds have held a soft spot for me ever since I had to rehome my first shepherd when deploying to Korea in 2016. Fast-forward to 2018 and once I knew that a service dog would be what could help me on my healing journey, I began searching for breeders and then a trainer who could ensure Rocky and I would become certified as a service-dog–veteran team.

A few hundred miles away in South Carolina, I found what I was certain was the right puppy. Unfortunately, the cost was not affordable for me and my family. And now here is a moment when thunderstorms and hurricanes are much better than rainbows and butterflies, literally. Because of a hurricane in the Carolinas, the cost for the puppy was reduced significantly.

While in a pet store to get supplies for this bundle of fur now named Rocky, I met a dog trainer for the local K9 sheriff's department who volunteered free of charge to train Rocky and me. While I began working with this gentleman, my wife found Northwest Battle Buddies. An application, a one-year wait, and another guardian angel crossed our path to finalize Rocky and me as a team. Shannon, the CEO of NWBB, agreed that Rocky could come to certification class though he had begun his formal learning externally. I am forever grateful to Shannon and her organization for helping Rocky and me.

I would love to tell you that every day is a great day now, and that I never know sadness or the struggle to rise out of bed sometimes. Yet, I do love telling you that I can be a part of all that my wife and children enjoy doing because I have Rocky by my side. If you are a reader who has children, you may struggle to read what I will now say. I will do the best I can to explain. Rocky gives me purpose to get up each day for the sake of my family. I know you might wonder why it isn't my family that is the motivation I need. It is another one of those oppositions we can find ourselves in as human beings.

Human beings have a gift that canines don't have, or at least don't exhibit if they do. Us human beings can judge and discern if we need to. Us human beings have these great minds full of voices that tell us how to perceive reality. And we determine that reality based on our experiences, our values, and our reactions to what we perceive. Some days my family needs me, and they are left to judge because of the expectations I can't meet. Some days when I am judging myself the most, I am not able to receive their love for me. Into the mirror I look and there is my family also judging me, my certainty. Canines don't judge, unconditional in their accepting. There is never the feeling that to Rocky I must explain anything.

I love my family with my whole heart and there is nothing I wouldn't do for them, including lay down my life. That is scary, you know, to love that greatly, and what makes it especially hard sometimes is when I think, *Do I have this right? Hey button, let's turn off for a moment until I can catch my breath. I'm watching my children laugh, play, and grow, and Sergeant can't because he's dead. Most days I know I'm living the way he would have wanted for me. And then some moments I just need to turn off the button for a short reprieve.*

I have hope again, and a confidence in myself that I had lost for a very long time. Thanks to Rocky I know it's possible to survive. You have probably heard others say how their service dog has their back, and of Rocky that is true, too. He is my companion—that battle buddy—who I know I can count on to get me through. He is there through the emotional waves and triggered images and memories. He holds me in his brown-eyed gaze and lets me wrap my hands—and sometimes my face—in his fur, while he just sits there listening. He doesn't try to solve or fix or understand, nor feel uncomfortable with what I am sharing. In his eyes I am accepted for being me.

If I could ask one thing of you who are reading my story... If I could ask on behalf of all of us who journey with PTSD... Please try not to judge our struggles and please try to hold a safe space for our vulnerabilities. Please try to challenge any stigmas or images you have of who a soldier or veteran is "supposed to" be. I know we signed up to serve, so that carries a certain element of ownership that it was the risk we took and the choice we made. And I know that the subjects of war, death, and traumatic experiences are ones we would prefer to keep at bay. Yet, underneath the uniforms are individuals who have something in common with you. We are human beings trying to do the best we can with who we are and with what we are able to do.

Hey Dad, I'm not sure I knew that there was a chance you might not have gotten me. I can't imagine what my life would have been if you and I weren't a team. I wouldn't be fulfilling my purpose, that much I know. I was meant to live my life serving you, a man the world knows as Armando.

Dad, do you think people could judge less if they saw that it takes pain and traumatic times to lead us to our callings? Do you think it would make people less afraid of such things as pain and grief? As I observe people, I think that it is because they are afraid to hurt that they judge those who are hurting the most. If people keep it pushed away, it won't have to become something they intimately know. Or at least that is what I feel people believe. Out of sight, out of mind, out of range of possibility. Yet, Dad, if there hadn't been a hurricane where I lived, I wouldn't have been led to home. I wouldn't have been led to helping you heal your pain with unconditional love.

Well, Dad, I think the best we can do is share our story and then live to the best of our abilities. When you have moments when you need the button to turn off, I will be right beside you patiently waiting. And when the button is on and a moment comes along trying to harm you, trust I've got your back.

Dad, one more thing, I'm certain Sergeant is watching how you are leading your life and he is glad.

JOE AND BAILEY

*When you look deeply into your anger, you will see
that the person you call your enemy is also suffering.
As soon as you see that, the capacity for accepting
and having compassion for them is there*

—Thich Nhat Hanh

*D*ad, I know it is not the same when a pup is weaned away
from its momma and siblings. Yet, for what it is worth, I
understand your hurt and your grief. There is such a comfort
having your family surrounding you, and not just figuratively, but literally,
too. I can still feel myself squished tightly with my brothers to my left and
to my right. And my little sister, well, her favorite position was smack on
top of me as she slept through the night. I didn't always get to lie next to
Momma, but I could hear her breathing. Even if there was physical space
between us, I could lull myself to sleep with the rhythm of her heartbeat.

Though it didn't make it super easy, Momma did prepare us for "the
day," that time when each of us would be permanently taken away. She
had let each of us know that we had a purpose to fulfill much bigger than
being her baby. That each of us had at least one human soul who was in
our destiny to meet. Someone we were meant to give our whole heart too,
unconditionally. Gosh, she made each of us feel so special, like we were
royalty. I felt so important, and I was so excited for when I would find this
human being.

Of course, Dad, we know it was you that Momma was talking about,
though I had to meet some other humans before you. I guess like you, Dad,
I had some of my own trials to go through. When Momma told me that I
had a purpose to fulfill she said, "My daughter, you have a gift the world
needs. You were put on this Earth to love unconditionally. My dear, your
heart only knows love and how to give it no matter the hate tossed your way.
Some people hurt so deeply, they will try to give to you their darkest, ugliest

pains. *They may raise their voice so loud you will shake in your paws and want to retreat. My dear child, they may strike out at you and they may bid you good riddance as they command that you leave. Do not let their self-hate turn you into someone you are not meant to be. Keep your faith, for there is someone you will find who will love you in return unconditionally. That person will know sorrows that run deep; yet into each other's eyes you will look, and you will know this is the home where you are meant to be. That each of you will be each other's family."*

And well, Dad, as we know, two peas in a pod, you and me.

The time of my life, from baby through childhood to eighteen. I had all that a young man could want—a job, a new car, a loving close-knit family. I graduated from high school in a small rural community. I got a job right away at a local foundry. Me, eighteen years old, able to buy a brand-new car with my own money. I was best of friends with ten boys and girls, my siblings. I was spoiled in love from a mother and a grandmother whose fierce strength ensured I never wanted for anything. Now graduated, free from studying, poised to begin life, I was on top of the world until that letter arrived.

Dear Joseph, we want you! Come be all that you can be! They left out one important detail—that it was not a choice up to me. I had been drafted into the Army. A tour in Vietnam would become my destiny. As I made my way to Detroit to then raise my hand to vow to serve my country, I opened the door to let in my internal pillar of strength for surviving. I would stand strong on the only foundation I could see beneath my feet. As I went through basic training, my best friend Anger accompanied me.

My siblings were not singled out for the draft as it seemed I had been, my certainty. My brothers were not drafted for this war that was becoming very good at separating. A separation of North and South, continents away; division between people and within families in our own US of A. From the moment I went to Detroit, and then Fort Knox, Kentucky for basic training, my homesickness was the jet fuel to keep Anger mounting. Instead of six weeks of hard, stressful training simulating life in a humid, mosquito-filled, war-raged country, I could have been completing back-breaking work at a foundry. Enjoying home-cooked meals and laughter sitting at the table among my family. *Dear Anger, if you would like, we can invite Hate to join us on this journey. No sense in us being a pair in misery. The more the merrier, don't you think?*

Hindsight is the blessing we find when our hearts are ready to rewind and replay. I did not know at the time that Anger was my protector to keep me safe. Perhaps A.N.G.E.R. could stand for Any way to Not Give Emotions Rein. By keeping Anger as my pillar, I did not let Fear and Despair cloud my judgment, Anger my armor against mind's thievery. I observed some dear souls whose minds shattered under the unending booming barrage of nighttime artillery. With Anger my sidekick, there was a certain *I'll be damned if you will get the best of me; you may have stopped the start of my life, but you I will beat.*

Don't get me wrong that I was immune to Fear—for I was scared—and I certainly looked for ways to escape my reality. Drugs of choice and alcohol accompanied Anger on our tour of duty. Yet, before I expand on my love of self-numbing, let me back up to my additional pre-Vietnam training. After more basic training at Fort Lindenwood, Missouri to become proficient in being ambushed in the night, I went to Fort Gordon, Georgia to learn how to install telephone lines. For eight weeks, I climbed telephone poles, stringing wire from the air to the ground. When some of the others I trained with went home for a seventeen-day leave, Anger got a workout when I was told, *No leave. You go to Vietnam NOW.*

I know we choose how to respond to what life brings our way. But, man, I got to tell you, to respond with anything but Anger was near impossible those days. I loved my family—and still do—with all my heart. That feeling that I was being ripped away from them—potentially forever—was very hard. I will be honest with you that the thought of going to Canada entered my mind frequently. Yet, to make the choice that I could never enter the States to see my family again was even harder than someone making a choice for me. As my nose communicated to my entire body, my deployment included *the most horrible, nastiest smell I must inhale for the next year,* the love in my heart nudged *365 days and you will be out of here.*

I didn't mark a calendar day after day as some guys did. Anger told me that I would do better to become oblivious. If Fear wanted to enter when I didn't know who a friend was or who was the enemy among the Vietnamese, I would conspire with Anger to hang out with some of the battalion or better yet, go find a drink.

Often, we are led to who we are meant to be in life through the experiences that tug us the opposite way. It is how well we dance between the opposing forces that is our purpose-filled grace. I did not want to be on this tour for one minute, one hour, one day. That is all I could see—how much I did not want to be in this place. Yet, the opposing force to not wanting to be here was because of how much I loved my family. Burning so very strong, no matter the distance between, was the bond of love felt for and among all of us collectively. Anger held the rope tugging on this tour and for many a year after my service was through. Yet, behind the scenes and fully front and center, my love for what it means to have family also grew.

Training didn't end once we were immersed in the war. We received training in-country on what to look for. We were led through simulation demonstrations to learn there is always more than we initially see. An enemy can be right in the front row and then sneak through parameters without us noticing. I mentioned earlier that I was not immune to Fear, for Fear certainly walked beside me. Especially each time I was on night guard duty. Just as I found a way to keep Anger from erupting like a volcano outwardly, I used drinking and drugs to silence Fear's nudging.

Those "vices" as people might refer to alcohol, marijuana, or cocaine are no longer part of my life. One thing that remains is my dislike of the Fourth of July. Don't get me wrong, it isn't Anger that hates this holiday. It's the fireworks that take me back to the yelling, screaming, and unending bombing from the war days. I love to go for walks, though I probably am still cautious with my step. I know there are no claymore mines in front of me, and yet… Memories may not be predominant, though they also don't completely fade. Like how I gladly retreat indoors from the outside humidity on certain days. Thankfully rain doesn't agitate me too much; then again, I'm no longer wading through the trenches of monsoon season mud.

I suppose I was one of the lucky ones to have days when boredom was the theme. Oh, but how time moves so very slow when you are waiting. I would work on a truck, performing preventative maintenance until telephone lines needed to be routed or repaired. I guess one can say it is a blessing and a curse when I'd get to perform the reasons I was sent there. The blessing to do something involving expertise to pass the time quickly. The curse was that if I was repairing, the war had been actively happening.

I was not a rebel before the draft—I was a "good kid" who didn't drink and who obeyed laws, rules, regulations, and authority. Oh, my mom and my grandmother had those eyes in the back of their head, which meant if I misbehaved, they would see. Anger likes to be a rebel, though, and lead one to places they wouldn't normally go. Like a bar, a fence line to buy a drug, a fistfight, and jail—all new experiences I would come to know. I found I could pass the time more quickly if I lived by these five essential things—women, booze, beer, cocaine, and speed! If I was sad, someone was there to offer a solution to lift me up, higher, and higher, *oh thank you, please.* Night guard duty running telephone lines, not able to shower for a week. Then a lull, back to the barracks to repair trucks, pass the time ever so slowly. Drink, eat sea rations, *ah, find a way to be higher, and higher still.* Minute, week, month, three hundred and sixty-five days this would be my drill.

I would watch guys head for home, their tour coming to a close. *I can't wait for that to be me,* I'd think each time I watched another one go. I knew I would miss them—close friendships work that way. Yet, I was glad to be envying the heck out of them when it became their time to return to the States. Calling home wasn't an option, for communications were not what they are today. A link to home was the letters mailed back and forth—probably a good thing my family couldn't hear what I might say. I could shelter them from what I was experiencing and what I was feeling, keeping my letters positive and upbeat. I know my mom would have worried herself sick if she had heard my voice speak. If I could have talked to her on the phone, I would have sheltered her that way, too. Yet, a mom is wise to what isn't said—that I was not myself when I wrote home, I anticipate she still knew.

If you ever wonder if a care package sent from home matters, let me tell you without any hesitation *it means everything!* Us guys would share with each other anything we received—a way to bring to all of us love from family. I would get an occasional letter from my girlfriend at the time—I thank the good Lord that she became my wife! Of course, just like my mom, I didn't let my girlfriend know I had made best friends with Anger and that I had found ways to push homesickness far away. I liked the fantasy I was still the Joe they knew, though I knew the Joe they knew had been replaced. I should rephrase that, for the Joe they knew was still inside. But he was just out of reach for a very long time.

I volunteered for any jobs, even if they didn't involve running telephone lines. The busier I was, no matter the task, the faster the spin of time. I dug auger holes, I hauled gravel, I was designated driver for leadership to black market meet-and-greets. Vigilant to the mines in the road, as well as to the bodies no longer moving. An obstacle course I don't wish anyone to maneuver through—but hey, at least I was busy. And at least I was one day closer to seeing my family.

If you think the world is vast, I will share it is smaller than we think. I can still hear someone who knew my family call out to me. We had decided to build makeshift walls around our barracks, a way to give us privacy. On a lumber run I had a gentleman call out, "Are you?" and "Hey, I know your family." It probably seems silly to you, or just an ordinary moment in an average day. Yet, for me, it was a nugget of connection to my favorite place so far away. Someone who knew where home was for me. Another scene in the fantasy that I was still the eighteen-year-old Joe before I had been mandated to leave.

When I first arrived in Vietnam, I had observed a group of guys who held the eeriest blank stare. I think I mentioned them earlier in my story, how their minds had thieved their capability to be present and aware. A few weeks before my tour was complete, I experienced a week when I thought someone might say the same of me. Where was I, where had I been, what exactly was my reality? I had been on another one of my volunteer assignments when bombs started coming in, and in, and in. All night, machine guns and bombs were our sky above as we sought cover in a water-brimmed ditch. A ditch which didn't include our normal netting as protection from the mosquitos savagely seeking food. And the worst part—at this point—is I hadn't had near enough beer to be soothed.

By this time, that is what drinking meant to me. Anger had invited in dependency as a coping buddy. Far more than I realized while in the thick of it, I had moved through my tour in a foggy state. People ask me where I served, and my response is, "I wonder that myself to this day."

With Anger in the driver's seat mightier than the pain and sorrow buried away, I saw each order and command as a further reason to grow hate. I can look back now and see the gifts in being told, "No, you can't go to Cambodia" or "You will go to this class, that is an order, immediately." Okay, maybe it is a stretch to say a gift, but my faith has helped me better see. I have faith that in the sergeant's dislike of me, I was kept physically safe to come home alive to my family.

Guys were putting in for early outs, to be done in fifteen months versus twenty. Of course, my rebellion had burned bridges with sergeants, so *denied* was the answer I received. The wastebasket makes a great catcher's mitt when someone wants to highlight *NO* boldly. My paperwork handed to the sergeant went in one hand and then shifted to the trash so very quickly.

At this point I began marking that calendar with an X for each day. *You can do this Joe, just thirty more days.* With each X, Anger dissipated a little bit, subsided by happiness that soon I would see my family. Day twenty-nine, twenty-eight, fifteen. Ah, at long last, for fifty-nine days, I was sent home on leave! Reunited with those who were the balance to my Anger deep inside me. No longer ripped away from those who meant everything!

The freedom of a motorcycle, just me and the road. And to my friends—*Yeah, man, let's get together now that I'm home.* Except, I no longer recognized my friends for they had changed since I had been away. Anger stepped into the limelight, again clouding the truth that it was I who had also changed. Okay, Any way Not to Give Emotions Rein. I'll push aside this further pain.

I took my time getting back to Fort Riley, Kansas where I would complete my service in the Army. I was considered AWOL for a bit, but that didn't anger them enough to punish me. Well, let me rephrase that for punishment I would receive. Just not in the form of jail nor immediately. Two days prior to the end of my service, I received a phone call through Red Cross that my grandma was asking for me so that she could say her goodbyes. She was in her final hours on Earth requesting to see me a final time. Because I had continued my rebellion, inspiring other soldiers at this base to implement heavy partying, the Captain under no circumstances would let me leave. It has taken considerable time to see myself as I know my grandmother has always seen me. Her love of me so genuine, so good, so accepting—a role model I try to emulate within my own family. A love a lot like my dear Bailey. My grandma never blamed me that I couldn't come to her side—she knew I would blame myself well enough for both her and I combined.

Hello, Anger, my familiar comforting friend who I can count on to never leave my side. What do you say we muscle through this thing called life? We survived a war by doing something we do best—care to join me for a drink, and another, and another, before we get some rest? Work, drink, get fired, work, drink, get fired a second time, yes, that was me. Have a company create a special shift to support my hangovers and my drinking, and still get fired from job number three.

Anger, I see what we are doing to my dear mom, but I cannot stop this rage. No more can I keep these emotions locked away. Nothing is the same as when I left, nothing and no one has stayed the same. I was outgoing, I loved people, and YOU, Anger—didn't even know how to speak! I was not someone who ever felt the unstoppable urge to throw and break things. I don't know who this person is you have taken hostage inside my dad's garage where I, too, hide. It is someone my own mom cannot even look into his eyes. My mom no longer likes me, and neither do my brothers or my sisters, and God rest her soul, I'm sure my grandma would hate me, too. I don't blame them, for I don't like who they see drunk the majority of the day through. Yet, the more I see sorrow in their eyes, the more I must look away. Their eyes reflect what I have been fighting so hard to keep at bay. The hurt too great to let Grief take a front row seat. To the bar I must go where I can find reprieve in a round or two or six drinks.

Tough love it is called when we need to protect our own hearts from completely shattering. When we reach a point where we can no longer witness the one we love self-destroying. My mom's unconditional love never wavered, though at the time it felt like once again it was being stolen by a dirty rotten thief. When my mom told my siblings to stay away from me, my worst fear during my time at war became a reality. I had died, figuratively, not able to return home to the ones I loved. The person who came back to them was a shell that led my family to shout, "We are done with you. Enough!"

On the deepest level where hearts know the truth, I know my mom was doing the best thing to do. She had taught me the power of choice and she had taught me responsibility. She had taught me perseverance and that family is our most valuable commodity. She knew me better than I knew myself, that within me was the capability to choose different steps from where I currently stood, or barely crawled, most days. She had to reject my actions so that I would decide a better path to take. She didn't have a choice, just as I didn't when I was eighteen. I had drafted her into my internal war, but unlike me she was going to desert and break free. Though it hurt deeper than anything I hope I never have to feel the rest of my life, I am grateful for my mom's tough love that was my beacon of light.

Of course, it was not an overnight trip to find forgiveness and peace. I would stay best friends with Anger held down and deep. I was no longer drinking, replaced by working seven days a week. I had a wife and a daughter to provide for, thankfully. My wife, the patience of a saint, a force to be reckoned with, and a beautiful thief of my heart, gave me the ultimate gift when she said, "Either, or else, you choose your drinking or your family." I was not a person to walk away from my children or the best thing that had ever happened to me. My wife was the one to lead me to that start of my life. This time, that start was so much better than what had started the first time.

I stayed working and we bought our first home. The vividness of Vietnam started to dissipate and go. Anger wasn't visiting like it used to, though occasionally it would come calling. I had grown good at not giving it much airtime to talk with me. There is a quote from John

Lennon that states, *Life is what happens to you when you are making other plans*. I wasn't necessarily making other plans, but life continued happening very fast.

I am proud of the forty years I worked for four different paper mills, considering there was a point in time when work and I didn't see eye to eye. Yet, working seven days a week didn't always have me fully present in my children's lives. Retirement has provided me the opportunity to be available twenty-four hours a day for my children if they need me to be. Yet, my heart feels the weight of my absence as they were each growing. There is a part of me that knows work was the strong arm to keep pain, trauma, sorrow, and despair (PTSD) from overtaking my days. There is also another part of me that knows I was working hard because of the way I was raised.

I've shared a little about my story with my children, parts I didn't used to want to share with anyone, not even me. I don't think I've ever told them, though, just how much they rescued me. If it wasn't for my wife and my children, I'm not sure I would be here to tell you my story. If I wasn't in jail, I think I would be next to my grandmother at the cemetery. As a child it can be hard to understand why dad isn't home and is always working. I hope my children can look past the times I was absent to see that they were my inspiration to be the best for them I could be. Because of them, and my wife, the shell of a person who came home was no longer lost or empty. The best fulfillment I have found is being husband and father for my family.

I wasn't all work, though it might seem that was my main activity. I didn't necessarily like a lot of social interaction for relaxing. Crowds were not my comfort, feeling an anxiousness in public settings. My outlets included caring for our horses and woodcarving. In the quiet with the wood and chisel or in the pasture is where I could find serenity.

I mentioned retirement and the blessing of being available for our children around the clock. This is where I should mention that retirement was also hard. I had plans to fish in my spare time, but Restless introduced itself instead. It took a little bit after Restless entered for me to see that Anger was trying to rear its troublemaking head. I needed to fill the void from work with more to do, so I began remodeling homes as one of my brother's crew. Any way Not to Give Emotions Rein, yet the emotion of meanness was not staying tucked away. I was mean to those I loved, though it did not feel good to do. I was starting to feel like that person who returned home from Vietnam was coming into view.

The Veteran's Administration tried to help, but in my mind, they were still to blame. How dare they offer to help when, if it wasn't for the government, I wouldn't feel this anxious state. Once again, my dear wife gave me a gift when she said, "Either, or else, that temper cannot stay. Make a choice, Joe, for your family's sake."

I started with a prescription to take the edge off anxiety. I then, surprisingly, found comfort in group therapy. I had kept my story under lock and key. After all, I had returned home from a war in which parts of society were not warmhearted in their homecoming. If upon returning home, it had been easy to talk about one's story, it would have been at risk for fostering further hate. I had enough of that within me already without anyone else pouring more my way. Now I have found a group forum in which I could freely be me, with others who understood what I was feeling. There is a powerful healing effect when one speaks about things they are certain no one else would want to listen to; and instead of judgment, one is met with acceptance, and finds belonging, too. I find, too, that I am able to help others on their healing journeys; I guess one can say that the gift of struggle is the wisdom we glean. That wisdom becomes someone else's inspiration to keep going. Perhaps one of the most life-giving aspects of being among my brothers in arms in our group therapy is that our tears are accepted as we each move past our deep-seated grief.

Life has a way of bringing us back full circle to a similar place, though as we come back around, we are no longer the same. In that circle that comes back 360 degrees, we are given the opportunity to find healing. I had felt the government had stolen my life when I was eighteen. It would be the government that would save my life when they diagnosed me. *You have cancer, Joe, but the good news is we have caught it early.* My gratitude to the VA for discovering this disease. When they did, Anger largely left me. The gift of traumatic news is the healing it can bring.

In addition to group therapy I have also found comfort in a faith I was missing. It has helped to also become part of a church community. There is no greater peace than to know there is a love greater than us all who accepts me unconditionally, even when I have gotten angry or even during the time my pain was significantly hurting my family. I find belonging not just in God, but among the members of the church, too. I find an enjoyment in visiting, no longer looking for the nearest exit so that I can quickly leave a crowded room.

When my wife and I relocated after retirement to be near our children, we also began living near a brother of mine. The exceptional closeness from childhood was never the same, though we have been able to find a semblance of reconnection with time. The family I cherished and missed dearly while in Vietnam never became that same family, yet we found a way to move past the estrangement to find a form of unity.

Forty-five years later I do believe Anger has grown old, tired, and ready to retire, too. I think Anger has figured out my time with it is through. The eighteen-year-old has found peace and understanding. It was not life that was taken, but life that was spared, thankfully. I had friends who didn't return home in one piece, and some didn't return home alive. I came home to raise two children and to be husband to an amazing wife. Life happened exactly as it was meant to be. I am so blessed with every moment the good Lord has given me.

I returned home to now relax and to cast that fishing line. Along with my other best friend by my side.

Dad, can we go to McDonald's first to get some chicken nuggets before we go fishing? Just a little snack to munch on before I supervise your casting. I love how Mom describes me as mini-you; how I try to replicate whatever you do. If you shake hands with someone, I raise my paw to shake, too. Remember when you thought it was your friend helping you lift that heavy log from point A to point B? You turned to see the person on the other end was little ole me.

I know I'm not a certified service dog, yet I am of service to you. 110 percent for you there is nothing I wouldn't do! I will gladly keep any enemies away—real or perceived. Just ask those snakes that think they can sneak in our yard how I am ever watchful of predators lurking. I know it is hard when you feel anxious, but know I've got your back there, too. I'll gladly go for a walk or for a ride in the truck when the walls feel like they are closing in around a room.

Dad, it has been my greatest pleasure watching your heart's expansion as it freed itself from the constriction of sorrow and pain's brutality. Don't get me wrong, Dad, your heart was already so very large, bursting with love for your family. It's just that now I can see your love is given like I strive to give, unconditional without caution that it could all be ripped away. There is a relaxation that shines bright now, a relaxation and a strong faith.

You know the other day when we went through the drive-thru and you got me those nuggets to eat? It was not just joy in eating that not so good for me snack that fostered that tear to slide down my cheek. In that moment, Dad, feeling your heart at such ease, well, in that moment I could hear those words my momma had said to me. "My dear daughter, you have a purpose to fulfill and I know you will make me proud in how you do. There is a human being who will need your unconditional love to help her or him through. You will know when you meet this person that you have found your reason for being on this Earth as a soul in a fur coat. Your heart will feel like it wants to explode, you will love this human so."

She was right, Dad, about my heart bursting at the seams. I am glad it was you that I was destined to meet. I could not have found any better human being to love with my whole heart unconditionally.

The mind is a powerful thing that can play your life like the poetic motion of a fishing line casting through the air. Or the mind can walk you toward a cliff edge relentlessly repeating, *You are better off to jump, go ahead, I dare.* I have chosen to turn around and no longer look over the edge to the rocks below calling my name. Do you know, it is such a beautiful view above—my eyes can't stop drinking in the sky's sun-filled haze.

A quote by Elisabeth Kübler-Ross reads: *The most beautiful people we have known are those who have known defeat, known struggle, known loss, and have found their way out of the depths. These persons have an appreciation, a sensitivity, and an understanding of life that fills them with compassion, gentleness, and a deep loving concern. Beautiful people do not just happen.* Beautiful people are created from journeys with such things as anger, hate, pain, sorrow, and grief. A purpose fulfilled when we take these and turn them into understanding, love, healing, forgiveness, and peace.

NAAMA AND BELLE

*It's okay to be a glow stick; sometimes we
have to break before we shine.*

—Author Unknown

*M*om, tell me again what led you to me. When you begin by
whispering "once upon a time," it's my favorite start to the
story. You put your right hand on my back, and you look into
my eyes. You then say: "Dear Belle, there was this little girl, once upon a
time…" And then you tell me how you have known your calling since you
were five years of age. A destiny with dancing, memorized lines, costume
disguises, and standing center stage. To be an actress one day was your
heart's longing. Oh, the sparkle in your eyes when you say "I, Naama,
actress, director, producer—oh Belle, I was certain the sky's the limit in
achieving all three."

Mom, I also see the tears you hold back as you feel you have taken a
detour away from your dreams. That's why I like this quote from Neil
Gaiman so much: "Fairy tales are more than true; not because they tell us
that dragons exist, but because they tell us that dragons can be beaten." And,
Mom, he is right, I do believe. After all, I look at all the dragons you've
defeated before your path was led to me.

You defeated the dragon of disappointment when you couldn't get into
the theater army. You defeated the dragon of not belonging when training
as a member of the military police. You defeated the dragon of vulnerability
when you became a mission to save, no longer seen as a person who valued
being discreet with her body. You defeated the dragon of lost innocence as
your mind tried to understand what your body was now experiencing. You
defeated the angel clothed in black extending a hand for you to walk his
way. "Come, my pretty girl, death is on your side," this angel was trying
to say. You defeated the dragons of multiple surgeries to repair and then to
beautifully mask the visible scars that will always be visible in the depths

of your soul. There is the dragon of depression you've beaten, too, and there is the dragon that has tried to tell you dancing makes you less than whole.

Mom, yes, I believe that fairy tales are more than true because of the dragons that are not stronger than dreams. The princess is always meant to one day become that beautiful Queen.

I was one of the fortunate ones, or so I once believed. Since I was five years old, I knew what I wanted to be. Most never know what they want to be when they grow up, and this was not me.

Since it is mandatory that my path toward becoming an actress must include time in the military, my certainty then was I would enlist in the theater army. Yet, life has a wisdom to it that we don't always know at the time it is redirecting our plan. Life felt I needed to learn disappointment first—and so much more I would soon come to understand.

In my senior year of high school I took tests designed to determine the best fit for me once in the Army. Taking a test for the theater was not an option given me. That I felt unhappy would be stating it mildly. Yet, I also deeply valued my parents' perspective, as they encouraged me to pick an option that would benefit me once I completed my service in the Army.

I began basic training, with the intention that I would become part of the investigative police unit after additional course training. As I trained with the military police, I felt this path as investigator was not a good fit for me. I had started down a path of being commander, then had stopped that for this branch of the police. I decided the commander path would be better suited, and thankfully, I was granted permission to return to commander training. I smile that I just said "thankfully." Sometimes I wonder what life would be like for me today if I had stayed in the investigative police unit of the Army.

I remember relocating back to where I had first completed my basic training. I remember pieces of the commander course that I was learning. I remember there were groups of girls and groups of boys that came through basics during the time I was commanding. I can't seem to remember much about being their actual commander, though; funny what details retreat from our memories. Except I do remember one specific day, seven months after becoming commander, quite vividly. I remember one specific day in which I, Naama, would come to watch scenes from a horrific movie. Or, at least that is what it felt like as I was bearing witness to the person on a stretcher being saved, while I lay on that stretcher being the person they were saving.

I remember being inside the shooting range with the next group of cadets we were teaching how to shoot. This process was somewhat like an assembly line, in which the focus was on getting everyone through. Each group of cadets would spend nearly a week inside the shooting range. It was the first day of the training week, this particular day. It was just before lunch, too, this I also recall. Yes, it's funny what memories retreat, and even more what ones stay at the forefront of them all.

I can still hear "Pull the trigger" and "Fire" from a commanding officer to the cadets. I had just taken out my phone and plugged it in so that it wouldn't go dead. Immediately after these words, I could no longer lift my arm. I didn't know that I had just been harmed.

Perhaps it was adrenaline or the gift of shock to protect our body from pain. My soul would tell you it is also the gift of being an actress to put yourself in another place. Whatever happened in that moment that my brain would not allow me to understand, my twisted arm with a hole and visible bone I could see actually enabled me to focus on one thing: I needed to get out of that range immediately.

I took two, maybe three steps before I fell to my knees. *Okay, if I can't walk, then I will crawl,* I told myself instantly. I started crawling when another commander came running toward me. Not any more experienced than I in a crisis, yet I commend her for her quickly formed expertise. Because of her reassuring manner, she kept me from absorbing my new reality. As I asked her what happened, she calmly stated, "You are fine" and "Nothing" and remained calm and determined while people came rushing to help me. She then proceeded to carry me to safety.

She and I haven't talked about those moments after the accident, and right now, that is okay. Perhaps we will one day. Right now, I don't need to know for certain if she told me what happened or if she saw the extent of my injuries. Right now, it isn't important to know how she remained so incredibly calm if she saw my organs protruding. What matters most right now is the abundant gratitude I feel for her being there in those initial moments, so reassuring with her *you are fine* and *nothing*. Because of her I could stay the actress watching movie scenes not fully integrating with the knowledge that my condition was life-threatening.

I remember being carried on a stretcher to the paramedic whose protocol it is to sit outside the range should an injury take place. I imagine paramedics never anticipated they would respond to something like this that day! I can still see the paramedic's tears when she looked at me. I also remember thinking, *Why is she crying?*

I think I may have passed out momentarily, to then wake up with so many heads surrounded above me. I remember, too, that these heads were male—or at least the majority. One was looking at my legs, one was looking at my left arm, and one was checking. For what, I wasn't sure at the time, though I kept hearing shouting. Fast, higher pitched in that excitable anxious way. All this feverish yelling above my head, so many heads standing in one place.

Can you see where they entered and exited, or is there only an entry hole?

What are they talking about "entry," "exit," and "hole," I didn't know.

My mind was trying to comprehend the meaning from all these voices and heads above me. *Find my phone, call my mom and tell her I'm fine, please.*

They didn't call my mom at the time, for they didn't know if I would live or if I would die.

The movie scene I watched, as I also lay on that stretcher while they assessed the severity. I remember seeing girls in the shooting range crying. I remember witnessing the girl on the stretcher getting physically sick. *I don't think something is right, but my mom will know how to fix this.*

This is that way that our experiences become part of a tool kit in which we can draw upon them when in need. I am grateful for the dance teacher who taught me special breathing techniques. She was my seventh- or eighth-grade teacher who taught us a meditative exercise in which we learned to breathe from one lung versus two. A lifesaving gift I received in how to be at one with one's body—to be that in tune.

I began to tell the nurse that I could not breathe from my left side. *Keep breathing out of your right lung and you will be fine.* My body kept communicating this to my mind. At first, the nurse thought it was my stress escalating as she encouraged me to take deep breaths. I continued to let her know something was not in alignment with the left of my chest. The Army doctor then saw that it was not only one bullet wound my body had absorbed on the range. A hole in my chest—on my left side—was an additional entry place. I received four bullet wounds that fateful day. One in my left arm, one in my chest, and one in each leg. Four entries, each their own dragon trying to slay me. They were not successful, though, for I am here to tell you my story.

If I thought the voices were fast and higher pitched before, now there was a heightened energy among everybody. Still all these floating heads everywhere above, now seeming to escalate into panicking. *We have to help her breathe, IMMEDIATELY!*

I think it is this moment that forever changed me. I think this is the traumatic moment that took away one of my most valuable commodities. Don't get me wrong, the accident itself drew that line in the sand in which life became before and never to be the same. Yet, this moment in which these floating heads decided they needed to help me breathe extracted from the air in my lungs my innocence and my vulnerability.

All my clothing had to be removed in order to help me breathe. There I was on that stretcher, completely exposed to the heads swirling above me. It felt to me that nobody was listening. Nobody was respecting my needs. *Soldiers I am supposed to be commanding are here watching. Please, please, PLEASE! Please leave my clothes on; please leave me with that dignity. Please...can't there be a respect of my privacy?*

I couldn't understand at the time that they were trying to save me from dying.

I felt like my body had been violated, and the pureness of life was no longer a possibility.

In this moment, fairy tales became only someone's made-up stories. Childlike wonder and believing in dreams became history.

I remember four paramedics in the ambulance, one of who was younger and kept asking me awareness questions as he continually talked with me. I believe he was an intern, and I remember telling him, "I just need you to help me breathe." That ambulance ride felt like five minutes, but it was probably closer to twenty-five in reality. I remember a glimpse of the trauma room, and a nurse with blond hair and big glasses saying, "Now we will put you to sleep." And the next thing I remember is waking up the next day not yet realizing the full extent of my injuries.

There is a quote by an unknown author that reads: *Good friends help you find the important things you've lost…your smile, your hope, your courage.* These things and so much more three of the greatest friends brought to me. I know my parents were the first people I saw when I awoke from the first of what would become many surgeries. Yet, one of my very first memories after the accident that day is three of my childhood friends standing around my bed supporting me. I couldn't talk due to the ventilator nor could I write due to my left arm injury— I'm a lefty when it comes to writing. I am certain it was a scary sight to see me in bandages and a machine to help me breathe. Yet, my friends didn't alter their facial expressions, acting so normal as if we were sitting at breakfast sharing over coffee. There they were to remind me I was not going to walk this journey forward on my own. Three of the greatest friends I am blessed to know.

It is the bond of a childhood friend that allows you to share the most private of things, and without question, they will react with the highest sense of urgency. One of my dear friends noticed my contacts had not yet been removed from my eyes. When she leaned in to confirm, I pointed her to my white board message that I needed help of a different kind. *I'm having my period* she started to read. Immediately she ran to the nurses' station to elicit help for me. They assured her they had taken care of the personal hygiene for me during the time of my surgery.

My mom brought me a whiteboard so that I could communicate. My first question I asked was, "Do I still have my arm and my leg?"

My mom didn't understand what I was asking at first as my mind kept thinking of what I had learned in basic training. If someone has had a tourniquet on for more than four hours, amputation is likely. I didn't know how long it had taken to get me from the accident into surgery.

I then asked, "Do I get a week off now?" which gave my mom a chance to do something I don't think she'd been able to do since she received the news her daughter had been wounded critically. She laughed at my question before she joked back, "Are you crazy?! More like a couple of months," which I still didn't quite absorb that meaning. I just remember being excited I was off for at least a week. I was confused, to say the least.

Nonstop vigil my parents held for me. Day, night, and every single moment in between. By my side together until it was time to sleep. Then one would be nearby in a room the hospital provided while the other slept next to me. There was not a second that they left the hospital for the first two weeks. Of course, the day my dad traveled home was a day I scared my mom tremendously.

I began coughing up blood, to the point of receiving seven blood transfusions consecutively. You may call me strong, but it is an inherited trait given to me. For my parents to go through what they did, they are the definition of what strength means.

I am filled with immense gratitude for the love that surrounded me. My aunt came without hesitation the night of my transfusions when my mom called her frantic at what was happening. Over the initial weeks, I was visited by many other friends and additional family. Many of my friends who visited were soldiers, coming in their uniforms, which included their weaponry. At first, I tried not to notice, and I also tried to keep silent my growing anxiety. I tried to concentrate on my friends and cousins and not what was hanging by their sides. Eventually it became too overwhelming and I requested my parents ask that all weapons be left outside the room, out of my sight.

My grandmother was my evening companion, a hand to hold as I would ask her repeatedly, "Grandma, will I be okay? Please tell me." Of which she would affirm every time, "My dear, dear Naama, you will be more than okay, honey. You will be great, just you wait and see."

I was in intensive care for five days before I was moved to the orthopedic department for the next step in my recovery. During my two-and-a-half weeks in this hospital, I went into surgery every two days, or nearly. I had many plastic surgeries. Yes, that's right, seven or eight during those sixteen or seventeen days for me. Oh, don't feel bad, for there was a certain fun to this. Well, I should rephrase: at the time it seemed fun as it became addictive. I developed an addiction to the anesthesia and found I started to wait for the next surgery. This didn't lead to serious long-term issues thankfully!

In fairy tales there are villains disguised as good beings, their ability to lure you into trusting. I had a specialized plastic surgeon who developed a technique to close shooting areas in a very aesthetic way. My parents and I trusted his sincerity until we learned more intentions were at play. Unfortunately, we were later informed that this surgeon photographs his surgeries performed and then presents them world-wide without patient consent to do so. The notion of being showcased this way creates an image in my thoughts I would rather not hold. There is a swirl of heads all gawking and peering at an image of me on screen. Not the way I imagined myself as an actress being watched by audiences around the world! Not the way I imagined it at all as that five-year-old girl!

After experiencing health complications while in the first hospital, I was moved to another, much bigger hospital, where I was returned to intensive care for several more days. I was then moved to the chirurgical department, or in layman's terms, for expert surgical care – more surgeries to face! During this time the focus was on healing my stomach, as I continued to have occurrences where I would heave up blood. This required seven or eight transfusions—I had lost that much! My dear parents—how worried they were, more than I probably realized. They have been my unending support through this entire time! It was only after more surgeries and when my bleeding events stopped that I was returned to the plastics department for a few weeks. And then from there, I was ready to start rehabilitating.

While in rehab, I started learning how to walk again, for my leg had sustained a crippling injury. I, a dancer, was now learning how to put one foot in front of the other again where I once could glide and leap with such ease. During my hospital stay, I was fortunate to have a psychiatrist who asked a key question that would enable me to finish my rehab from home. "How do you sleep at night?" to which I replied, "I don't!"

The nurses would come into my room at night when they thought I was asleep and use that time to try to give medicine via infusion to me. I have thin veins, and very sensitive skin, which makes needles painful—actually rather excruciating. There is another aspect to this, too, that made these night visits hard for me. Since I was a child, I have been very scared of a needle's viscous poking. When I was having to have the blood transfusions, I would pass out as fear washed over me. To avoid these needles during the night, I found I could use the TV. I believed that if I turned on the TV, they would come to my room and think me awake. If I was awake, I didn't have to experience the sudden awakening of needle pain. So, the TV and I became close friends while another friend began keeping us both company. This third friend was called Depression, and it started to visit more frequently.

I am blessed to have an aunt who took me under her wing. She not only visited daily to help administer shots or draw blood from me. She helped me overcome my fear of needles as the very gigantic enemy. She helped me slay the dragon of this fear so that I can administer my own medicine effortlessly. My aunt works in the oncology department at the best children's hospital in Israel and has the gentlest touch. I am forever grateful for her daily visits when I was in the hospital and for her unconditional love.

During my rehab, one of my childhood friends who was studying to get into the university would come visiting. She would bring her study materials with her to help distract me. Idle time was really starting to feel suffocating. Though I had rehab appointments daily, I wasn't learning or experiencing new things. Wake up, eat, learn to walk, eat, help a friend study, eat, go to sleep. Depression enjoyed this rhythm, but it was not liked by me.

I recruited my parents to help me go back into the Army, to the same location where I had been commander before my accident and injuries. The Army was kind to me—perhaps a little too much, as I didn't have to develop a disciplined routine. I could come and go and only "work" three hours if that suited me. I was physically present, yet not engaged in my responsibilities. I was buying time, or hindsight would say wasting it significantly. Yet, I think it was also part of my healing journey. I needed to go back to the place in which life changed for me instantly. I needed to face that dragon lurking in my memories.

An officer who meant well tried to help me face that dragon by encouraging me to go back to the range—to that movie scene. Bless her heart, she wasn't trained to know if that is how one slays a dragon or if there is a better way. I respected her authority to not say no, and perhaps a part of me wanted to prove I was mightier than the memories lingering on this range.

The dragon was stronger than I anticipated, teaching me what a panic attack means. It didn't defeat me, but it let me know I wasn't ready to confront this beast. I needed more time to heal the traumatic moments that had seared through the all of me. I needed more time to process this life-changing event's meaning. I almost lost my life, and my dreams feel shaken from their base of certainty I once stood on so confidently. That this accident was a distant memory with no side effects or lasting scars—oh, how I wish it could be!

Hello, Panic Attacks, why you might as well join, too. You complement Depression well as I try to figure out what I'm now supposed to do. I'm trying these acting classes, yet I'm not finding comfort in them as they used to bring. Maybe I don't have anything left inside to give on stage; I barely have anything left inside to give to me. Assisting in directing these plays is nice; yet, I feel like I am going through the motions—acting. Isn't it ironic that I'm now doing what I dreamed? I didn't imagine faking interest was acting. Maybe I'll just skip school for a bit; after all, I don't know what I want to do anyway. Staying in bed feels better—a safer place. Thanks Doctor, I'll give this medication a try. No, wait, I'd like to take a break from medications, if you don't mind. Ah, there you are Depression, please come sit and stay a while as my thoughts in my head run relentlessly. I think I'll try a marathon of watching Friends *as that will most certainly cheer me. Ah, sweet pillow, let's forget TV.*

Earlier I mentioned the blessings of friendships that appear at just the right time. Two friendships formed while in college have become two meaningful parts of my life. How fortunate we are to have people who notice when we are absent and miss us, too. While I was busy hanging out with Depression, my friends were noticing I was not at school. They came with food, they came with their company, and they came with pajamas to stay the night. They got me showered, they enlisted my mom, and they got me to share what was weighing on my mind. They took turns for the next week being my shadow, slaying the dragons of despair that were trying to engulf me. Once again, I was lying on the stretcher of vulnerability, but these two were treating my wounds differently. They were helping me to start stepping back to my self-worth and my dignity. They were helping me back to believing in my purpose and in my dreams.

When they asked me what I felt would help me, I immediately responded, "I think I need to get a dog to be emotional support on my journey." I had grown up with dogs as a child, thankfully because of my father's dream. Though he didn't actually realize his dream to be a vet, dogs and rabbits were an integral part of our family. When I moved back home during my rehab, I convinced my family to get a dog, which was not an easy step for everyone to take. The family had lost a dog a few months before my injury in a traumatic way. To endure grief again was not what anyone was ready for. Yet, to have a dog to give me hope as I recovered was what I longed for. Seven years later and this beautiful fur child has completely taken over my parents' home. I now knew I needed one of my own.

I saw Belle's story on a social media page, the remaining puppy of eight who had been found in the middle of nowhere in a box. She was with a foster family and oh, I worried when I arranged to meet her—*would we bond, or not?* Instantly. The best word I can say when our eyes met—instantly Belle was rescuing me! Sure, I was getting her from a shelter, but it was I who Belle was saving. She is my reason to wake up each day and my comfort when it is time to go to sleep. She is my inspiration to revisit my dreams.

A quote by T. D. Jakes reads: *A setback is a set up for a comeback,* and

I think perhaps, thanks to Belle's unconditional love and support, I'm coming back to me. I should say that differently, for I know that I will never be who Naama was seven years ago before my injuries. Yet, the Naama who believed in her dreams and in life is starting to step onto center stage. No longer backstage do I stand frozen in place.

Hey Mom, is this where we'll tell them about how we become foster parents for dogs as part of a scholarship you applied for approximately eighteen months ago? And how that led you to being manager of the scholarship program, and your dreams for how the program will grow?

You are a natural leader, Mom, and we sure had fun coparenting, didn't we? You could teach all those puppies we had how to be good puppies for their human families. I could teach them how to do what they do best—listen, love, protect, and comfort unconditionally. I could teach them how to do what they do best—hear their human's heart and then provide what their human needs. Caught tears, laughter, reminders not to give up…hope. To help their human once again to feel whole.

Mom, I read a quote by someone they call Rumi who said, "The wound is the place where the Light enters you." Have you ever thought about your injuries as being the catalyst for your radiance to shine through? I know you are now working on your master's in cinematography. I can't help thinking that because of your accident, you are going to be able to see colors and imagery in ways no other can see. I can't help thinking you had to crack open to expand into your capabilities. You are capable of so much more than that five-year-old could even begin to dream. And the only way to discover that was to let more light in so that all you are meant to be had enough room to become…the Queen.

SHAI AND TOFI

Your heart knows the way. Run in that direction.

—Rumi

Perhaps you know these words from the Tanakh that read:

> *To everything there is a season, and a time to*
> *every purpose under the heaven:*
> *A time to be born, and a time to die;*
> *A time to plant, and a time to pluck up that which is planted;*
> *A time to kill, and a time to heal;*
> *A time to break down, and a time to build up;*
> *A time to weep, and a time to laugh;*
> *A time to mourn, and a time to dance;*
> *A time to cast away stones, and a time to gather stones together;*
> *A time to embrace, and a time to refrain from embracing;*
> *A time to seek, and a time to lose;*
> *A time to keep, and a time to cast away;*
> *A time to rend, and a time to sew;*
> *A time to keep silence, and a time to speak;*
> *A time to love, and a time to hate;*
> *A time for war, and a time for peace.*

These words my dance with destiny, as I ran to it while it was running to me. Now I can unconditionally love someone who is certain love is not theirs to know because I have felt self-hate to the very depths of my soul. I have held new life in my hands at their birth. I have held the hand of someone taking their last step from Earth. I have known tears of sorrow that I thought would never stop pouring down my cheeks. I have celebrated the kind of laughter that begins at one's toes, like a baby joyfully giggling. I have been intimate with a time when I could only speak to the paper beneath my pen tip, certain the paper would not judge me unworthy. I have felt the freedom of unleashing the chains around my heart as I find the courage to share my story. To every moment a reason, a purpose, a destiny. At long last, amid this war that will always be within me, I am finding peace.

I am father to seven children: sons and daughters my blessed family. Two of my children have given me the sacred gifts of a family legacy. I have two granddaughters to make our family whole. Beautiful innocents of life who teach us how not to grow old. My youngest child—my son—is my wisest teacher, my strong and brave sage. His destiny to guide me in fulfilling my purpose the rest of my days. Our son is a reflection of my beautiful wife, equally her strength of spirit to never give up, to always fight. Sometimes I pinch myself to make sure I am not in a dream. My tears of gratitude flow that I have been given such an amazing family to surround and love me.

Before I share with you about my soul mate in fur who became my lifeline to hope, I would like to share with you the hopelessness I've known. I will express my gratitude to you in advance of looking into my eyes as I tell my story. What I mean by that is I know to hear someone talk about the depths of despair is not easy. Yet, by you reading this, you are looking into my eyes, handing me back a piece of my self-dignity. Even more important, you are honoring all veterans, not just me. With my humble appreciation for your listening ear, I will begin with how I was following my heart toward my destiny. This was before destiny would reveal it had bigger plans than I could first see.

Believing my destiny was to be a leader in the military doing what I could to protect from the enemy, I reenlisted after eight years of being outside of the Army. My mission was to help build a new unit and my responsibilities included responding to emergencies. An explosion the catalyst, a siren the signal, and now a run to soldiers and civilians with utmost urgency. To attend to their injuries and save their lives was my priority. I couldn't see destiny standing in the background keeping watch where I ran to. My focus was on running to where my heart whispered, *Here, right here, this is what you need to do.*

Imagine a young toddler who has a set of building blocks in front of them, learning dexterity and thinking skills as they create a new shape. I can see your smile as you think about the look on that child's face. The child may start out with individual blocks scattered all around and then one by one, they start bringing the blocks together to make that tower rise high. The child might even knock the tower over for the joy of rebuilding that tower in a new direction to reach the sky. Imagination is so beautiful to watch in young eyes. If only it were this easy to put other things back together in life.

A time to be born and a time to die. I ran to save, but that was not always the outcome destiny had in mind. Destiny knew I would be doing my part to rescue souls in need one day, but first I would need to learn what it felt like to not be able to keep death at bay. I would first need to integrate with dying and profound grief. I would first need to let death put me in a chokehold to squeeze all feeling out of me. A time to break down and a time to build up others who are struggling to stand. I first had to break apart to then be able to offer my outstretched hands.

My heart called, *Run* to the shouts *Over here, hurry, please*, on a path in which part of a life was displaying the way piece by piece. A young Bedouin boy, sixteen years of age, had been herding his sheep. He witnessed what at first appeared to be a homeless man dropping something on the street. It was not a drop by accident, but a planned enemy attack. The power to maim—or kill—held in this now dropped sack. This brave young handsome soul tried to hurry this missile outside. In that brief moment in which life becomes before and no longer the same, both this sixteen-year-old soul and I would learn what it meant to die. His literal, he without hands and legs as I felt his pulse retreating. I, emotionally, feeling the full weight of reality that I was unable to do anything. This experience not new to stand beside another as they prepared to leave Earth sooner than we think is appropriate timing. This time, with destiny's hand firmly on my shoulder, beside this sixteen-year-old boy I, too, started to leave. Both of us no longer mobile, no longer free to move effortlessly. Death had its muscular arms tightly around my neck as it walked this dear boy to final rest.

There are times in life when we are witnessing ourselves at the edge of a cliff, about to leap. We can feel the bottomless air below one of our outstretched feet. It isn't that we want to step off that edge like a bungee jumper might do for the thrill. It is more that we know it is going to be bad if we do, but we don't know how to stand still. After this experience with this young Bedouin boy, my officer wanted to get together for a debrief. For thirty minutes, I sat frozen in my room in a chair unable to meet. In that moment, I knew I was starting to let go, falling somewhat slowly, but falling, into the darkness below. As I began falling, I split in two, leaving part of me still standing at that edge. Destiny had another lesson plan for me while my back was being pushed down by death.

Two years later, in 2008, I was a student at the university. With the alarm came the shouts again, "Hurry, this way, please." As soon as my friend and I ran outside, I could smell that someone was in need. Our senses of our body are like that in their unifying. We don't just hear someone's pain, we can smell their injuries too. I knew from the smell that someone was in serious need. I see the student lying on the ground as I direct my friend to call for a helicopter before I am fully at the scene. Ensuring no time is lost in rescue is critical in an emergency. His heart was still working, though I knew it was preparing to slow its rhythmic beat. I knelt beside him with my hand holding his heart as his eyes stayed fixed on me. Once again, as with the sixteen-year-old soul, this student and I were beginning to walk the same path. As he prepared to take his last breath, I was letting go of any feelings I had. As his blood became my skin, my heart started to become still like his heart was doing, too. Death would become the victor of both of us soon.

A few short months later, death would finish its squeeze on me. Again, I ran as my ears heard *Shai come help, Shai come help,* and my soul was responding to my destiny. My legs were running fast to a woman lying on the ground, no longer alive. To make sure, I checked twice. That, too, is a necessity when responding with urgency. If you are running and you feel another pulse, you need to make sure it isn't your own accelerated heartbeat. Death wanted, though, to be a trickster with me. As I was checking for life, I saw her stomach moving. Could there be a baby inside that needed saving? A time to die and a time to be born no more integrated than this possibility that as she left Earth, a baby would be born on this street. Though she wasn't pregnant, the moments I thought she might be felt like another hand pushing me. Down, down, from that cliff I fell faster awaiting the rocks below. *Hurry up and catch my body for I'm ready to let go.*

The bottom I reached, the rocks now my bed. Down here I was not alone, for I walked with the dead. My physical body was still at the cliff edge with family and friends holding on to me. I could feel them there, yet, truthfully, I couldn't really feel anything. It was more comfortable to me to be down here in this cool air among the jagged rocks that made my steps dangerous to take. Actually, if I slipped and fell and could then leave Earth, that would be okay. I can hear my loved ones weeping, but their cries are out of my reach. Louder is the quietness of those beside me who no longer have voices to speak. At least not in a language those alive can hear, though I can hear them quite easily.

Dear young man, I know, you died so very young before you would know what it is to have a wife and children like me. Dear woman whom I initially thought was pregnant with another child, please know I am sorry I could not help your son as he shouted into the phone his deepening grief. And dear girl whose curly hair I can still see in that car seat, the picture in the paper of you was so breathtaking. I wish that your drive that morning did not end with a terrorist reaching out his window with a gun. I hope the last thing you saw before you closed your eyes was the radiant and beautiful sun. And woman who ran to me pleading me to help your father and your brother who you loved so dearly. Please know, to be wrong that your father had died was my yearning. I bent down to read your brother's lips as his soul was leaving you behind. I hope that in these past sixteen years, peace you have been able to find.

I write letters to you, dear souls, whom I could not save. You are close, which I am comforted by, and yet, equally I try to push you away. I can't tell others about you as much as I would like to sometimes. I want to protect you from their sights. For you are too sacred for me to let just anyone see. I also know people won't be able to see past your brokenness to your extraordinary beauty. Sometimes I am haunted by the million pieces you shattered into. And other times, I feel safe among the fragments that were once the whole of you.

I don't know how to let you finish your journey in peace. I feel that

I need to keep you right beside me. Yet, I want you to leave—would you do that, for me, please? Wait, don't go, please stay. Without you beside me I am so very afraid. You are the only ones who understand what I feel in this unending night. Wait, who am I kidding, there is no feeling—only a hollow shell I am inside.

I have children and I have a wife who I once loved with all my heart. I don't know how to tell them, I too, shattered into a million parts. They say they love me, but how can they love someone who is no longer the man they once knew? I may look like their father and their husband, but Shai as they knew him is through. It would be better for them if they could come to see me as I lie beneath a buried grave. At least then they wouldn't have to look into a blank and unseeing face.

Because you can no longer live, I will best honor you by remaining dead, too. My destiny to fill my soul with sorrow, to pay penance for how I have failed each of you. I couldn't save you and enable you to grow old with your families. If you can't hear your family in sweet laughter, then to hear mine the same I am not deserving. I will push my family away by raging anger on their love. Like a volcano it erupts flowing forth beside my certainty who I am is not enough. I am a fighter, and my warrior strength I will use in a way I have never known before. Self-hate, I have a solid hold on this majestic sword. I am ready to swing it then turn the shiny blade into my own heart. Perhaps, then, I will have made it matter the lives war and hate tore apart.

I am sitting here among these jagged rocks and I am standing up above at the edge of the cliff. I am one person, yet I am split. I want to integrate those who have died into how I live. Yet, I don't think I can let the sadness move in. I am certain I can be stronger if I keep this pain out of reach. This pain, out of reach, that is consuming the all of me. Grace comes in the angels that destiny brings to our path on our rebirth journeys. One of those angels before Tofi was a wise soul who said this to me. *Shai, stop being afraid of the sadness; stop trying to remove it from who you are. Let sadness have a seat in your big and good heart. The sadness only needs to have a small percentage of room. By you trying to bury it out of sight, it is devouring all of you. Make peace with sadness, Shai, and it*

will shrink its hold. It will mean you are giving purpose to deceased souls.
These dear souls had to shatter for you to fall into place. As you do, destiny
is going to bring other broken souls your way.

Like the changing of seasons, so, too, us as souls living as human
beings. We can know the winter months when leaves are barren from
the trees. Equally, we can know the blossoming of new beginnings in
spring. Like the changing seasons that continually repeat, so, too, does
our journey in finding peace. Despair has knocked me down and kept
me away from sunlight. And hope has lifted me up and kept me holding
my own against enemy lines. I have experienced not knowing where
the next meal would come for my family. I have known what it is to sit
in the dark when our power was turned off for lack of money. I have
received the grace of my father's unconditional love when he bought me
a caravan for my soul-nurturing retreats. I have been blessed to talk with
veterans whose listening ears helped me heal my own story. I have felt
the pride of being a brave warrior in the Army. I have felt shame and no
dignity. I have used prescription medicine to cure my pain. I have said
no to medicine so that my deepest pain I could bravely face.

I share this with you especially if you are a veteran reading my
story. I will not tell you that the trauma leaves. It is an up and a down
journey where sometimes you feel you have just come back full circle,
and nothing has changed. But, my dear comrade, know that you are
no longer in the same place. You ARE stronger and better able to walk
with sorrow by your side. Sorrow is no longer more powerful than your
willful spirit to fight.

I have mentioned grace that destiny brings in the form of angels
who guide our way. I would now like to tell you about my very young,
yet very wise sage. His name is Itamar, and he is our youngest son who
also has a rare blood disease. Hemophilia keeps our son at risk that his
blood will not clot appropriately. Every day I must care for my son to
ensure he does not bleed. Every day I must focus on making sure his
life is not in jeopardy.

When my son Itamar had just left the safety of the womb, but was
still as one with my wife, another angel helped me step from death into
life. The nurse guided my hand to hold the umbilical cord that courses

life through our veins. I felt the blood of my wife, and of my son, and of my own heart in this moment of Divine grace. In that moment I did not hear, see, and smell that blood equaled dying. I felt new life take the driver's seat.

We knew in the first week of Itamar's life that he was not completely healthy. A circle of life revealed through ritual that our son had an incurable disease. On an honorary day of cleansing mind, body, and soul through fasting, from his circumcision that had just taken place, Itamar would not stop bleeding. His body purging too, but in this we knew things were not as they should be. Three days later, we would learn for his entire life Itamar would have a life-threatening disability. Once again destiny was standing in the wings as I absorbed the reality of what at first glance seemed a cruel irony. I needed to leave home for a few days to stop thinking, *How could my son being a wounded soul who now needed me to ensure there was never bleeding? Was someone playing a trick on me?*

We have a choice in every moment that life brings our way. We can respond with bitterness from our pain or we can respond with faith. I started to see that death was not trying to keep me sprawled among the jagged rocks below. Life was desiring that of it I would take hold. In the way that life teaches us through opposites, my son has been one of the angels to save me. Every day when I give my son a shot, I know that his life is bringing me healing. Every day that I save Itamar's life, another deceased soul gently walks away from my side. I can look up and see their radiant light as it shines.

In that up and down of life, I found I needed to leave home. Itamar was about two-and-a-half-years old. I was walking that circle still very much sharing the path with those deceased. I was hurting deeply, and so was my family. In that six-month separation, I would still come for Itamar's daily shot routine. Sometimes I am in awe of how destiny works behind the scenes. I hadn't yet realized to the extent Itamar was saving my life through the sacred vulnerability of his own. Through his soft tears, with each shot he required, something was touching the depths of my soul.

I began to look into the mirror, directly into the eyes looking back at me. I questioned, and I found answers as I began to further see. As I looked in that mirror seeing so many hands reaching out to me, I started to notice in their palms were gifts for unwrapping. I opened one and found the words imprinted on paper: *Forgive you.* I opened another one and found the words *You did your best you could do.* I reached for another and found inside this tiny package the words *Thank you for being the one by my side.* And then another said, *Because of you, I crossed in peace to the other side.*

I opened a few more, doing my best to hold these papers between my shaky hands and away from my runaway tears. *It is okay to have fears. It is part of what makes you human when you have uncertainty. A time for doubt and a time to believe.* I can still feel how my shoulders shook as my sobs took control of my body. These following words filling my entire being. *Your heart is good as it was with each life you ran to. With each run you were fulfilling what your heart knew to do. We are so very proud of you for how you always listened and ran with all your heart toward the shouts, "This way, hurry, please." For Shai, when you did, you were not only fulfilling your own destiny. You were fulfilling the plans we had for every soul your path intersected with. Shai, your heart is so very good for how well you did this.*

I know I haven't yet told you about my dear and beautiful Tofi. I am saving the best for last in my story. I would like to tell you a little bit more about my father and his unconditional love for me. I had mentioned a caravan he bought—well, make that many. He could see the benefit not only I was gaining, but other veterans, too. For I had started to take veterans for nature retreats for four days or two. He could see that I was finding a purpose in helping other veterans also suffering from PTSD. He was becoming the receiver of gaining his son back as I continued healing. I can still see my father's outstretched hand as he handed me a piece of paper from the post office that read, *Nonprofit business*—a notification from the government I had been anxiously awaiting. *Dear Dad, I will do my best to pay forward the goodness of your heart; thank you for always—oh so unconditionally and always—believing in me.*

My father gave me the most sacred gift any person can give another when he let me hold his hand as he said goodbye to life. The strongest man I knew who held my hand each time he saw fear in my eyes was now asking me to hold his as his own fear crept in to his eyes. *Not by accident, Dad, I now sit with you. I can see the fear in your eyes, so this is what we are going to do. Together we will take this walk, me by your side. I will not let go until I know you are ready to step across the line. It is okay that you go—you may go in peace. I promise I will not let go until it is time for us to part company. When I know you feel safe, I will come back to Mom, my wife, your grandchildren, and your great-grandchildren—we all love you so. Dad, I've got you and I promise until you feel safe, I will not let go.*

Rest in peace, Dad, and thank you for this most precious gift you have given me. To be your son has been an honor and a most amazing privilege.

Because I now have given sadness in me its rightful place that it is no longer fighting for, tears of sorrow and of compassion flow much more. A quote by Washington Irving reads, *There is a sacredness in tears. They are not a mark of weakness, but of power. They speak more eloquently than ten thousand tongues. They are the messengers of overwhelming grief, of deep contrition, and of unspeakable love.* Slowly, steadily I am starting to embrace all tears with the help of angels on Earth and above. My daughter told me words similar to this on the day she married. *Dad, because of your big heart, tears flow freely. People feel safe crying with you because they know you hold their hearts in safekeep. Your tears speak what words do not need to say. "I believe in you and all things will be okay."*

Now let me share with you about my hope in fur named Tofi. Tofi and I met when she was a puppy. About five years ago Tofi and I became an inseparable "we." I looked into her eyes and asked, *Do you want to come with me?* I felt she deserved full transparency, so I let her know this too. *If you come with me, it is going to be a long and hard journey you will do.* I talked to her about destiny, even though I wasn't sure exactly how that purpose might unfold. And then once again I asked, *Do you want to stay here on your own?* One lick of my hand said, *Okay, Shai, here we go, you and me.* No matter how hard that journey, Tofi stayed right beside me.

If I got angry and saw the only option was to shatter something to see it break, in an instant Tofi would gently but firmly get close to my face. At first, I was so far into my darkness I would resist what Tofi was trying to achieve. My wife also gently but firmly helped me better see.

My wife gently but firmly stated *Tofi and I both know the big heart that is inside you. Tofi is trying to pull you through that tunnel you sometimes feel safest crawling into. I know it is hard for you to let me pull you to the light. Trust that Tofi can hear you in a way that no other person can in your life. She can hear the rhythm of your heart when it is not beating evenly. If you let her, she will help that heart beat again regularly.*

Tofi would not only calm me, but she would also relax my children and my wife when sirens would alert us to find the bomb shelter quickly. Tofi, our fearless commander who knew when to take the lead of our entire family. Because of her, we are now focused on creating a center to train service dogs to help other veterans suffering from PTSD. This my dear Tofi's legacy.

My dear Tofi also reached her time to leave this Earth so very recently. That circle that sometimes feels like we are back to where we stood—that is some of my feelings. My heart feels shattered into a million pieces that will never be whole. Yet, that I am no longer at the same place of that circle I also know. It is because of Tofi that many more fur and human lives will find hope and healing. In every life we serve through our center will be Tofi in the lead. I look into the mirror and standing with other souls is my dear Tofi. Oh, how her light does shine so very brightly.

If we pause long enough, we can see the most incredible circles that wrap us tightly. I had shared with you earlier about the angel that helped me feel life's heartbeat. How I held the life force of my son, my wife, and I as cocreator of his life. There is another very powerful circle I was wrapped in through the interlocked arms of Tofi and my wife. My wife opened my heart to let Tofi fulfill her purpose in how she was meant to help me. Tofi opened my heart to better see that I had another soul mate waiting patiently. My wife is my partner, once again the half that makes me whole. Together, in the most unconditionally loving conspiracy, both Tofi and my wife handed me hope. My heart is open wide in compassion for veterans journeying with PTSD. And *together*, side by side, my best friend, my wife—we will serve those in need. Together, my wife and my beautiful family.

My dear Shai, it's me Tofi. I'm not sure if I told you enough, thanks for taking me. Sure, it was a hard journey sometimes for I didn't always know what to do to ease your deepest grief. But that feeling of powerlessness comes as part of my destiny. Yes, I have a destiny to bring hope, to calm, to hear what your heart speaks without words needed for me to understand. Yet, who I am meant to be is part of a bigger plan. My purpose is to give love unconditionally. It is also my purpose I am meant to teach. It was my time to let go because I knew you, my dear student, was ready to spread compassion and love to humanity. It has been one of my greatest joys watching the love you have been extending.

I miss you, too, and I would have loved to stay physically with you until you were of a very old age. Yet, we both know life for dogs doesn't work that way. Because your heart knew what is was like to no longer feel love, you are now able to give such goodness to others who seek feeling worthy. It is unconditional love to give not because you have but because you know what it means to not have such things as hope, compassion, love, and dignity.

In every service dog that finds their veteran, know this truth. Even though you don't physically see me, I will be right beside you. It was the most wonderful journey I could have ever taken, and I am so grateful I listened to my heart whisper, "Run to him, hurry, please." There will be no greater one to fulfill then this destiny. My heart was right, Shai, so very right when it nudged me to say "yes." Being by your side has been the absolute best.

JOY AND SARA

And the day came when the risk to remain tight in a
bud was more painful than the risk it took to blossom

—Anaïs Nin

*S*ome say that in order to fulfill our purpose in life, we must first experience the opposite of our destiny. I can share with you an example, or perhaps two, or maybe even three. One would be growing up as an apple of a father's eye: an only daughter among brothers, receiver of my father's adoration and pride. I was safely wrapped in the protection of his love when I relied on him to take care of me. When daddy's little girl grew into her independence, his self-worth began floundering. Not able to "make it all better" as he could when I had a skinned knee or a boy made me cry, he chose to build a wall around his feelings of helplessness thick and tall enough to push me out of his life.

I could no longer be my father's favorite little girl he adored completely. Broken from my heart was another piece, though it wasn't the reason for my heart's shattering. Because I was trying to glue the broken pieces inside me back together again was the reason that being my father's daughter came to an end. Like that bud that reaches a point where it must begin to bloom, I had reached a point where I had to honor what was my own authentic truth. I had experienced pain and trauma that had stripped me of my self-trust and my sense of security. That I couldn't flip a switch and move forward easily my father struggled to understand and support my needs.

Before I share the third experience, let me share the second experience that has greatly influenced who I am meant to be. The second example is being a teenager who experienced seizures frequently. Imagine studying for a test, and then in an instant the material you studied has been wiped from your memory. If only it could be as humorous as the movie

Fifty First Dates, but that isn't reality. There is a gift in this, though, for it led me to serve others in need. First as a 911 dispatcher and then training as a technician assisting during surgeries.

Let me first talk about being a dispatcher, for that will lead me to my third puzzle piece, the piece that snapped "perfectly" into place to guide me toward my wholeness that had been stripped away from me. When you become adept at living with an unknown, you become a calm voice when others experience significant uncertainty. Never certain when a seizure would render me to a blank stare, I was never aware of the exact timing of my mind's erasing. I became a 911 dispatcher receiving incoming calls: *Help me, I don't know what to do, she's unconscious from her fall.* Or, *He's not breathing, I can't get him to wake up, please hurry, help me, please!* Or, *I'm scared, I'm so very scared he's going to find where I'm hiding.*

Sure, not all calls were of such gravity, yet for the more distressed ones, I knew I was where I was supposed to be. That I would enter a career in the medical field had been calling since I was a patient, too. When you have unexplainable seizures, you become a specimen to test, trial, and prescribe medications to. My choice to respond to these experiences was to develop a gift of empathy for what others who are ill go through.

I met my first husband while in college, while both of us were in need. I, with my seizures; he with a kidney disease. Illness was our bond until my seizures ceased. No longer being dependent on him unveiled a deeper sickness I did not see when I said, "I do." His sickness in the form of verbal, psychological, and borderline physical abuse. It began on our honeymoon, though I didn't realize it at the time. After all, I was still a *for better, for worse, until death do us part* blushing bride. Though our honeymoon was eleven months after our wedding due to a restriction on vacation days, I was still focused on *happily ever after* per the vows I had made.

How is it said *two sides to every coin*, or said another way, two ways we can look at signs we receive? It is hindsight that often provides us our best wisdom, to see more than what we initially see. Our honeymoon was bumpy from the moment we flew to our destination, flying over

Hurricane Rita's tumultuous energy. In my naïveness, and my dutiful wife love, I thought our honeymoon experience about the tests that marriages endure and rise above. Now I realize it was symbolic of the massive storm that would soon rage, a storm that would try to erode my self-worth and dignity in every way.

The storm began as near misses, meaning a thrown remote control that avoided my head, yet caught my arm. An immediate second later was the "make it all better" by his expressing he meant no harm. *I'm sorry, I didn't mean to do that,* I believed had been spoken with sincerity. Until a coffee cup, an office chair, and then a fire extinguisher were at later times hurled toward me.

Though I was familiar with first-response processes and procedures, I was not knowledgeable about how to work around the rules meant to be in place. The man I was legally married to was very savvy in leveraging relationships to sweep his actions away. The marks he was leaving on me were invisible to the naked eye; the rips and tears I was experiencing were administered deep inside.

The psychological wounds took place in public by the continued monitoring of my whereabouts while I was working. If only those were the only wounds I had received. Pieces of my soul were pierced when in the privacy of home. Behind closed doors where the only witnesses were the walls who couldn't communicate what they know. Actually, I take that back that the concealed injuries only took place in what was supposed to be a safe haven from harm externally. There was also an experience while at the Mayo Clinic after he received a new kidney. Not at home, yet still a shattering that nobody, except my dear mom could see.

About four years before the fire extinguisher met with my strength to leave, we traveled to Mayo Clinic for the transplant operation as more than a two-person family. I was pregnant, though my condition was not of importance in his mind. In pre-op, during-op, and post-op, unwelcome tones and words by him and his family communicated it would be best if I remained out of sight. My mom, always only a phone call away, flew eight hours to offer moral support to me. If it wasn't for her, I would have been alone during a time of increasing grief.

It is said we have guardian angels that keep us in safe keep. Yes, my mom is one, but there was additional guardianship that took place, or at least how I believe. A child I was not meant to bring into this world and myself were angels to give each other what would be best at that time. I had a miscarriage while in Arizona, so a baby that would not know this life. I was not able to fully grieve the loss, yet I was also at peace. I know that it was best for this little soul and me. My mom taught me well that unconditional love is about loving another over one's own needs. As much as I would have loved this child, this soul was safer not becoming part of our family.

After a three-month recovery period at Mayo Clinic, we returned home where once again we were hidden behind closed doors and out of sight of closed support systems like the police. It was during this time my second guardian angel was conceived. This time my child was meant to enter this life and our family; twelve years ago, my son Benjamin entered this world to complete me. My son Benjamin, whose name symbolizes strength of the right hand, is without a doubt my right-hand person who inspires my strength to believe I can.

In the beginning, I talked of opposites and how we must experience one extreme to then fulfill our destiny. I am thankful every day for the gift of my son I received. He was conceived from fear for my life—and his—that I would then learn I would give my all for my son and I to live. My son was conceived from a deep hate directed at me, that I would learn there is no greater love than the one I have for my son and his well-being. Benjamin entered this world full of smiles and laughter, exhibiting the joy I had locked tightly away. My emotional pain and my despair have been anchored from drowning me by Benjamin's giggles and radiant smiling face. Benjamin my right-hand strength, anchoring me in the moments when the rest of my life has felt in such disarray.

There are things I haven't been able to shelter him from, innocence my son is losing far too quickly. Yet, unlike his miscarried brother or sister, I know Benjamin—and I—are better that his soul entered this life to experience it with me. Benjamin's biological father had tried to develop Benjamin into a weapon of control since he was no longer able to yield domination of me as if I were a puppet on a string. It is not easy to share joint custody with an individual who views his son as a chess piece. Yet, true to Benjamin's strength and his wisdom beyond his tender age of twelve, Benjamin knows that he is close to setting his wings in flight. He can already discern between genuine love and love that comes with a price. I strive to bring a foundation to Benjamin that fosters his independence and his safety; in turn, Benjamin gives me the bricks on which to build a solid foothold beneath both our feet.

And now let me tell you about my third experience in which—at long last—my heart has found home. I first had to know the depths of loss, frightened to the brink of death, and feeling completely alone. To know what unconditional love feels like one must know conditional hate. If I hadn't experienced someone's hatred, I may not have recognized when I found my soul mate. Though our souls are very old friends, we have been newlyweds every day since August 7, 2011 formally. Informally, it was the day Ken offered to cook me dinner and our voices and text messaging became a face-to-face meet.

My husband experienced his own storm, his opposites to guide him to his destiny. Though his journey was not filled with emotional abuse, his experiences were guiding him to me. A military veteran, well-versed in serving those at their most vulnerable time, my dear husband has saved lives and has graciously held dignity for those who reached the last moments of life. Both of us calming voices for those who are struggling. We have been brought together to heal within ourselves as we walk toward a purpose to serve humanity.

I'm not yet able to go back and work in an operating room because I still need Sara—my service dog—beside me, and her fur is currently a barrier for sterility. I know we haven't yet talked of Sara. I promise I will share more about Sara shortly. My husband has paused his role as sheriff, currently serving people in a different capacity. My dear husband—the kind of unconditional love that puts first above all else my well-being. I need more time to heal the sight of uniforms and sidearms from my memories. That my husband can wear plain clothes to his job is helping reframe the images that equal my T (for trauma) in PTSD.

What do you think when you hear the numbers 9-1-1? Maybe you think *emergency* or perhaps you think *September 2001*. For my husband

and me both meanings resonate equally. I was dispatcher when my husband and I began communicating casually. My husband was at the Pentagon when life became before and no longer the same for all of us nationally. This number so significant to us, it formed the development of my wedding ring. Some interpret the number nine as symbolic of living one's life committed to being of service to humanity. The number one is about unity and new beginnings.

Our four sons—three from Ken's first marriage and of course, Benjamin, who I've already introduced to you—are the center of our committed service in all that we do. Our extended family, such as my mom, my brother Mike, and my niece, are the next layer of who I strive to service and who equally give back to me. As Ken and my servanthood expand, we wish to inspire others on their healing journeys.

I know what it means to fight for my life, not just in my past, but each and every day. Fear is such a powerful force that threatens to imprison one from believing they are no longer in harm's way. I also know what it is to fight not only for that inner voice inside me that has a will not to give in; I know what it is to fight for one who is an extension of my flesh, blood, and each of my limbs.

I didn't understand the depths of the cuts when objects were being hurled at me, nor the depth of the trauma the day my son was conceived. I could apply a simulation as if I was a teenager again having a seizure to render my mind a blank. Only this time I was still alert, opting to erase any feelings that might distract my focus on staying safe. Being scared was allowed only enough to keep me on my toes; caring that my dignity and self-security were slipping away, I swallowed and then buried whole.

I did not know the pain that would sear me and nearly cut me in two while in the throes of fighting for my son and what he had been through. Like a person whose adrenaline leads them to extraordinary feats despite the fire raging around them nearly burning them alive, I was oblivious to what was creating scar tissue inside me as I focused on ensuring my son would be all right. This time I could feel emotions—feelings stronger than anything I had ever known. What I wasn't feeling were the flames burning into my flesh and bones.

Like that bud whose petals can no longer remain tightly wrapped around its soul, the pain and trauma I had experienced needed a place to go. It started to rise to the surface in a place where I felt safe. Thankfully it was caught by unconditional love and gentle strength. Ken was wise enough to look beyond a wall I was building to not take my distance personally. Adept at calmly breaking down barriers, Ken guided me to people who could help me.

One such "person" is Sara, who I briefly mentioned above. Yet another to enter my life giving me unconditional love. It is said that we have experienced a fortune if we are blessed to have one great and true love in our life. I thought my cup overflowed to have two great loves in mine. It was love at first sight when I held Benjamin in my arms after his first breath. It was love at first sight when Ken was peeking around the curtain to see his dinner guest. Somehow despite the darkness that makes up a significant portion of the life I've lived, I have found not just one, nor two, but three great and true loves to share my heart with.

I think of that rose still a tight bud and I think of the so very prickly base in which it rests atop the stem and waits. The thorns a protection that no harm will come to its delicate petals before they are ready to unfold and captivate. My physical self-cutting moments in which I was trying to release the core-to-my-bones pain of not feeling worthy. My panic attacks and my anxiety heightened in crowds I was certain were full of people who wanted to further hurt me. These crippling fears my thorns to protect the fragile yet strong heart tightly tucked inside. Through many layers of believing I was not lovable my soul was whispering, *There are three angels who will be your guides.*

Sara and I met for the first time when she was a mere four weeks of age. Another love at first sight when her tongue and my hand integrated that day. No, it wasn't a puppy teeth bite, but a kiss she gave me. In an instant I knew she was the service dog for me. We have been inseparable since she could come home. I am convinced she can read every whisper of my soul. Without words, Sara can hear my body and my heart when either or both are in need. She senses my emotional fears and she is in tune to my hypoglyccmic crashes before I know they are about to happen to me.

Sara is my crowd control to be my front or my back, ensuring people don't step inside my box of comfort when I am in a public domain. Sara turns lights on and off and presses the button to open a handicap-assessable doorway. Before Sara, I found the risk of leaving home greater than my bravery to leave. Now the petals around my heart are unfolding ever so slowly. Thanks be to Sara who is my guardian, my eyes, my ears, and my even breathing. Sara enables me to believe again in my own bravery.

Both Ken and I have had individuals try to tarnish our reputations, to discredit our integrity. We chose not to fuel the lies printed about us as a result of court proceedings. It would also be easy to keep my personal story tucked away—after all, most aren't comfortable listening to another's pain. Yet, the more I bravely risk stepping out of that bud, and the more my petals unfold, the more I fulfill my destiny. If one person finds the strength not to give up because I have found the courage to share my story, then I have made it matter and given purpose to the pain, trauma, sorrow, and despair that have engulfed me.

Mom, it's me Sara, and have I told you lately that I am proud of you? I know it isn't easy, yet I continue to watch you pushing through. You give me credit, believing I am the one that has given you your life back since my paws entered your life. I would like to remind you it isn't until a student is ready does a teacher arrive. You and Dad consider me a guardian angel to keep watch over you. I appreciate that, yet your forward momentum is at the hands of YOUR bravery, too.

I know I alert you before you can hear that the sirens are about to get louder and nearer to our home. Yet, it is you who makes the choice in how you will respond as the frightful noise draws close. You could choose to flee, to hide, to ask Dad to sell our home so that you could find a place even more isolating. Yes, I know we live in seclusion now, but it is not being hermits to an extreme. I am your strength, I know, but please don't diminish the strength that is growing in you because of your own courage to boldly and beautifully bloom.

Mom, do you know what one of the best things about our relationship is to me? How you and I can communicate so much without my ability to speak to you in English. I know you feel there aren't enough words in a dictionary to communicate how much I have helped you find your gentle petals waiting to beautifully unfold. It can be hard to adequately express what a heart feels and knows. Yet, Mom, that is the joy of our relationship—yours and mine. You and I don't have to try to find words to express the rhythm of our hearts that beat in perfect unified time. It's like the beautiful roses you talk about in your story; when the petals of a rose unfold, they can take someone's breath away because of their beauty. And in that intake of breath, someone doesn't need to try to verbally convey their awe and reverence of a most miraculous grace. We are like that rose that has unfolded to steal a breath or two; such is the power of our love and how I show you the courage that is YOU.

Mom, you know what else I can't wait for is to see what number forty-five, forty-six, and even eighty-eight might be! I love how your tattoos also communicate your story. They contain beautiful colors and imagery and they are the healing art to release your deepest-to-the-bone once-held belief that worthlessness was your only deserving. In their messages they communicate your invisible scars are what enhance your radiant beauty. Forty-four petals visibly showing your bravery; forty-four tattoos telling a most extraordinary story.

I would also like to say thank you for equally giving to me what you so lovingly say I provide. Unconditional listening and love you give back to me every moment of my life. I see it in your eyes, I hear it in your voice, and I feel it each time you touch me. I feel it in the home that you, Dad, and Benjamin have created for all of us as family. I know the song "A Thousand Years" by Christina Perri is one you and Dad share to signify you are each other's everything. There are certain words to that song that my heart also sings. "Time stands still, beauty in all she is; I will be brave; I will not let anything take away what's standing in front of me. Every breath, every hour has come to this."

Mom, you are everything to me and there is nothing I wouldn't do for you. Thank you for the honor you've given that I would have the privilege to keep watch over you. I could not think of a better person to be a guardian angel I was sent to. And, Mom, as much as I wish you had not experienced the pain, trauma, sorrow, and despair you've known as part of your story, I am grateful only in that because of your journey I have been able to fulfill my own destiny.

EPILOGUE

Between stimulus and response there is a space. In
that space is our power to choose our response. In
our response lies our growth and our freedom.

—Victor E. Frankl

A veteran is someone who, at one point in their life wrote a blank check
made payable to "The United States of America," for an amount up to and
including their life.

And we survived; Perhaps now, as veterans, we will show civilians how
to do the same.

Hope and resilience are ours for the taking. We've got this, don't you
worry. We will reach the other side of this uncertainty. Have faith, never
give up, believe. We've got your six, you are in safe hands.

—J. Vanata

SOURCES

DEAR READER:

Dickinson, E. (1890), *The Collected Poems of Emily Dickinson*, Reprinted: Digireads.com Publishing (2016) (p. 64).

Unknown author *In my darkest hour*. Retrieved May 2 2020 from https://www.pinterest.com/pin/191473421634508214/

Walker, S. (2019), *PTSD and Service Dogs: Beneath the Surface*, TEDX Mount Hood 2019 (November, 2019), Retrieved from: https://www.bing.com/videos/search?q=ted+x+talks+shannon+walker&docid=60802258 5464260302&mid=DE840F1C1F976036AE63DE840F1C1F 976036AE63&view=detail&FORM=VIRE

Newman, M. (2014), *Suicide rates in the IDF hit record low*, Times of Israel (January, 2014), Retrieved from: https://www.timesofisrael.com/suicide-rates-in-the-idf-hit-record-low/

Richardson, C. (2014), *Week 41—A letter I wish I could send to every 'checked out' healthcare provider*, (October, 2014), Retrieved from: https://cherylrichardson.com/newsletters/week-41-letter-wish-send-every-checked-healthcare-provider/

EPILOGUE

Latin Phrase (1894), *ad astra per aspera*, Finland.

JACOB AND TRACER

Stein, Garth (2008), *The Art of Racing in the Rain*, New York: Harper Collins Publishers.

JENNIFER AND ONYX

Unknown author. *Sometimes God will put the Goliath in your life*. Retrieved May 2 2020 from https://www.pinterest.com/pin/3541659 58180690620/

Unknown author. *Sometimes Fear Won't Go Away. Retrieved August 2, 2020 from* https://emilysquotes.com/sometimes-the-fear-wont-go-away-so-youll-have-to-do-it-afraid/

KRISTOPHER AND SHERA
Thomas, I. S. (2017) *I Wrote this For You: 2007-2017*. Washington: Central Avenue Publishing.

DESIREE AND CHUNKY
Bob Marley. (n.d.). AZQuotes.com. Retrieved May 02, 2020, from AZQuotes.com Web site: https://www.azquotes.com/quote/515457

BRYAN AND ROXEY
Rudyard Kipling. (n.d.). AZQuotes.com. Retrieved May 02, 2020, from AZQuotes.com Web site: https://www.azquotes.com/quote/372441
Roger Caras Quotes. (n.d.). BrainyQuote.com. Retrieved May 2, 2020, from BrainyQuote.com Web site: https://www.brainyquote.com/quotes/roger_caras_104849

TOM AND ZOEY
Mary Anne Radmacher. (2013). *She: A Celebration of Greatness in Every Woman*, New Jersey: Viva Editions.
A.W. "Smokey" Linn (1958). *Firefighter's Prayer*. Retrieved September 4, 2020 from https://www.aspiringfirefighters.com/coaching/firemans-prayer/
Williams, A. D. (2008). *Inside the Divine Pattern*. New York: Gemini 11, LLC

DONALD AND CHARLEY
Unknown author. *At the end of the day* Retrieved May 2 2020 from https://www.pinterest.com/CountryThang/

DUDLEY AND BRUTUS
Ephesians 2:10. New International Version. Biblica, https://www.biblehub.com/nlt/ephesians/2-10.htm Accessed 2 May 2020.
Unknown author. *Angels Walk Among Us*, all-greatquotes.com, Retrieved May 2 2020 from all-greatquotes.com web site: https://www.all-greatquotes.com/angels-walk-among-us-but-there-very-hard-to-see/

NICK AND DINKY

Betty White. (n.d.). AZQuotes.com. Retrieved May 02, 2020, from AZQuotes.com Web site: https://www.azquotes.com/quote/312899

Anonymous. *A Dog's Plea*. Retrieved May 2, 2020 https://www.all-creatures.org/aro/p-adogs.html

JON AND JAEGER

Pablo Picasso. (n.d.). AZQuotes.com. Retrieved May 02, 2020, from AZQuotes.com Web site: https://www.azquotes.com/quote/489887

Chumbawamba (1997) *I Get Knocked Down*. From Album: Tubthumper. Universal and Republic Records

Unknown author. *Kindly the Father said to him*, Retrieved May 2 2020 from https://www.pinterest.com/pin/121738614724428138/

REBEKAH AND FROG AKA TRIGGER

Brené Brown. (n.d.). AZQuotes.com. Retrieved May 02, 2020, from AZQuotes.com Web site: https://www.azquotes.com/quote/1024551

Barnum, P. T. (1880) *The Art of Money Getting or Golden Rules for Making Money*

Audre Lorde. (n.d.). AZQuotes.com. Retrieved May 02, 2020, from AZQuotes.com Web site: https://www.azquotes.com/quote/788062

GLENN AND CAMPBELL

Benjamin Disraeli. *The legacy of heroes*. Success.com. Retrieved May 06, 2020, from https://www.success.com/11-quotes-about-leaving-a-legacy/

Storm, J. M. JMStorm Quotes. Retrieved May 5 2020 from https://www.facebook.com/Jmstormquotes/photos/a.1594812220755534/2524649197771827/?type=3

Sonny and Cher (1985) *I Got You Babe*. From Album: Look at Us. Atco Records.

Adichie, C. N. (2009), *The danger of a single story*, TEDGlobal 2009 (October, 2009), Retrieved from: https://www.ted.com/talks/chimamanda_ngozi_adichie_the_danger_of_a_single_story#t-1064

ROBERT AND BRINKLEY

Unknown author. *Do not judge my story*, Retrieved May 2 2020 from
https://www.paintedteacup.com/mental-health-awareness-quotes/

DOUG AND JETT

John 15:13. New International Version. Biblica, https://www.biblica.
com/bible/niv/john/15/Accessed 2 May 2020.

TOM AND RYDER

Unknown author. *It's okay to be a glow stick*. Retrieved May 2 2020
from https://www.all-greatquotes.com/its-okay-to-be-a-glowstick-
break-before-we-shine-cute-quote/
J. K. Rowling. (n.d.). AZQuotes.com. Retrieved May 03, 2020, from
AZQuotes.com Web site: https://www.azquotes.com/quote/365401
Unknown author *As soon as I saw you* Retrieved May 2 2020, https://
www.pinterest.com/pin/421086633912528068/

JEFF AND ABLE

Elsie de Wolfe. (n.d.). AZQuotes.com. Retrieved May 03, 2020, from
AZQuotes.com Web site: https://www.azquotes.com/quote/357659

PHIL AND RAVEN

Unknown author. *The wolf in my heart*. Retrieved May 2 2020 from
https://www.pinterest.com/pin/78953799705499419/

FELIX AND STRYKER

Donoghue, E. (2017). *Room*. United Kingdom: Oberon Books

ARMANDO AND ROCKY

Henry Wadsworth Longfellow. *Every man has his secret sorrows*. Retrieved
May 24, 2020 from https://www.brainyquote.com/quotes/henry_
wadsworth_longfello_109285

JOE AND BAILEY

Nhat Hanh. (n.d.). AZQuotes.com. Retrieved May 03, 2020, from
AZQuotes.com Web site: https://www.azquotes.com/quote/479607

Elisabeth Kübler-Ross. (n.d.). AZQuotes.com. Retrieved May 03, 2020, from AZQuotes.com Web site: https://www.azquotes.com/quote/395280

NAAMA AND BELLE
Unknown author. *It's okay to be a glow stick.* Retrieved May 2 2020 from https://www.all-greatquotes.com/its-okay-to-be-a-glowstick-break-before-we-shine-cute-quote/
Neil Gaiman. (n.d.). AZQuotes.com. Retrieved May 03, 2020, from AZQuotes.com Web site: https://www.azquotes.com/quote/348682
Rumi. *The wound is the place.* Retrieved May 2, 2020 from https://www.goodreads.com/quotes/103315-the-wound-is-the-place-where-the-light-enters-you

SHAI AND TOFI
Rumi. (n.d.). AZQuotes.com. Retrieved May 03, 2020, from AZQuotes.com Web site: https://www.azquotes.com/quote/1352153
Ecclesiastes 3: JPS Tanakh (1917) Jewish Publication Society Retrieved from: https://www.biblehub.com/jps/ecclesiastes/3.htmAccessed May 5, 2020.
Washington Irving. *There is a Sacredness in Tears.* Retrieved May 2, 2020 from https://www.brainyquote.com/quotes/washington_irving_149294

JOY AND SARA
Anaïs Nin. *And the day came.* Retrieved May 2, 2020 from https://www.goodreads.com/quotes/876911-and-the-day-came-when-the-risk-to-remain-tight
Christina Perri. (2011) *A Thousand Years.* From album: The Twilight Saga: Breaking Dawn—Part 1. Walt Disney Records

PROLOGUE
Frankl, V. (1946). *Man's Search for Meaning.* Boston, MA: Beacon Press.

ACKNOWLEDGMENTS

I have a personal perspective that each person who crosses our path is a puzzle piece to complete the picture of our lives. Where to begin expressing my gratitude for all the puzzle pieces that are a significant reason you have just read *Hope Has a Cold Nose*?

To my professors, who taught me in mind that I would bravely step onto the path that was calling my soul. I especially thank those of you who became my ongoing mentors!

To aka Viola Shipman, you shine by example. You are always just a mentor moment away, and I will forever be grateful that you are one of the border pieces of the puzzle that complete the picture of my life.

To many wonderful organizations that supported the development of this book by trusting me with your most precious commodities—the veterans you serve. I have included links to their webpages at the end. Please note that a couple of organizations do not serve veterans; yet, their missions serve broken spirits, both human and of fur, and both touched my heart in such a way I could not leave them out.

To Jona, thank YOU for your open heart to that "God instance" whisper when our paths first intersected. We are both holding a copy of *Hope Has a Cold Nose* because you listened.

To a special team of individuals willing to come together to climb Mount Adams. Because you said "yes," this book is in final form, available to read. To Adrian and Kelsey, it has been my privilege and honor to be part of the "A team" with you!

To the Wing of Rehabilitation, thank YOU for your belief. I believe our paths are intersecting for us to be a collective support of rehabilitation far greater than you and I can see at this time. I look forward to the ripples we will cascade together.

To Nancy. You, more than most, know my love of words, for you have given your heart and soul to read each one for grammar, punctuation, clarity, and reader engagement. As I now find myself at a loss for those words, and I love to be able to adequately express my gratitude, I will turn to the hummingbird that has just graced my path for inspiration. It has been a pure joy having you as my editor. I smile when I think of the dear soul who said to me, "Oh, something tells me you will be back," as she referred to a slice of heaven on the West Coast. How right she was indeed! I am so grateful that the reason I did was because of you.

To Nikki. My heart's work has been in the safest of hands thanks to you. Whether you have held my heart in your own hands or guided me to Nancy, I am blessed that you, too, are another very significant piece of the puzzle that completes the picture of my life. Thank YOU for being able to find a way to be a part of HHCN!

To dear friends who walk beside me, and when necessary, who give me a gentle push from behind or a tug from ahead, thank you for being some of the most vibrant puzzle pieces of my life! No matter the duration you have been snapped into place, there is one certainty. Each of you are key pieces that complete the picture of me.

To my biggest cheerleaders, both humans and fur, that are the border to the puzzle picture of my life. My family. I am the luckiest girl in the world! Thank you for being my wings.

To a friend from long ago who once so wisely said, "Christine, you will make it [pain and sorrow] matter in how you live," if only you knew what a significant ripple you cast. Thank you for being a Divine messenger. Please know, I listened.

And to each storyteller in *Hope Has a Cold Nose*, you gave me the most sacred gift you can give another and that was your trust with your hearts. It has been my honor to serve each of you as each of you have served us all. Namaste.

ORGANIZATIONS

https://www.northwestbattlebuddies.org/
https://www.mission22.com/
http://www.doggoneexpress.com/
https://www.quantumleapfarm.org/
http://www.thebigfixuganda.org/index.html
https://livelikeroo.org/

ABOUT THE AUTHOR

Christine Hassing is the author of her memoir, *To the Moon and Back to Me: What I Learned from Four Running Feet* and a compassionate mentor, teaching individuals to find a centeredness in life, in their leadership, and within themselves. It was while Christine was using her intuitive listening skills as a life story writer and earning her MA that her path intersected with a veteran and his service dog. In that way that no moment in life is coincidental, this encounter would guide Christine to write *Hope Has a Cold Nose*. Christine is a passionate advocate for holistic well-being, animals as healers, and the integration of pain, trauma, sorrow, despair, and grief into living a "hope-full" life. Christine's capacity to listen and recount the words of storytellers create compelling testimonies to engage and endear support for veterans struggling to integrate back into civilian life and for anyone who is suffering from pain, trauma, sorrow, or despair. Her stories enlist the support of service dogs as an effective healing methodology for people journeying with PTSD and encourage listening, understanding, and compassion. Her other goal is to inspire hope. In addition to her legacy and healing life story writing, Christine is also a self-employed mentor of transformational leadership tools and techniques to organizations and individuals. Christine resides where her loudest neighbors are the bull frogs and blue herons, alongside her husband and their four-legged souls, each with a cold nose.